AN ADAMS BUSINESS ADVISOR

Marketing Magic

Other titles in
THE ADAMS BUSINESS ADVISORS

Accounting for the New Business by Christopher R. Malburg
The All-In-One Business Planning Guide by Christopher R. Malburg
Entrepreneurial Growth Strategies by Lawrence W. Tuller
Exporting, Importing, and Beyond by Lawrence W. Tuller
The Personnel Policy Handbook for Growing Companies by Darien McWhirter
Service, Service, Service by Steven Albrecht
The Small Business Valuation Book by Lawrence W. Tuller
Winning the Entrepreneur's Game by David E. Rye

AN ADAMS BUSINESS ADVISOR

Marketing Magic

INNOVATIVE AND PROVEN IDEAS
FOR FINDING CUSTOMERS, MAKING
SALES, AND GROWING YOUR BUSINESS

DON DEBELAK

BOB ADAMS, INC.
Holbrook, Massachusetts

Published by Adams Media Corporation
260 Center Street, Holbrook, MA 02343

ISBN: 1-55850-352-8 (hardcover)
ISBN: 1-55850-351-X (paperback)

Printed in the United States of America.

J I H G F E D C B A (hardcover)
J I H G F E D C B   (paperback)

Library of Congress Cataloging-in-Publication Data
Debelak, Don.
    Marketing magic : innovative and proven ideas for finding customers, making sales, and growing your
business / Don Debelak.
        p.   cm. — (An Adams business advisor)
    Includes bibliographical references and index.
    ISBN 1-55850-352-8 — ISBN 1-55850-351-X (pbk.)
    1. Marketing—Management. 2. Advertising. 3. Communication in marketing. I. Title. II. Series.
    HF5415.13.D376   1994
    658.8—dc20   94-8711
                                                                                    CIP

This publication is designed to provide accurate and authoritative information with regard to the subject matter covered. It is sold with the understanding that the publisher is not engaged in rendering legal, accounting, or other professional advice. If legal advice or other expert assistance is required, the
services of a competent professional person should be sought.
    — From a *Declaration of Principles* jointly adopted by a Committee of the American Bar
                Association and a Committee of Publishers and Associations

COVER DESIGN: Marshall Henrichs

This book is available at quantity discounts for bulk purchases.
For information, call 1-800-872-5627.

Table of Contents

SECTION 4
MOTIVATING CUSTOMERS

SECTION 5
COMMUNICATING WITH CUSTOMERS

SECTION 6
MAKING THE SALE

Introduction

WHO IS THE BOOK FOR?

Marketing is a particular challenge for owners of small businesses and new business ventures. These companies don't have the resources, name recognition, existing distribution networks, or established customer base of a larger corporation. What their owners and marketers do have is a close relationship with their customers, the ability to quickly experiment with different programs, and the commitment and desire to make sure that their companies succeed.

I've worked for big firms and I've owned two smaller ones. I find that marketing is more fun at smaller companies. One reason is that you are in control. At big companies you sometimes have to wait six to nine months to see the results of a major marketing campaign. At a small firm, you can see a campaign's results in two to three weeks. Second, you don't depend on anyone else for your results. You decide what to do, and you get results or you don't. Third, you can run a variety of programs and see which ones work best. At a big company, you need to convince a whole array of people to go along with your programs. Getting approval for one program is hard enough, let alone trying to win approval for three or four. Finally, at a small firm you know that your efforts resulted in a program's success. That's a direct correlation that is difficult or impossible to get at a larger company.

Of course, a small company doesn't have the same resources for marketing its products as bigger competitors. That's all right, because the ways a small firm markets its products and services can be more efficient, more cost-effective, and easier to execute than the marketing methods available to large corporations. The goal of this book is to help marketers in small businesses and new business ventures not just even the odds against big corporations, but actually turn the odds around so that they're in their favor. Is this difficult to do? Not at all, because the small business marketing tactics covered in this book are easy to execute, low in cost, and quickly implemented. Large businesses don't have these advantages.

WHAT IS THE BOOK LIKE?

I know that 90 percent of you are picking up this book to learn how to make more money. If you have a marketing problem, you want to start solving it today. If sales are slow, you want to boost them now. If a competitor makes a move that hurts you, you want to respond before you miss a payroll. The important thing is that you want to implement marketing programs quickly and decisively.

This book is not going to teach you everything you would learn in an MBA course, nor is it going to cover complex marketing theory. What this book does is break down marketing strategy so that it is straight to the point and easy to implement. Once you've decided to improve your business, I want you to know what to do, then start doing it—all within one day.

I want to change the way you think about marketing. You don't need elaborate focus group studies, or expensive consultants, or an in-depth knowledge of customers' buying behavior. What you need is action. Getting customers to actually buy your product is what counts. This book is designed to start making you money today. Every chapter explains how to execute one or more tactics and provides immediate, low-cost action steps you can take to start implementing those tactics.

Throughout the book I use the term "product" to refer to manufactured products, retail store concepts, virtually every type of service, and anything else you might sell to a customer. The principles and tactics discussed throughout the book apply to all of these types of products and all types of businesses.

How to Best Use the Book

Marketing has two major elements: strategy and tactics. Strategy includes deciding who your target customer is, choosing the right product and distribution channel, creating a reason why people should buy from you, and developing a consistent marketing focus. Tactics are the means by which the strategy is carried out. There are dozens of them, including brochures, promotions, advertising, events, publicity, and referrals.

The first two sections of this book, "Discovering Where the Money Is" and "Being Better than Everyone Else," cover strategy. They discuss how to create a marketing focus. The book's last four sections are tactics oriented. They are organized by small business' four main marketing objectives: finding, motivating, communicating with, and selling to customers. Each tactics section starts out with a chapter that explains which types of tactics work best for various kinds of businesses. The following chapters explain how to use each tactic.

This book is designed to be used in two ways: as a blueprint for immediate action, and as a long-term reference work.

First, you can use it to create or clarify your marketing strategy. As you read the book, you can decide on your key marketing elements: target customers, products, distribution channels, product advantages, key selling points, and your market identity. Then you should read through the tactics sections and pick out three to ten tactics to implement in the next six to twelve months, including one or two that you want to implement immediately. This should give you a marketing plan and focus for the next year.

Once you're happy with the marketing focus, you can go back to the tactics sections and see if you overlooked any key steps. The most common marketing mistake (which I still occasionally make) is to believe that your product is so great that all you need do to get sales is to tell people about it. No matter how good the product, people need to be motivated to buy it. If your message doesn't create enough desire, you may have overlooked a key implementation step.

The appendix of the book includes a glossary and a list of helpful sources, but its most important part is the section titled "The Marketing File Drawer." Throughout the book I mention different files and forms that marketers can put together to make their job easier. "The Marketing File Drawer" lists the files and key forms you should keep in a marketing strategy file.

The book is also designed to be a day-to-day action guide and marketing problem solver. When you are ready to use a tactic, check your marketing thrust form (page 109), then decide what your objective is, and create your program after referring to the appropriate chapter for implementation advice.

When your marketing programs are not going well, always start with your marketing focus form. Three-quarters of the time problems are caused by a marketing strategy. If you see a flaw in your strategy, go back and reread the relevant pages of the first eight chapters. If you are not sure where the problem lies, read Sections 1 and 2 again to create a better strategy.

Don't read the book and then put it on the shelf. Use it often, and refer to it every time you get ready to prepare or implement a new marketing program.

The most important way to use this book is as a call to action. Start implementing the tactics that follow, and I'm convinced you'll have a marketing program that will be the envy of all your competitors.

Chapter 1

The Six Steps to Marketing Success

If you're going to be action oriented, you can't get bogged down in theoretical marketing concepts. Instead, you need to look at marketing in a straightforward way that's easy to understand.

The most profitable way to look at marketing is to consider it as just six steps:

1. Discovering where the money is
2. Becoming better than everyone else
3. Finding enough customers
4. Motivating customers to take action
5. Communicating on a regular basis
6. Making the sale.

You can use these six steps to address virtually every marketing problem. They give you dozens of ways to improve business and increase profitability. They offer you an easy-to-follow format for developing an effective marketing strategy and plan.

This chapter will describe each step and give several examples of how it is used. Each of the six main sections of the book focuses on one of these key steps. The last chapter will show you how to put everything together into a marketing plan. The goal of this opening chapter is to let you know what the six steps are, and to help you realize how they can speed you on your path to success.

THE MONEY-MAKING STEPS

Discovering Where the Money Is

There are always profits to be made when you find underserved customers and provide them with products that they want or need. Wal-Mart, the nation's biggest retailer, started out with mid-size discount stores in small-to-medium-size cities that had been overlooked by Kmart and other major retailers.

Philtec Instrument Co. learned that automotive manufacturers were having trouble measuring the depth of nitriding on parts. (Nitriding is a hardening technique used for critical metal applications, such as transmission rods.) Manufacturers couldn't be sure if parts were hardened as deep as specified, and they were afraid to use the parts because of the product liability risk. Philtec designed special equipment for this application and was able to pick up a new, very profitable customer group.

Kodak took a different approach with its disposable cameras. It knew from its film business that people who went on short trips were a lucrative target. But tourists could buy all the film they needed at tourist locations: they were hardly underserved. Kodak asked the question, "What group of tourists isn't getting the products it needs?" The answer was people who forgot their cameras. Kodak met this need with a disposable camera that sold for $12, which was cheap enough for people to buy, yet still allowed Kodak a profit.

Becoming Better Than Everyone Else

You don't have to be better at everything, or in every market—you just have to be better in one aspect of your business and in one market. If yours is a small business, that market doesn't even have to be large for you to succeed. The secret to being better is to have a sustainable advantage. For example, Toyota had a quality advantage over GM and Ford in the 1970s and 1980s. It took the American companies more than ten years to match Toyota's quality, and that delay gave Toyota a sustainable edge that it was able to turn into a significant market share.

Rubbermaid has a sustainable advantage because of its broad product line and its extensive retailer network. Park Tool Company is a small manufacturer that uses the same tactic. Park makes tools for repairing bicycles. It has a broad product line that covers most bicycle repair problems. Its large product catalog gives Park Tool an edge on any potential competitor. What's the difference between Park Tool and Rubbermaid? Just the size of the market they've chosen to attack. Rubbermaid's market is large, and Park Tool's is small.

Pick out the market leaders or fast-rising firms in any market, and you'll always find they have one or more strong competitive edges. The edge might be quality, status, innovative image, a combination of product features, a unique sales strategy, or in-depth technical support.

Finding Enough Customers

Big companies that sell to broad markets don't usually have to worry about finding customers. Their only problem is getting their products in enough locations so that customers can find them. But a small company serving a niche market may have trouble finding potential customers in a cost-effective manner.

Landcovers Design is a landscaping design firm. It acquires some customers through contractors, but it depends on individual customers for much of its business. Finding those customers makes the difference between success and failure. Many small industrial suppliers of equipment, such as machine shops or production equipment suppliers, have the same problem: the constant need to locate customers in the market at any given time.

I once helped a small consulting company that was close to going out of business because it couldn't acquire customers. The company used a proprietary osmosis process to correct problems in water purification systems. Its potential customers were companies or municipalities with an immediate problem they couldn't solve themselves. The company didn't have any trouble finding potential customers—it just couldn't get them to call when they needed its services. Its direct mail letters were typically tossed aside, and it couldn't find a cost-effective way to advertise. We generated business by simply giving prospects a reason to remember the firm. We offered a free sample evaluation and a quarterly newsletter. This information was of real value to customers, and people referred to it when a crisis occurred.

You'll find businesses in every town that have the same problem. An upscale jewelry store may generate a certain number of customers from walk-by mall traffic, but it still may need to find another group of customers to survive. A new restaurant may be able to attract diners from a one mile radius, but it may need customers from a five mile radius to survive.

The second part of finding customers is that customers have to be able to find you. This means that you need to have your product in a good distribution channel. Procter & Gamble, Coke, Pepsi, and other consumer giants all fight for shelf space to be sure customers can find their products. By the same token, a great housewares product isn't going anywhere until a store or catalog stocks it.

Motivating Customers

You have the right product, the right market, and several features that make you better than competition. At first glance, you may think you'll have an easy time selling your product. But that's not the case. Customers are bombarded with thousands of messages. There are hundreds of products that they could buy. You still need to find one or two things you can do that will actually motivate customers to take action.

Blue jeans advertisements in the 1993 Super Bowl telecast are examples of great motivation. Levi Strauss set its sights on teenagers and young adults. Its commercials showed Levi's as an item that every teenager is wearing. Levi also supports this image with frequent product changes. However, I was particularly fond of Lee's jeans commercial. It had people sucking in their tummies trying to fit into a regular pair of jeans. I'm forty-three and slumping, and those commercials really motivated me.

Every type of business has motivation problems. How does a car repair company convince people to trust their cars to it? How does a manufacturer convince another company to place its equipment in a new production line? Or how does a day-care center or preschool motivate people to entrust their children to it? All these products need emotional and logical motivation. People have to feel that a business will "do right" by them.

Small industrial suppliers often have the hardest time motivating customers. A tool and die maker might find plenty of prospects, but not be able to motivate them to actually buy. The prospects are reluctant to change suppliers, in part because of the paperwork involved and in part because they have an entrenched relationship with their current supplier. But there are ways for companies to break through, and when they do, they will have a steady supply of business.

Communicating on a Regular Basis

Once you know how to motivate your target customers, you have to communicate with them often enough to get them to take action. For some smaller purchases, this might take only one or two contacts; for larger purchases, you may need to contact customers ten or more times.

Most people think that communicating means advertising. But that's not true. You have dozens of other ways to get your message across to customers. I have to confess that I'm not a big believer in advertising. One reason is that ads are cost-prohibitive for most small businesses simply because they need to be run often before they are effective. Another reason is that ads are not nearly as effective as most people think. In fact, most advertising people won't even use an ad's sales results as a measure of how good the ad was.

Most effective communication programs employ a mix of different tactics. For example, Campbell Soup has a well-balanced program. It runs some TV ads, mostly to promote new products, and newspaper and magazine ads that are aimed at mothers. It has created a strong, well-known identity through its logo, its can design, and its use of the Campbell's Kids in its advertising programs. Campbell also uses newspaper and direct mail coupons to keep its message in front of consumers.

My favorite Campbell Soup tactic is its computer program for schools. Schools that collect enough Campbell proof-of-purchase seals can receive computers, monitors, printers, and other related products. Campbell's furnishes each participating school with four-foot-high soup barrels to remind kids and parents to bring in their labels. This tactic keeps Campbell's name in front of its prime target customer, parents with children, and reinforces its message that "Soup is good food."

Small- to medium-size companies can't afford a big advertising budget. They have to use other tactics, such as store signs, sales calls, newsletters, free speeches and seminars, classes at local colleges, membership in trade associations, direct mailings, personal letters, phone calls, and a host of others to communicate their message.

Finding, motivating, and communicating with customers are three distinct tasks, but all of them have to be done well if you are to succeed. As an example, look at the marketing strategy of Media Exposure, a service business that helps people get on radio and TV talk shows. Its target customers are authors, marketers, company spokespersons, and anyone else who wants a chance to sell or promote a product or service on either local or national talk shows.

Media Exposure first has to find people who have a product or service to promote that would interest a radio or talk show host. To do this, it can run ads in local business newspapers, give speeches, attend trade shows, follow up on newspaper and magazine stories, or do direct mailings. Next, Media Exposure needs to know what will motivate people to spend $100 to $1,000 to get a radio or TV appearance. People's expectations and desires, the type of sales a company can generate from an appearance, and how to use an appearance to generate future publicity are just a few of the factors the company should look at in order to create motivation.

The last step is to communicate with the customers. You may wonder why this step is needed. The reason is that in most cases, people start to look around for possible products or services well before they actually need them. A new author may check out publicity angles six to twelve months before his or her book is actually published. Media Exposure needs to keep in contact with prospects during that six to twelve months so that they will call when they are ready to buy. It can do this with newsletters, seminars, speeches, and direct mailings.

Making the Sale

Why has Wal-Mart crushed Sears and taken over as the nation's number one retailer? There are many factors involved, but one of the biggest is that Wal-Mart knows more about making a sale. Stand-alone stores, superior customer service, easy-to-understand store layouts, and an image of caring about the customer all lead to both more sales when people enter a store and more repeat sales.

The first five steps are all designed to get customers predisposed to buy your product or service. All that work is worthless if you can't make the final sale. Knowing how to trigger that final sales decision is a critical marketing tactic.

This is my third book, and I'm interested in what makes people buy a particular book. My last book was *How to Bring a Product to Marketing for Less Than $5,000*. My business assists inventors, and I've been surveying the two or three people a week who call me after reading the book. What I've learned is this: People initially pick the book up (finding customers) because it is in the store; they like the title, and they have an idea to introduce. They are motivated to open the book because of the copy on the cover, which promises a unique, low-cost method of introducing a product. But over 70 percent of them don't actually buy the book until they look at the index and see that the book offers a solution to their specific problem.

What does Wal-Mart really do? It puts people into a buying mood. Every business has a few final details it needs to deliver in order to get the sale. But there is more than that involved in getting the final sale. People are typically apprehensive just before they make a purchase. A salesperson is usually needed to get the customer to make the final decision to buy. Knowing how to handle that person-to-person contact can make the difference between success and failure.

Boyd, Tammney, Cross is an advertising agency in Philadelphia. It provides high-quality service, but so do dozens of other agencies. Customers can't really know which agency will give better service, so Boyd Tammney Cross' success depends on its ability to close the sale.

THE SIX STEPS TO SUCCESS: REAL-LIFE EXAMPLES

A&P

For years the country's largest grocery store chain, A&P slid into a deep decline in the 1970s. The chain did everything wrong. Stodgy, run-down stores, poor customer service, and lackluster displays all hurt sales. A&P's strategy was simply to put products on store shelves and wait for people to buy them. A&P's tactics may have worked fifty years ago, but they certainly didn't work in an era where fierce competition is a marketer's daily reality.

A&P is growing again, and currently has over 1,000 stores. It achieved this remarkable turnaround by following the six key steps:

1. It targeted working couples as its customers. To meet the needs of this group, A&P remodeled and enlarged stores, and added food items and store features (delis, seafood bars, and bakeries) that appealed to high-income, very busy working couples.

2. It created a sustainable product edge by devoting management time and effort to its delis and seafood bars. The result was that targeted customers preferred A&P's stores because of these two areas.

3. It directed mailings, ads, circulars, coupons, and publicity to business and residential areas where upscale working couples could be found. These efforts were designed to encourage people to visit the store at least once.

4. It motivated customers with carefully chosen product selections and with locations in targeted residential areas.

5. A&P communicated with customers through its store layouts and product selection. It also placed signs in appropriate residential neighborhoods and became involved in community projects to keep its name visible.

6. A&P put people into a buying mode with its stores' ambiance, location, product selection, and greatly improved customer selection.

Chrysler Mini-van

No company seems to go back and forth from the brink of disaster more often than Chrysler. But there is no doubt that its mini-van was one of the great product introductions of the 1980s. Chrysler, too, followed the six marketing steps:

1. Chrysler targeted families with children, a large group that had specific, unanswered product needs. The mini-van was ideal for these customers because it provided space and easy access for families that had to cart around baseball equipment, playpens, cribs, and an assortment of their children's friends.

2. There was nothing like the mini-van on the market. Station wagons didn't offer the room or accessibility of the mini-van, and full-size vans didn't offer the same passenger space or comfort. Chrysler's advantage was sustainable because a lead time of three to four years is needed to put a new car on the market.

3. Chrysler didn't have to worry about finding customers, but it did run extensive publicity and direct mail programs.

4. People are usually reluctant to buy a new product. Chrysler built confidence in the mini-van by orchestrating an incredible publicity program, with positive reviews from virtually every magazine and newspaper critic. In addition, Chrysler priced the mini-van below most station wagons so that it was a particularly good value.

5. Chrysler's communication plan called for dealer displays and promotion, advertising, publicity, and sponsorship of certain key community events.

6. Momentum is almost irresistible to many people, and Chrysler certainly had it. Chrysler's dealer network was also in place to close sales.

Southwest Airlines

At the end of 1992 virtually every airline was losing money, and lots of it. Southwest Airlines bucked the trend and actually made money. Again, part of the reason was that it had a sound program that covered all six key marketing steps:

1. Southwest targeted smaller, underserved cities with frequent, inexpensive trips to a nearby city, such as low-cost flights from Sacramento to Los Angeles.

2. Southwest's differential advantage was both flight frequency (it had three to four times as many flights as competitors) and low prices (often only half as much as other airlines were charging).

3. Southwest found customers through campaigns directed at travel agents, large companies, and affluent residents. Another tactic it used was billboard advertising in locations near the airport.

4. Confidence is one factor that motivates people to choose a particular airline. Southwest inspires confidence with friendly, helpful employees. Southwest has those types of workers because of an intensive employee training and screening program.

5. Southwest communicates through its airport presence, billboard ads, newspaper publicity, and travel agent contacts.

6. Convenience and price are the two tactics that Southwest uses to close the sale. Southwest has automatic ticket machines that dispense tickets in just twenty seconds, and it doesn't require people to buy a ticket in advance to qualify for the discount.

All three of these companies also had strong financial management and effective operating divisions. But the third leg of the triangle is an effective marketing program that includes all six steps to success.

Section 1

Discovering Where the Money Is

This book will show you how to use many effective marketing tactics. These tactics will work, but you still will not make any money unless you choose to compete in a profitable area. This means that you must target the right customer, with the right product, through the right market channel.

This first section helps you choose a playing field where you can be successful. Section 2, "Being Better than Everyone Else," helps you create a sustainable advantage. Sections 3 through 6 show you how to find, motivate, and sell to customers. But profitable marketing always starts with discovering where you can make money.

Chapter 2

Finding the Right Customers

In Minneapolis, Target discount stores and Cub Foods, a large food retailer, have successful stores in some of the most down-and-out neighborhoods, while Saks Fifth Avenue and Dayton's, two upscale department stores, have profitable locations in a downtown business district. These stores have radically different customers. Finding the right customer doesn't necessarily mean finding prospects with high incomes. You have to find customers who will let you charge more for your product or service than it costs you to produce it.

You can find the right customer for any type of business, no matter how competitive it is. Lionel Sosa decided to quit his job and start his own advertising and specialty promotion agency in San Antonio, Texas. Advertising is a tough business; there are dozens of agencies fighting for business at every medium-size large company in America. But Sosa's billings have grown more than 600 percent in just a few years, even though his target customers were big companies such as Budweiser, Coke, and Burger King. To find his perfect customer, Sosa segmented these customers by objective, such as motivating young adults or appealing to people over fifty. Competition in most of these was stiff, but one area where competition was light was motivating Hispanic prospects. That was the opening that Sosa used to develop his business.

Some readers may have the flexibility to target any set of customers; others will be tied to a geographic location and will have to find the best available customers. This chapter will show you how to do both. It's divided into three sections: how to find underserved customers, how to determine which customers are profitable, and how to determine if a customer segment can support your business.

FINDING UNDERSERVED CUSTOMERS

Munsingwear, the knit shirt manufacturer best known for its penguin logo, recently came out of Chapter 11 bankruptcy. Sales are up, and profits are recovering. Munsingwear came back because it started to focus on an underserved customer segment, golf pro shops. Those shops are always looking for high-priced, high-margin products. Munsingwear provided just that, with shirts with the famous penguin logo that could be sold for $25 to $50.

Munsingwear's target customers were golf pro shops. Golfers are the final customers, but they are hardly underserved. Hundreds of stores and catalog houses are anxious to sell the golfer whatever he or she wants. Golf pro shops can't compete on price with those outlets because they are small and don't have enough volume. So they need products that are different from those that can be bought at regular stores.

As the examples of Lionel Sosa and Munsingwear both show, you need to keep segmenting potential customers until you find a group that isn't getting the products or services it needs. At first glance, both companies are competing for their target customers with dozens, if not hundreds, of other companies. However, both companies knew that competing in a crowded market can be suicide, so they looked at different ways to segment customers until they could find a group with unmet needs.

Ways to Segment Customers

There are hundreds of ways to segment customers. Some of the more common ways are:

- Size
- Usage
- Benefits
- Lifestyles
- Occupation
- Predispositions
- Distribution channels
- Geography
- Process
- Company versus individual
- Income
- Social class
- Personality
- Family size.

Size

Joe Sugar sells clothes to people who have trouble finding clothes that fit because they are tall, small, wide, or skinny. His business grossed $2 million in 1992, despite the fact that his store is in a small town with only two stoplights. Sugar's motto is, "If you have a figure, I can fit it," and he carries clothes in every conceivable size. His stock includes more than 11,000 pairs of pants, 8,000 suits, and 5,000 shirts—in a town of 2,000! By concentrating on a customer segment that couldn't get clothes anywhere else, Sugar draws customers from a huge radius and consistently outsells stores in much bigger cities.

Other firms might segment by how large a business is, the dollar amount of a contracting job, the size of production equipment, or the size of production runs. For example, the target customer of one company I consulted for was companies with production runs of 1,000 to 3,000 PC boards with over 400 components.

Usage

Industrial suppliers often segment customers by usage. One manufacturer of equipment that measures coating thickness might specialize in chrome coatings, while another manufacturer might specialize in gold coatings. Each application has a different set of problems that a supplier could work to resolve.

Service businesses such as engineering firms, architects, or marketing consultants also often specialize by usage. An architectural firm might specialize in designing the interior of retail stores, an engineering firm might specialize in pavement testing and evaluation, and a marketing consultant might specialize in new product introductions.

Benefits

Some people who buy back support devices want less pain. Others engage in heavy lifting and buy a device to prevent injury. Chiropractors might want to offer these devices to generate income or to provide better patient care. Each of these customer groups has a different set of product requirements. Frequently, most competitors concentrate their efforts on the biggest customer group, leaving the needs of some of the smaller groups unmet. Those are the groups you want to focus your attention on.

Lifestyle

Eddie Bauer sells high-quality products for people who want to look good, but who are also active outdoors. Therefore, Eddie Bauer needs well-constructed clothes that can take the wear and tear of hiking and camping expeditions.

Predisposition

In 1993, there was a large group of people who were predisposed to buy items made from recycled products. Other people usually buy the same products as their parents. Manufacturing companies are predisposed to stick with a production method, an inventory control system, or certain product features. For example, one company may prefer injection-molded parts, whereas another might use a rotational molding process to make similar parts.

Distribution Channel

Devee Philpot introduced the Junk Drawer Organizer and turned it into a million-dollar product. She targeted one market channel, organizational stores such as Lector's, The Container Store, and Mjeir's, to sell her product through. She could have targeted discount stores, mail-order catalogs, home centers, or large drugstore chains. But she chose organizational stores because those stores didn't have as many products to choose from and were actively looking for new products.

Other plastics manufacturers might sell through hardware stores, large discount stores, smaller chains such as Woolworth's, mail-order catalogs, or a network of distributors or manufacturers' representatives.

Geography

Minnesota is a fishing hotbed, with a large number of experienced, dedicated fishermen and women. A new fishing lure supplier might choose to enter the

Minnesota market, where competition would be fierce, or it might choose to enter a smaller, less competitive market in the South or on the East Coast.

Family Size
While many hotels cater to business travelers, not nearly as many cater to families traveling with children. So Holiday Inn responded with a promotion that lets kids traveling with their parents eat and sleep free.

Income, Occupation, and Social Class
I have two children, aged ten and eight, and I've spent some time looking into day care. The choice always seems to boil down to a nanny, who is expensive, or a understaffed, overcrowded day-care center that is supposed to appeal to everyone else. This is an example of poor customer segmentation. There should be different types of day-care centers, each appealing to a different group of people.

Process
Service businesses and industrial suppliers can segment customers by the type of manufacturing process they use; for example, plastics manufacturers might use vacuum forming, injection molding, rotational molding, or hand layup processes. Suppliers can specialize in any one process.

Company Versus Individual
Some carpenters, masonry contractors, and electricians will work only for builders or large companies. Others work primarily for individuals. Each customer segment will have different needs.

Finding the right customer is important if you want to break through the communication clutter that surrounds most people. For example, how many times do you need to see a Hardees commercial before you remember it? Probably quite a few. But why should you remember the commercial? You can already buy from McDonald's, Burger King, and Wendy's. You really don't have a compelling reason to pay attention. What happens when high-income gadget lovers see a Sharper Image ad? They pay attention. Finding the right customer lets you communicate more effectively, and with better results.

Segmenting Your Customers

For Consumers
1. Segment your customers by broad categories that reflect the most important differences. For example, a jewelry store might decide that the most important difference between categories of shoppers is income. High-, medium-, and low-income buyers look for different types of jewelry. A computer manufacturer might feel that usage is the most important characteristic, and a radio station might consider age its key consideration. In some cases, you may have two or three equally important characteristics—for example: income, usage, and lifestyle could all be key points. Then use them all to segment customers—for example: Eddie Bauer might segment customers by lifestyle, income, and image. Your

goal is to find a customer group with unmet needs. You might need to divide customers into twenty groups to find one group that is underserved.

2. Next, take each customer group and determine the reasons why those customers buy. For example, people might buy because of price, a product feature, status, quality, or a variety of other factors. The best way to find out why a group buys a certain type of product is to take a survey. List every possible reason people might buy on a form, then ask people you know or people who have bought your product to indicate their top three considerations in buying a product. Figure 2.1 shows such a market survey for a business phone system.

Figure 2.1

MARKET SURVEY: NEW PHONE SYSTEM

Reason for Purchase	Important		Priority Rating
	Yes	No	(List Top Three Reasons Only)
Low cost	_____	_____	_____
Brand name	_____	_____	_____
Ease of installation	_____	_____	_____
Ease of use	_____	_____	_____
Appearance	_____	_____	_____
Product features	_____	_____	_____
Intercom	_____	_____	_____
Speakerphone	_____	_____	_____
Ability to add music	_____	_____	_____
Switching capabilities	_____	_____	
Fax and modem compatibility	_____	_____	_____
Service	_____	_____	_____
Warranty length	_____	_____	_____
Repair capabilities	_____	_____	_____
Past performance	_____	_____	_____
Recommendations	_____	_____	_____
Past experience	_____	_____	_____
Other reasons	_____	_____	_____
	_____	_____	_____
	_____	_____	_____
	_____	_____	_____

3. Group the answers into categories, such as applications, personality, status, style, performance, and new technology. These categories will differ for different types of products. You should end up with twelve to twenty groups, such as companies testing incoming materials; companies using the product for final testing; and companies using equipment as a process monitoring device.

From these customer categories, you want to find groups of people whose needs aren't being met. As an example, I'll go through the three steps for the Tattered Cover bookstore in Denver, Colorado. This store covers four floors and stocks a wide variety of books on virtually any topic—over 5,000 books in all.

1. The owner might decide that the most important way of categorizing customers is number of books purchased in a year. A large purchaser might buy twenty-five or more books per year, a medium buyer five to twenty-five books, and a small purchaser fewer than five books.

2. A survey conducted to find out the reasons people buy books might show that high-volume book purchasers buy because they enjoy reading, want to be up-to-date on the newest technology, like to give books as presents, want an impressive-looking library, have specific problems to solve, want to understand what's happening in the world, enjoy best sellers or romance novels, and want to expose their children to fine literature.

3. Using these answers, customers could be grouped into buyers of self-help books, occupation-related information, history and current events, best sellers, and fine literature.

The owner could then see which of these customer groups weren't able to buy the products they want.

FOR INDUSTRIAL ACCOUNTS

Businesses make three different types of purchases. The first is one-time or infrequent purchases. A new phone system, like the one in Figure 2.1, is an example, as is new production or packaging equipment to handle increased or new production. Companies make these purchases for a variety of reasons, and their behavior is similar to consumers'. You can segment customers into groups by the reasons they purchase and look for a group that isn't having its needs met.

The second type of purchase is recurring purchases—raw materials, a consulting service, or office supplies, for example. Companies do not like to switch suppliers if they are happy with their current ones. For this type of purchase, you want to know what customers don't like about current suppliers and what additional features they would like to have.

1. Discover all the buying influences for the product. This could include buyers, production managers, line workers, engineers, inspectors, and even the marketing and sales managers. Most people don't think of marketing and sales people as buying influences, but I have requested, and received product or vendor changes any time, I felt they gave a sales advantage.

2. Talk to people in every type of company that uses your product to see what needs they have. Buyers are often the worst source of information; they usually say everything is okay. Production managers, engineers, and marketing people are usually your best sources of information.

3. Contact manufacturers' representatives who have been in the industry a long time. You can find their names in the *Directory of Manufacturers'*

Representatives. You may need to pay a fee for their help in interviewing people, but they can often get through to people that you can't reach.

Companies make other purchases because they have a critical need. A production problem, a breakdown in an inventory system, a quality issue that must be solved, and a customer's demand for immediate shipment are all situations where such a need exists. This is the type of sale you want to look for. In my industrial experiences, at least half of all new clients were gained because a supplier solved a problem. It could be a new problem or a problem with current products. You need to keep your antennas up to find these needs.

1. Keep up your membership in industry associations. Also have an employee be a member of ASTM, which sets standards for material testing. You pick up key information about current needs or problems from these groups.

2. List your company under a vague heading in product directories. For example, if your product measures gold thickness, list it under gold thickness measurement, but also list it under thickness testers. This way you'll get inquiries from people in trouble.

3. Provide a troubleshooting department that will look into, and attempt to solve, any customer problem.

4. Set up an engineering council or advisory board that can meet periodically to suggest product improvements, or new problems or needs that you can address.

ACTION STEPS

1. Create a chart entitled "Customer Segments," and list five to twenty customer groups for your type of products.

2. Rank the customer segments by how well they are served. Give your top ranking to the customer group that has the fewest products offered to it. However, don't automatically take this group as your target customer, as you still need to determine which customer groups will both be profitable and match your profit objectives.

WHICH CUSTOMERS ARE PROFITABLE

Back in the 1970s, Timex lost its market position in low-cost watches to digital watches. Yet by the late 1980s Timex was back, and was claiming one-third of America's $1.5 million watch market. Timex engineered this amazing turnaround by targeting young people involved in sports activities, such as running, swimming, jogging, and bicycling. It created sports watches for each activity that helped athletes fine tune their performance.

Timex's target had the two key characteristics of a profitable customer group: its members are easy to find, and they allow you to charge a profitable price. Timex could find these sports enthusiasts through sports magazines aimed at runners, bicyclists, swimmers, and triathlon athletes, or by purchasing entrant lists for relevant sports events like a local community's marathon. Sports enthusiasts will pay top dollar for products that will help them in their hobby. Many of them consider their commitment to sports an important part of their lives, and they buy premium products for every aspect of their sport. They are ideal target customers.

Customers That Are Easy to Reach

Fortunately, marketers rarely start from scratch in trying to find and locate prospects. Instead, they have several methods available that let them reach customers easily, including dealer networks, other distribution outlets, location, specialized magazines, mailing lists, exhibits and shows, and networks of clubs and associations.

Dealer networks

Toro and LawnBoy have been major brand names in the lawn market for years. Targeting lawnmower customers can be difficult because there is no way of knowing who will buy a lawnmower in any given year. At $200 to $300 each, lawnmowers also don't support an extensive advertising budget. Toro and Lawn-Boy overcome this handicap by selling through an established network of highly visible lawn and garden equipment dealers.

People in a neighborhood drive by a dealer for years, then visit it when they are ready to buy. Appliance makers, carpet producers, and TV manufacturers are other businesses that use a dealer network to reach customers.

Other distribution outlets

Flight Time is a small airline that provides emergency charter service to virtually any destination in the world. Its clients are typically celebrities and business executives. At first glance you might think Flight Time would have a hard time reaching potential clients in a cost-effective manner. But it does it through travel agents. In 1991 Flight Time did over $6 million in business without spending a dime on advertising.

Location

Many businesses simply reach customers through their location. People drive by, see the company's sign, and stop in when the time is right. Drugstores, gas stations, appliance dealers, carpet stores, and small convenience stores all depend on location to generate business. Other stores, such as Musicland and B. Dalton bookstores, depend on a mall location to reach customers. Of course, premium locations are expensive, and virtually every person driving or walking by must be a prospective customer for this strategy to pay off.

Specialized magazines

One reason Timex was able to reach its targeted customers was that there are magazines for runners, for walkers, for swimmers, and for participants in virtually every other sport. A recent issue of *Popular Mechanics* had ads from well over 100 small companies. People advertise in *Popular Mechanics* because it goes out to more than 5 million home handymen, which is a well-targeted customer segment.

Mailing lists

A direct mail campaign that John Deere directed to 20,000 farmers drew 5,000 of them into dealer showrooms and sold $40 million of equipment. The campaign consisted of four mailings that included a variety of giveaway items such as toy truck banks, magic kits, and stopwatches. The program was expensive, but it was effective because most, if not all, of the 20,000 farmers were ideal target customers. How did John Deere get the names of 20,000 farmers? From mailing lists. These can be gathered from county tax rolls, ownership records at co-ops, or customer lists of other farm suppliers. The point is that a mailing list of farmers is easily obtained because farmers identify themselves in many ways. You can also buy an accurate mailing list of dentists, homeowners, or small business owners, because those groups also identify themselves in a public way.

Shows

A landscape architect recently told me that he found 80 percent of his customers through a spring lawn and garden show. Some businesses, especially industrial suppliers and manufacturers that supply a small retail market, such as party supply stores, have conventions, trade shows, or consumer shows that may supply 50 percent or more of a company's business.

Clubs and associations

Some customers, especially hobbyists, are members of clubs or other groups, such as computer bulletin boards, engineering or accounting trade groups, or coaches of youth sports teams.

Will Customers Be Profitable?

Are your targeted customers going to be willing to pay more for your product or service than it costs you to deliver it? Important points to consider are: Is the purchase important? Do features dominate the buying decision? Are you meeting a specialized need? Do customers have a predisposition to buy your product? How much choice do customers have?

Is the purchase important?

Cub Foods has profitable stores in low-income neighborhoods. Cub can always get a fair price because people need to eat. Products sold for hobbies, status, or adventure also represent something important to buyers and can generate a profitable price.

Lisa Kanarek started a company called Everything's Organized. She could have targeted either people in companies or homeowners. She decided that organizing offices would be more profitable, because people were much more concerned about being efficient at work than they were about being efficient at home.

Do features dominate the purchase decision?

When you buy gas, you buy it at a convenient location that has a low price. You don't worry about the features of gas; you just worry about the price. When you buy products such as paint, household furnishings, or word processing equipment, however, your first concern is features. These products allow you to charge a higher price.

Some customers, such as engineers, are typically more interested in features, whereas other groups, such as accountants, are often most interested in price.

Are you meeting a specialized need?

At one time Bethlehem Steel sold steel primarily to traditional large users, such as car companies. After a brush with financial disaster, Bethlehem started concentrating on smaller customers with specialized needs, where it could add value and generate more profit.

Are customers predisposed to buy your product?

Mike Wing owns Info Plan, a company that offers customized market research for small- and medium-size businesses. Mike didn't target large companies, even though they had more money to spend, because they were predisposed to use big market research firms. Mike could break into that market only by offering extremely low prices. Small firms, in contrast, are owned by entrepreneurs who are sympathetic to another small-businessperson.

How much choice do customers have?

Prices are always higher in small towns where customers don't have any choice. Drug companies often have to drop their prices substantially when generic versions of their products become available. And price wars are common on airline routes that several airlines fly. You will always make more money if you alone can provide a product or service.

ACTION STEPS

1. Refer to your list of customer groups. Place an X by each group for every one of the following characteristics that make customers easy to reach that is has:

   - Readily available dealer networks
   - Helpful distribution outlets
   - Highly visible locations
   - Availability of target specialized magazines
   - Access to well-defined mailing lists
   - Currently operating shows and conventions
   - A large network of clubs and associations.

2. Go through your list again and place an * by each group for every one of the following characteristics that will make customers profitable that it has:

   - The product is important to them
   - Features dominate their purchase decision
   - They have specialized needs
   - They are predisposed to buy this type of product
   - They have few alternatives to your product

SUPPORTING YOUR BUSINESS

General Mills recently opened the Olive Garden chain of moderately priced Italian restaurants. Chilli's Grill and Bar, Applebee's, Fresh Choice, Shoney's Big Boy, and Bob Evans are just a few of the low- to medium-priced restaurant chains in America—all targeted at similar customers. These companies are definitely not focusing their attention on underserved customers.

The problem these restaurant chains have is that they need a big market to support their corporate expenses and profit objectives. And most Americans are middle class, so that's the segment these chains have to go after. Big companies may have some advantages, but they are also forced to compete in large customer segments where competition is intense. Small companies have a definite edge because they can select smaller segments where competition will be light.

Peggy Glen is a small entrepreneur who started and still owns the Firefighters Bookstore, a mail-order catalog business. She supplies about 100 different books to a mailing list of approximately 10,000 firefighters. Glen's income matches her goals, but her market is far too small for someone looking for big profits.

Earlier I wrote about Munsingwear and its target customer, golf pro shops. This segment worked for Munsingwear only after it cut its work force from 2,000 to 350 employees. If Munsingwear wants to expand, it will have to find a bigger customer base.

Estimating Profit Potential

You want to choose a segment that is big enough for your profit objectives. To determine profit potential, multiply your potential sales revenues by the average industry margin. Margin is the amount of profit divided by actual sales. For example, if the potential sales to a customer group are $2 million and the industry margin is 10 percent, then your expected profit is $200,000. This does not mean you will make $200,000 per year, but instead that $200,000 is your potential profit.

You'll know right away that some customer groups are big enough to support your goals. For example, if your target group is the million or more engineers interested in drafting software and your profit goal is $250,000, you can easily achieve your goal. But in other cases you might not be so sure, and you'll need to learn to estimate a customer group's potential.

Sales potential

The most dependable way to estimate sales is to check the sales volume of other companies selling to the same customer group. For example, Munsingwear might look at the volume of pants manufacturers are selling to golf shops. To find another company's sales volume, you can:

1. Call the company's headquarters and ask for a copy of its annual report.
2. Call the local paper in the company's home town and ask for copies of any stories run on the company.
3. Call the company and ask how many employees or salespeople it has.
4. For retail locations, spend a few hours a day for a week or so observing the number of people entering the store and the number purchasing prod-

ucts. Try to get an idea of the average purchase amount. You can also talk to the store's employees to get a feel for the volume.

5. Ask salespeople or manufacturers' representatives in the market for their estimate of a company's sales. You can get the name of a contact by calling up and asking for sales information, then calling the person whose name is on the cover letter you receive with the brochure.

To find the number of target customers in a market, you can:

1. Check the size of the mailing lists of trade magazines and associations. Most associations and virtually all magazines will sell mailing lists. You can find out quite a bit of information by looking at the sales materials for the list.

2. Buy the list of attendees at past trade shows. This will also give you information about different types of customer groups.

Some businesses don't have other companies to compare themselves to. They can still estimate their sales potential with a three step approach:

1. Find five or six other products, services, or retail stores that cater to the same customers.

2. Get a group of five to ten potential customers and ask them to rank the products, services, or stores by their likelihood of buying or using them.

3. Estimate sales by finding out the volume of products ranked just above or below yours.

Average Margins

Most industries have a margin that is reasonably consistent. You can find that margin in several ways:

1. Through articles in industry trade magazines. A trade magazine is one that deals with an industry; for example, *Hardware Age* written for manufacturers and retailers in the hardware business. Ask people in the same type of business what magazines they read. You can also find the names of trade magazines in *Gale's Source of Publications*, which can be found in major libraries. Subscribe to trade magazines for your industry; they will often have articles on typical industry financial data. You can also call up the editor or staff writers and ask for the information.

2. By contacting salespeople and manufacturers' representatives that are experienced in the industry.

3. From industry-wide associations. Call and ask them for any industry financial data they have. You can find the names of associations at your local library in the *Book of Associations*.

4. From the *Almanac of Business and Financial Ratios* (published by Prentice-Hall), which is available in most large libraries.

ACTION STEPS

1. Go back to the chart you prepared that listed underserved customer segments with X's for the characteristics that make them easy to reach and *'s for their profitable characteristics.
2. For the groups that this chart indicates will be profitable, estimate the total profits that the group could generate.

Chapter 3

Uncovering the Right Product

The $3 billion shampoo market is shared by over 100 brands. Yet Helene Curtis launched a new shampoo, Vibrance, and quickly had over $25 million in sales. Helene Curtis succeeded because it discovered that customers wanted radiance and shine, two qualities they didn't think they were getting from available products. Sheri Poe believed that Nike, Reebok, and L.A. Gear were offering women scaled-down versions of men's shoes that didn't give them the features they needed. She started her own company, Rykä, which sold shoes geared to the specific needs of women. Sales rose to $8 million in just three years.

New products, services, and retail stores succeed every year, sometimes in what appear to be very crowded market areas. They typically owe their success to the fact that they discovered a product that supplies a feature or benefit that their target customers want or need, but that no other competitor supplies.

You can find the right product for your business by following four steps:

1. Determine possible products you could offer to your targeted customers.
2. Prepare a short product questionnaire.
3. Get a sampling of customers to answer the questionnaire.
4. Decide which of the products that customers want you can make a profit from.

DETERMINING POSSIBLE PRODUCTS OR SERVICES

Sheri Poe developed Rykä to provide shoes for women who exercised. She felt she had the right customer segment, women who bought sports shoes. Her next step was to determine the right product for this market. To do this, she needed to get a rough idea of what her targeted customers wanted by talking to people and using her own experiences. Then, just to be sure she was right, she needed to develop a questionnaire and take a more formal survey.

Factors to Consider

The best way to get product features is to develop your own list from the information you obtained when you were looking for a customer group to serve, then get additional information from outside sources. When looking for ways to develop the right product, consider product features and benefits, solutions to customers' problems, and services customers would like to receive.

Features and benefits

You might meet targeted customers' unmet needs with a new feature, a new mix of features, or a modified feature. Whirlpool identified as a customer group people who wanted a clean, almost aseptic-looking kitchen. This group didn't want knobs, handles, knickknacks, toasters, or anything else cluttering up their kitchens. Whirlpool found that these customers wanted, among other things, Corning Ware stove tops, flat fronts, and clean touch-pad controls on their stoves.

Solutions

People often buy a product to solve a problem. You may be able to add additional products, or even other features, that will help customers solve their problems. Cyndie Bender runs the Meridian Travel Agency. She chose corporate accounts as her target customers. She discovered that corporate accounts' main concern wasn't getting employees from place to place—that was easily done. Instead, they were looking for a way to keep employees within corporate travel guidelines. So Bender started providing the reports and controls that companies wanted, and her business took off.

I consulted briefly for a small company that sold a new, improved system for waterproofing basements. The product's primary market was contractors. The company felt it was solving a big problem by eliminating wet basements. But that wasn't the contractors' worry at all. They wanted to sell more houses. The company switched its efforts to solving what contractors perceived to be their problem. It offered a lifetime guarantee and a sales documentation package that helped contractors sell houses.

Service

Auto dealerships, computer stores, heating and air conditioning services, appliance outlets, and technical schools all include services as a part of their standard sales package. But they can go further and use service as a way of meeting a customer segment's needs. For example, a downtown car dealer could target busy executives that work in the downtown area. It could offer free shuttle service between its dealership and nearby office buildings for warranty repairs. Or a technical school that targets recent high school graduates might offer three Saturdays of follow-up training after graduates get their first job.

Ideas from Outside Sources

Your initial review should give you a list of ten to twenty features, services, or new products to include. Before you develop and administer a questionnaire, you should talk to other people from outside sources, who will give you ideas you wouldn't think of otherwise. You can get ideas from advisory boards, trade shows, and customer suggestions.

Advisory boards

An advisory board is a group of potential customers, or even a group of vendors, who can meet with you every month or two to give you ideas about ways to improve your business. People really enjoy being on a board, and they'll offer you a steady stream of features you can add. Vendor advisory groups can give you information about things other companies are doing that might affect your plans.

Trade shows

Trade shows are conventions for people in the industry. Trade shows are where most new products are introduced, and where you can see the trends in the industry. I like to attend trade shows because I like to see what new product features are well received by customers. That information can help you choose the features you will offer. Trade shows also give you the opportunity to talk to customers about what types of products they are looking for.

Customer suggestions

I used to get some of my best product ideas from warranty cards. At the end of the card there were a few lines for customers to list either features they'd like improved or features they'd like added to the product. Not all of the ideas were valuable, but every now and then someone had a great suggestion. Be alert to customers' suggestions, and write down the ones you think are best.

Once you finish this exercise, you should have a fairly extensive list of possible product features and services that you can offer customers. For example, consider a builder who has targeted high-income families that like to entertain. Some of the features it might consider are:

- Large, multi-level deck
- Center islands in kitchen
- Wide-open layout between kitchen, dining, and family rooms
- Heated Jacuzzi for eight on deck
- Built-in bar in family room
- Built-in large-screen TV in family room
- Speakers for stereo system on deck and throughout home
- Wooden hanging racks for holding glasses.

The builder might actually end up with fifteen to twenty features that could be included in the final product. Before actually adding those features, however, the builder needs to survey customers further to see which features will make them buy and which can be profitable.

ACTION STEPS

1. List features, additional products, or services that you could offer that you feel your target customers might want.
2. Even if it's only on a one-time basis, set up an advisory board of your targeted customers and see what features they'd like you to have.
3. Set up a system to receive routine comments from customers. Ask questions on warranty cards, or call people one or two months after they buy to get their suggestions on how to improve your product.

PREPARING A PRODUCT QUESTIONNAIRE

At this point you have found an underserved customer group, and you know some of the features or services they might want. You now have to spend time, money, and effort to produce your new product. Before you make that commitment, it makes sense to prepare a short product questionnaire to be sure you are on the right track.

Rules to Follow

You have to prepare a questionnaire carefully in order to get accurate results. After all, everyone will tell you that he or she would like a big deck with a Jacuzzi. What you need to determine is whether he or she will buy one. The four rules you should follow with a questionnaire are:

1. Use other products as comparisons.

2. Offer people options to choose from.

3. Ask people to rank their choices.

4. Find out if people will really buy.

Comparisons

If you ask people if it is important for a lawnmower to have a starting primer, almost everyone will answer yes. But they will also answer yes to virtually every other feature you ask them about, and you won't know any more than you did when you started your survey. You'll get much better information if you ask people to choose from five mowers, two with a primer and three without. If people consistently choose the mowers with a primer, even at a higher cost, you will know that the feature is important.

Choice

A comparison is made between two similar products, and a choice is made between two different products that provide the same benefit. For example, Little Caesar's, Domino's, and Pizza Hut all offer the same benefit, pizza. But they all operate differently. Domino's specializes in delivery, Little Caesar's in carry-out pizzas at a low price, and Pizza Hut in sit-down restaurants.

Little Caesar's would want to ask people to choose among the three concepts in three or four situations in which people might buy pizza. For example, the situations might be: when a family is going out for an evening and doesn't have time to cook; when people come home late from an outing and everyone is hungry; or when a family is going to stay home and watch videos.

Our builder of luxury homes for entertaining should offer a choice between a home set up for casual entertaining and one designed for more formal parties.

Prioritizing

When you buy a breakfast cereal, what is most important to you? Taste? Price? Nutritional value? How much the kids like it? Coupons? Or premium offers on the back of a package?

You may have found from a taste comparison that people like nuts, raisins, or apple chips in their cereals. Those ingredients add costs. Which is more important to customers: low cost or good taste? Or is there a compromise between the two? Different target customers, such as families, professionals, and health-conscious adults, will have different sets of priorities.

When you are doing a survey, ask people to rank all of your features, with the most important feature first. Also ask them to weight each feature on a scale of one to ten. A person might give an important feature a weighting of eight and an unimportant feature only a two. Finally, ask people to indicate the features a product has to have before they will buy it. Customers may rate some features as relatively unimportant just because every product has them. Your sales might never take off if you leave those features off.

Leave one or two blank spaces in case people feel that an unlisted feature is their top priority.

Will they really buy?

Customers like a lot of products that they don't buy. After all, people have only so much money, and only so much time to use the products they do buy. So, at the end of a survey, it's good to add a reality check to see if people will really buy your product. Again, you need to offer them a choice.

This is easy to do if people can make a direct comparison between your products or services and competitors'. Examples would be a clothing store, a divorce attorney, a dentist or physician, a barbecue sauce, or a baseball glove. You just have to let people compare your products to competitors', then ask them which one they'd buy.

If you have a totally different product, you can't do a direct comparison. Then you need to compare your product to other somewhat similar products and ask people which they would buy. Recently I did an evaluation of the Dish-Net, a net with hooks that holds down small items and plastic cups in the dishwasher tray. It prevents cups from overturning and filling with dirty water, and keeps small parts from falling out of the tray and into the heating element.

I had seventeen people list the likelihood of their purchasing these items: the Dish-Net, a set of microwave cooking dishes, an apple corer and slicer, and an easy-to-pour spout for milk cartons, and a lint removing roller. These products were similar in that they were housewares that sold for from $4 to $7. Four out of seventeen people listed the Dish-Net as their top purchase priority, and eight out of seventeen said they would buy it.

Creating the Questionnaire

Figure 3.1 shows a questionnaire for a knock-down awning system.

FIGURE 3.1

KNOCK-DOWN AWNING SYSTEM PRODUCT QUESTIONNAIRE

Product description: A new, less expensive awning alternative. The system has a permanently attached top holding bar and side holders, but the rest of the awning can be quickly detached and stored. The awning would have a life of four to six years, versus a life of six to ten years for a standard heavier canvas awning and ten to fifteen years for an aluminum or steel awning. This light-weight awning would require less maintenance, especially in colder climates where it could be removed in the winter.

Your name (optional):

Age:	20-30	30-40	40-70	
Do you currently own awnings?		Yes		No
Have you owned awnings in the past?		Yes		No
Do you have windows where you'd like awnings?		Yes		No
Have you ever considered buying awnings?		Yes		No

Consider the following options for the next questions:
A. Vertical, insulating window blinds; price for a double window, $150.00.
B. Standard heavy canvas awning; price for a double window, $450 to $600.
C. Knock-down, light-weight awning; price for a double window, $200 to $350.
D. Aluminum or steel permanent awning; price for a double window, $500 to $800.
[If possible, show shots, drawings, or actual products so that people can get a better understanding of the product.]

Rate the four options in the order you would buy them. Give a 1 to the one you would buy first:
___A ___B ___C ___D

List your top three reasons for choosing this model:
Appearance
Ability to remove or open in winter
Ease of maintenance
Ease of installation
Ability to raise or open on cloudy days
Product life
Familiarity with product
Price
Blocks out the most sun
Blocks out the least sun
Other. Please describe

Rate the models below 1, 2, and 3, with 1 listed next to the option you like best:

1. ___A ___B ___C
A. Light-weight, easily removed aluminum awnings, $650 to $800.
B. Standard canvas awning that snaps onto an aluminum frame. Awning can be removed, but frame stays on house. $550 to $750.
C. Aluminum or steel permanently attached awning. $650 to $800.

2. ____ A ____ B ____ C
   A. New, knock-down, light-weight canvas awning. $200 to $350.
   B. Heavy canvas awning, with horizontal bars that can be detached so that the awning can be rolled up against the house. $550 to $700.
   C. Heavy canvas awning that stays down all year long. $450 to $550.

3. ____ A ____ B ____ C
   A. New, knock-down, light-weight canvas awning. $200 to $350.
   B. Heavy canvas awning on the same frame as the new knock-down awning. $450 to $550.
   C. Light-weight, easily removable aluminum awning. $650 to $800.

4. ____ A ____ B ____ C
   A. Heavy canvas awning that stays down all year long. $450 to $550.
   B. Heavy canvas awning that can be easily rolled up on cloudy days. $500 to $600.
   C. Heavy canvas awning on the same frame as the new knock-down awning. $450 to $550.

5. ____ A ____ B ____ C
   A. New, knock-down, light-weight canvas awning. $200 to $350.
   B. New, knock-down, light-weight canvas awning that can be rolled up on cloudy days. $275 to $425.
   C. New, knock-down canvas awning with extra material layer underneath the canvas for extra sun protection. $275 to $425.

Look at the features below and rank them 1 to 12 based on their importance to you:

Appearance
Ability to block out the sun
Can be rolled up on cloudy days
Can be removed in the winter
Durability
Price
Ease of Maintenance
Ease of Installation
Heaviness of Fabric
Metal or Aluminum
Past performance history
Recommendations of friends

Rate the following prospective purchases from 1 to 6 based on the possibility of your buying each product. Rate your most likely purchase 1:

Storage shed for the back yard. $300 to $350.
Insulating, high security steel front door. $325 to $400.
Low maintenance aluminum gutters. $300 to $700.
New, knock down, light-weight awnings. $200 to 350.
New curtains for the living room. $300 to $450.
Storm doors for sliding double doors to patio. $300 to $500.

Opening questions

To begin with, you want to ask a few questions to determine how viable a prospect is and to understand that person's perspective in answering the questionnaire.

Choosing concepts

Create four concepts for meeting your customers' needs, then ask customers to choose the one they like best:

1. A concept similar to the one people are currently using to meet this need

2. A concept that goes about halfway towards the product you intend

3. A different approach to meeting your customers' needs

4. Your projected product concept.

For example, the builder of luxury homes designed for entertainment might have the following options:

1. A home similar to ones he was currently building, with separate living, dining, and family rooms

2. A home with a larger deck and a more wide-open family room, dining room, and kitchen area

3. A home with large formal dining and living room areas

4. A home with all or most of the product features the builder is considering.

Asking people to choose among these options will let you verify that this customer group is underserved and determine what degree of change people are willing to accept to meet their needs.

Comparisons

Take your list of product features and services, and add to it currently available features. From this list, develop six to ten different models, store variations, or service concepts. All of them should be items that you could offer. These models shouldn't contain all the possible features, just 30 to 60 percent of them, so that you can see which features make people want to buy.

Take these models and set up five comparisons of three variations each. Some of the variations can be used more than once. Ask customers to look at the three variations, then indicate (1) which variation they would prefer, (2) why they chose that variation, and (3) any features they wish their top choice also had.

These comparisons will help you determine which features will hit customers' hot buttons and which features are most important.

Prioritized list

Take all of your potential features and benefits, and also currently available ones, and ask customers to either rank them sequentially or, if there are more than fifteen features to choose from, divide them into groups, such as highest priority, middle priority, and lowest priority.

The final choice

Decide on the product you think you will want to offer, list it with three or four other choices, and ask people which one they would want to buy. Be sure to include prices.

After taking a few surveys, you may find that you have chosen the wrong product. People aren't choosing your idea in the concept or comparison stage. If that happens, adjust your survey's final choice to reflect the product that people seem to want.

TAKING YOUR SURVEY

Once you've developed a survey, you need to get out and use it and talk to people. You don't need expensive focus groups or sophisticated analyses. Amy Sandquist is a buyer for Nordstrom's, one of the nation's most profitable retailers. She spends half of her time talking to customers and salespeople and just getting out and observing people so that she can hear and see what people want and get a feel for what's going on.

You can actually give the survey to people at parties, or to past customers, or to people in groups you pull together. You can even talk to people who call you for quotations, or who stop in to talk to you. Another ideal survey location is at local conventions or trade shows.

Oshman's Sporting Goods recently opened four superstores with ten large demonstration areas where people can try products out before buying them. Oshman's gets feedback about this concept by interviewing customers as they leave the stores.

Are these scientific, statistically perfect surveys? Of course not. But they still give meaningful information that can help marketers decide what direction to take.

You need to take advantage of the fact that people are fascinated with the concept of market research. If Hasbro has a new toy, it can test it with a group of Boy Scouts, or a class at a local grade school. Next time you have a party, use a market survey as a party mixer. I occasionally give talks to people about introducing new products. When I do, I often run a little market survey with the people present. The audience is always fascinated with the process.

Some products are specialized and used by only a small percentage of people. You can find users of these products for your surveys in any of the following ways:

- Send out fliers or circulars, or make personal phone calls to areas where potential customers might live.
- Offer a club or association $50 to $100 if it will help you sponsor a survey of their members.
- Post a sign or offer at a store or other business asking for survey volunteers.
- Run an ad in a local paper or magazine.
- Set up a booth at a relevant trade show or convention in order to survey people.

For industrial companies:

- Contact local manufacturers' representatives or company salespeople to get the names of possible users.
- Ask for help in locating names from industry associations or your local Chambers of Commerce.
- Look for company contacts in your state's *Industrial Directory*.

ACTION STEPS

1. Following the chapter guidelines and the example in Figure 3.1, prepare a questionnaire to find out what type of products your target customer wants.

2. Give your survey to a group of target customers. You do not have to give the survey to all of them at once. You can collect surveys over a one- to two-month period.

PRODUCTS THAT WILL PRODUCE PROFITS

You make money when you can sell a product for more than it costs you to make and sell it, including your marketing and administrative costs. For products or services, the two prices you need to consider are the demand-based price, which is the price people are willing to pay, and the cost-based price, which is the price you need to charge to cover expenses. You'll make money if your demand-based price is higher than your cost-based price. Later in this section I'll cover retail stores' situations and explain ways for you to change the perceived value of your product or service.

Demand-Based Price

When you ask people how much they think a product is worth, they almost always give you too a low a number. If someone asks you what a Buick is worth, you might say $15,000, but you will still pay $20,000. To determine a product's perceived value, you should show people four or five similar products. Then ask them to list the products by value, with the top product listed first. This will position your product or service in between two products or services with known prices.

Cost-Based Price

Industries typically have a standard markup that covers the cost of running the business and gives the owner a profit. A drugstore might markup its products 50 percent, which means that if it buys a product for $1, it will sell the product for 50 percent more, or $1.50. A manufacturer of consumer products might set its wholesale price at twice its manufacturing cost.

You can determine the typical markup by talking to other people in your industry, contacting manufacturers' representatives, calling industry associations, or contacting your local Small Business Administration office. To calculate your cost-based price, increase your cost by the industry markup. If your cost-based price is lower than your demand-based price, you will be able to make money.

Retail Stores

When you add a feature to a product or service, you give that feature away every time someone makes a purchase, so it is an ongoing cost to you. When a retail store or a service business adds a feature, such as a new color coordinating center, a demonstration area for woodworking products, or a more luxurious decor, that feature stays with the store no matter how many products are purchased.

Calculating the percent increase needed

A retail store doesn't raise its prices to cover increased costs. It still has to be price-competitive with other stores. Instead, it has to make up the cost of its new displays with increased volume.

The way retail stores allocate their expenses can vary greatly depending on the type of store and the store's volume, but a typical allocation is listed below.

RETAIL STORE EXPENSE ALLOCATION

64 percent	Merchandise (including freight)
15 percent	Payroll
8 percent	Overhead
8 percent	Marketing
5 percent	Profit

A retail store can't afford to change its cost percentages, as the only percentage that can go down is profit. So if you add extra features and you want those features to be profitable, you need to increase your volume so that your percentages stay approximately the same.

To find the percentage by which your business will have to increase, add up the money you spend on overhead and marketing, then calculate how much your changes will cost. For example, your current marketing and overhead expenses might be $25,000, and your proposed changes might cost $7,500. Divide the $7,500 cost of the new concept into the $25,000 you're spending on overhead and marketing to get the percent volume increase your business needs. In this case, business would need to increase about 33 percent for the change to be profitable.

Can you generate the necessary increase?

There is no precise way of determining whether your business will increase enough. You have to weigh three considerations: First, will you increase your share of current customers' business? Second, will you be able to attract new customers? And third, will you be able to attract *enough* new customers?

Many retail businesses receive only a portion of each customer's business. For example, a customer might purchase 40 percent of his or her music from Musicland. The remaining purchases are made at other stores. You can find out from your surveys if people will want to shop at your store more after you make your proposed changes. You might find that current shoppers will buy 10 to 20 percent more often.

Getting new customers is more difficult than increasing sales to current customers. Your surveys will tell you if your new concept can attract new customers, but it won't tell you how many new customers you'll get. That depends on how many people you can make aware of your changes. Since this is a subjective area and there is no formula that will give you a reliable answer, I recommend that you simply figure out how many new customers you need and decide if that number is reasonable given the number of new people that stop by your store every week.

Improving Your Price/Value Ratio

Hopefully the perceived value of your product or service is greater than your cost-based price. But if it's not, you can still work to put value back into the product. One way to do this is to add additional features that have a high perceived value, but that do not cost much. My most successful product introduction was a dental chair that cost $3,500. Initial testing indicated that dentists weren't sure the product was worth that much. So we added fabric cushions to the product, a feature that was previously available only on top-of-the-line chairs. With this new feature, which cost very little, our product went from an uncertain value to the market's value leader.

The traditional way to add value is to borrow features from more expensive products. For example, GM designed its Saturn car with sleek styling, a feature typically associated with more expensive cars. The styling didn't add much to the car's cost, but it significantly improved its perceived value.

1. Review the features of various products in the market and list the ones that have a perceived value higher than the cost-based price of the product.
2. Based on your surveys, list the two or three products or services that target customers want or need.
3. Evaluate those products to determine which could be profitable to you.
4. If necessary, add high-value features to your product, then retest your new product with customers.

ACTION STEPS

1. Select a product the target customers indicate they would buy.
2. Determine an approximate cost-based price. If you're not positive what that would be, find products with similar technology, composition, and complexity that are already on the market. For example, if you want to provide a landscaping service for homeowners, you could use estimates of the design fee for firms that put in retaining walls or walkways for your cost-based price.
3. From customer surveys, determine your approximate demand-based price.
4. If your demand-based price is lower than your cost-based price, add high-value features to bring your product's price/value relationship into line.

Chapter 4
Locating the Right Market

Famous Amos chocolate chip cookies has sales of close to $100 million, and its name is known by most people. Yet I don't remember ever seeing a Famous Amos commercial or ad of any type. This is in sharp contrast to Oreos, on which millions of advertising dollars are spent every year. Famous Amos was able to bypass advertising because it found the right market for its products: vending machines. Famous Amos puts its products into attractive two-ounce packages to serve that market, and it has been moving ahead ever since.

"Market" is a term describing how a product is bought and sold. Usually people think of mail-order markets, retail store markets, an industrial market such as maintenance cleaning supplies, small convenience store chains markets, or the consumer electronic superstores markets. Retail stores' and service businesses' market channel is defined by their location. A large mall location, a stand-alone store, a store on a busy intersection, and a store on a side street are all different market channels, and each one has different characteristics that can make it the right or wrong market channel. Professionals have the market channel options of offices in small storefronts, in large downtown buildings, or in a medical or professional building.

Famous Amos chocolate chip cookies hit the three ingredients for finding the right market. First, it found a market where it could afford to stimulate customers to buy. Vending machines have only so much product selection, and the Famous Amos chocolate chip cookies' bulky package looks bigger than Oreo's tight little packages. Famous Amos repeated this strategy when it landed a big order from Burger King, which sold the cookies as a dessert. Again the distribution channel limited the selection, and Famous Amos's packaging was enough to motivate customers to buy.

Second, Famous Amos found a market where competition was light. Vending machines are not nearly as ferocious a market as supermarkets, where dozens of companies fight for precious shelf space. Third, Famous Amos found a market that was big enough for its sales and profit plans, and in which it could be a significant player with the resources it had.

No matter what size your business is, finding the right market will cut your promotion costs, substantially increase your sales growth, and dramatically improve your profits. This chapter shows you how to determine what market channels are available to you, how to recognize markets in which you can create enough stimulus to get customers to buy, how to find markets where competition is light, and how to know when your resources match the market opportunity.

YOUR MARKET OPTIONS

To find the right market, start by listing all the market channels open to you. This applies whether you are a retailer, service provider, or manufacturer. Every business has a variety of channels open to it, any of which might be right for you.

Key First Steps

Go through your local Yellow Pages and find all the listings for businesses of your type. Then group them into different market channels.

If you are a retailer, you might include people operating out of their homes or at flea markets, as well as stand-alone stores; strip mall stores; stores operated jointly with another store, such as a hardware and lawn and garden store combination; telephone sales; and door-to-door sales.

If you own an engineering service, your distribution channel might be engineers selling through networking contacts, a telemarketing sales force that sells over the phone, an engineering broker firm that has key contacts with three large companies, a partnership agreement with an architectural firm, or a network of company salespeople or agents.

If you are a manufacturer, your distribution channel might include the type of stores you sell through, such as kitchen shops, and whether you have a company sales force, use manufacturers' representatives, or sell over the phone. Other distribution channels might include mail order, catalog sales, telemarketing efforts, networking contacts, or selling through another manufacturer. A manufacturer might even sell through a technical service department that customizes equipment for individual applications.

Read six months' to a year's worth of trade magazines for your industry. Write down the market channels discussed in articles or reported on in industry surveys. You can find the names and addresses of trade magazines in *Gale's Source of Publications* at your local library.

Subscribe to business magazines such as *Success, Inc., Nation's Business, Forbes, Entrepreneur,* and *Fortune,* or read them at your local library. These magazines carry articles about new companies, and many of those articles will list market channels you might not have considered.

Talk to your vendor salespeople, and ask them about businesses that use unusual market channels.

Call up the Small Business Administration for your state and get the local number for S.C.O.R.E. This is a volunteer group of retired executives who are available to help you. If you can't find the phone number of the SBA's office, you can get it from your Chamber of Commerce.

Market Channels You May Not Have Thought Of

These first steps should get you a pretty good list of market channels. In reality, there are almost an unlimited number of ways to take your product or service to customers. I've listed just a few alternatives you might not have thought of:

1. Rent space from an existing retailer. Sears and J.C. Penney both rent out space to jewelry retailers, eyeglass companies, and a variety of other merchants. Smaller merchants will do the same thing if they have available space.

2. Combine independent businesses at one location. Insurance agents, lawyers, and doctors commonly do this. They share office expenses, plus they all benefit from looking like a bigger operation. Mechanics, auto body repair people, gift retailers, and a variety of other businesses can benefit from this tactic.

3. Combine two separate market channels. For example, Olan Mills photography studios combine a national telemarketing sales force with local walk-in studios.

4. Sell through other companies. Smaller manufacturers commonly sell through larger manufacturers. Small distributors (called rack jobbers) rent space from retailers and stock it with their products. They collect money only as products are sold.

5. Sell your product as a premium or promotion item. These are the giveaway items you see on the back of cereal boxes or items packaged together with another product. Examples are a tennis wristband that comes free with a can of tennis balls and a small bike windmill with a 12-pack of soda.

ACTION STEP

Put together as comprehensive a list as possible of possible market channels.

CREATING ENOUGH STIMULUS

Nike, the sports shoe giant, recently opened two gigantic Nike Towns, with wall-size aquariums, enormous video screens, and of course row after row of Nike sports apparel. Nike is creating excitement and fun, and as a result more stimulus to generate more sales. Nike also advertises. But in this highly competitive field, with competitors like Reebok and L.A. Gear, creating enough stimulus is tough and expensive.

Stimulus is an even bigger problem for service providers. Consider a cleaning service business. Customers don't make a new purchase decision very often. Instead, they keep buying from their existing supplier. You need stimulus to overcome that inertia. Furthermore, industrial buyers are usually aware of the products available, and they feel they've made the right choice. Customers are easy to sell only when they have a problem. The best choice for a cleaning service might be a telemarketing force that can call a large number of people and find out who is having trouble.

Industrial suppliers are in the same situation: They need to find customers when the time is right. A sample service, seminars, demonstrations, direct mail, and telemarketing might all be appropriate ways to find the people in whom stimulus is easiest to create.

All of these companies are in competitive businesses where you need a lot of stimulus to dominate the market. Most businesses need to look for markets where stimulus is easier to create. A telemarketing force might be effective for a cleaning service because everyone else is making personal calls. A seminar with technical experts will work only if few other companies arrange such things.

Unless you have unusually deep pockets, your best bet is to find markets where you don't have to generate a lot of stimulus in order to get customers. Competition has an impact on the amount of stimulus you need to create, but other factors that determine how much you need are product requirements, the amount of motivation customers need, whether or not customers are aware that they need your product, your location, customers' predispositions, and the amount of advertising support needed. You'll want to concentrate on markets where stimulus requirements are low.

Product Requirements

In some markets you need extensive product features, a broad product line, or expensive product support. Federal Express's chosen market is pickup and delivery for companies who want overnight shipments to locations anywhere in the world. Federal Express signs contracts with companies and individuals, and also has drop-off stations in major metropolitan areas. It needs airplanes, trucks, buildings, and a large employee base. The assets Federal Express needs to generate stimulus are expensive. Famous Amos chocolate chip cookies needed only a two-ounce bag of cookies to compete in the vending machine market. Some consumer products manufacturers sell through mail-order catalogs like Harriet Carter, Miles Kimball, and Taylor Gifts. That market is happy with small one-line suppliers, and the companies need only a simple product line. A stucco contractor may be able to get all the work it needs by signing an agreement with a general contractor.

Motivation Needed

When you decide to buy a computer, you need a great deal of motivation to visit and buy from any particular store, because there are many dealers that sell computers. Many people aren't completely familiar with computers, and they consider it a major purchase. Price or location won't be enough to motivate people, as it might be for a grocery or convenience store. Instead, customers will be looking for a helpful sales force, backup training, a wide choice of computers, and a strong service department.

P.C. Express has a full-page ad in the Minneapolis Yellow Pages in which it boasts that it is Minnesota's largest computer source. It promises an extensive line of computers, printers, and other hardware and accessories. It also offers training, service, assistance in upgrading systems, a five-year warranty on parts and labor, and a toll-free telephone troubleshooting service. Most computer stores have large ads because it's difficult to motivate customers to come into their stores.

Contrast this situation with that of a color printer that sells through the mail to small businesses that occasionally need color printing. The printer offers low prices, quick delivery, and guaranteed work. All that printer needs to do is to give away a free advertising specialty so that people can remember to call for a quote when they need color printing.

A decision doesn't have to be a major one to require motivation. Changing banks isn't really a big decision, but it's one that people just don't think of making. So banks need to provide a lot of motivation to attract new customers. Twin City Federal runs a new customer campaign that includes advertising, free checking, longer hours, and premium gifts.

Needs Awareness

Devee Philpot introduced her product, the Junk Drawer Organizer, through organizational shops that sold products such as closet organizers, kitchen organizing products, and baskets and boxes for organizing toys. All Philpot needed to do was to have the product packaged with a label that let people know its name. She didn't need stimulus to let people know they needed to organize their junk drawers because the market channel created the stimulus for her. Philpot would have needed a large promotional campaign if she had sold through discount stores, as she, rather than the market outlet, would have had to make customers aware that they needed her product.

Greenwood Plaque Company makes building plaques and large granite-like signs for the fronts of buildings. Its prices range from $3,500 to $7,000. It would take a tremendous amount of effort for Greenwood, on its own, to influence the architects and corporate people responsible for choosing the plaque vendor. Another distribution choice for Greenwood is to sell through manufacturers' representatives or distributors. In this case Greenwood would not have to provide as much stimulus, as the representatives would know what buildings were going up and would be able to personally contact key parties in order to bid on these jobs.

Location

Starbuck Coffee Co. sells thirty blends of coffee, primarily through retail stores. Starbuck's first store was located in Pike Place, a landmark Seattle fish market. In this location, Starbuck's ideal target customers walked right by its door. All it had to do is put up a few window signs.

A quality control consultant or high-tech manufacturing consultant can generate extra business if it is located in a technology center or a business park with appropriate businesses. Lawyers or accounting firms will generate more business if they are in buildings with similar firms than they would in a building with insurance agencies.

Taking the best location works only for certain types of businesses. In Chapter 3 I discussed how much a retailer would have to increase sales in order to cover the cost of a new marketing program. The same principle applies to increased rent for a better location. If you are going to pay double or triple the rent of your competitors, you need to almost double your sales to stay price-competitive. Starbuck Coffee doesn't really have to worry about being price-competitive, as it is a specialty retailer and so can charge a higher price. The same would be true of an accounting firm, a law office, or a consulting firm. People expect these firms to give better service if they are in a more prestigious building, and therefore they can charge more. A liquor store, on the other hand, has to worry about being competitive and probably can't afford a higher rent.

A service company, however, might find that certain outlets that don't have a cost premium provide better market stimulus. For example, an insurance agency might have the same rent in a storefront office as in an office building. But the storefront office would give the agency a spot for a big sign that could help stimulate customers.

Customers' Predisposition

People are creatures of habit, and they get into a routine of buying certain products at certain locations. For example, my sons want to go shopping for toys only at Toys "R" Us. Manufacturers in a town may all buy office supplies from a local company. And many marketers will only put their advertising-related work through a full-service advertising agency.

You need to create a great deal of stimulus to get people to break their routine, and this is often a tough task for a small business. I helped introduce a new inspection microscope that had a 4- by 5-inch TV-type viewing area instead of the traditional two little eyepieces. Operators liked the product after a two-week trial, as it eliminated neck strain and eyestrain. But companies were reluctant to switch any part of a critical inspection process. We really couldn't afford to offer all the support needed to sell the product, and we ended up settling for the much smaller inspector-training market.

Amount of Advertising Required

The Adomizer, a plastic seat that you do sit-ups on, is sold almost exclusively through large discount stores such as Wal-Mart, Kmart, and Target. That is advantageous in many respects. Only the one product is needed, and sales costs are minimal. But these stores require big advertising support before they put a product in. Large general market distribution channels require big advertising budgets.

Small, narrowly-defined market channels require much less support. Famous Amos didn't need to advertise. Black & Decker chose to sell its Handy Steamer through department stores and kitchen specialty shops to avoid advertising expenses. Toro chose to sell its mulching mowers through specialized lawn and garden dealers that required little advertising support. And industrial equipment suppliers often use distributors to avoid having to advertise.

For retailers, there is a trade-off between advertising and location. For some businesses, a location can generate all the customers they need. Other retailers that are more specialized and have fewer buyers, such as a waterbed store, find that a location alone doesn't attract enough customers. Those retailers usually take a less expensive location and then advertise.

A retailer or a service company can reduce the amount of stimulus needed by locating near similar businesses. For example, a wallpaper store located near a tile store, a paint store, and a furniture store is going to need less stimulus than one located near unrelated businesses. The store could cut its costs further by combining ads or even putting out a catalog with those nearby businesses.

Examples of Companies Choosing a Market Based on Stimulus

Maureen Barton thought party confetti was just too dull. She thought young people who like to throw parties would like confetti in different shapes, such as hearts, ghosts, or dinosaurs. Her target customers, middle- to upper-income party hosts, were identified, as was her product: confetti in a variety of fun shapes. What market should she use? Mail-order catalogs were one option, but party purchases are often made at the last minute, and she would miss out on these purchases. Her business was too small to be considered by large retailers. Barton's best choice was to sell through retailers and distributors from the balloon, party, and gift industries. This market has its own trade show, which attracts 2,000 to 3,000 attendees, and its own trade magazine. That market is always looking for fun ideas, and people in it don't mind buying from a new supplier. Barton could get all the buying stimulus she needed just by having the product on the shelves of key stores.

M&M Hydraulic rebuilds and repairs hydraulic pumps and cylinders for heavy equipment, special manufacturing equipment, hoists, and farm equipment. M&M runs an ad in the Yellow Pages and has a trained repairperson handle phone orders. M&M's competitors also advertise in the Yellow Pages, so M&M needs another way of signing up customers. Catalog sales, telephone sales, and direct mail would all require a tremendous amount of advertising and other support to build the customer's trust and confidence. Sales through nontechnical salespeople or manufacturers' representatives would also call for a high amount of stimulus to support the company's services.

M&M has two low-stimulus channels open to it. One is to send experienced repairpeople into the field who can estimate a job's cost, order parts, and schedule the repair into the shop. These salespeople could call on major accounts and offer to come out and bid on repair jobs. The company's credibility would come from the expertise of the salesperson. Another distribution channel option is to hire retired or part-time people who are well connected to the company's targeted customer group, such as retired crane operators or farmers. They would still need support, but not as much as a nontechnical salesperson. The company's best strategy is to send repairpeople into the field to make on-the-spot bids and sales.

North Central Schwinn is a retail store that sells bikes and accessories. A bike shop does not get enough business from drive-by traffic to support it. It needs to pull from a larger area. North Central Schwinn put its store on a side street about 150 feet from a major highway. To attract customers, the store has a large sign that is easily visible from the highway, a park entrance, a Burger King restaurant, and the exit of a busy gas station. The store has almost as much visibility as it would in a prime location. But because of its lower rent, the store is able to hold bike rodeos for schools and other community groups, have a reasonable-size ad in the Yellow Pages, and advertise in local papers. It is in the right type of location for its type of store.

ACTION STEPS

1. Take the list of possible market channels that you put together. For every channel, list any factors that may make it difficult to stimulate. Some of the factors to consider are product requirements, motivation needed, customers' awareness of their needs, customer predispositions, and amount of advertising required.
2. Put an asterisk by the markets that will be hard to stimulate given your resources. Don't eliminate them yet, as you may learn how to solve the problems later in the book. Just remember that your chances of making money will increase as you get around obstacles to stimulating customers. Figure 4.1 shows a total market analysis, including evaluating the stimulus required.

LIGHT COMPETITION

Melanie Franklin and Anthony Lee were shocked to find that no one in their New York apartment building had a fire extinguisher, or knew where to buy one. They opened a retail store and mail-order catalog business in 1989, and it did $6 million in 1992.

There is some competition in almost every market, but you'll find it easier to succeed in a market channel with few competitors. Melanie Franklin and Anthony Lee certainly benefited from that in both of their market outlets, retail stores and mail-order catalog sales. There are many ways to find, or create, a channel with light competition, including selling in a different way, selling to customers in a different market, singling out a small customer segment, adjusting your professional association, and creating a new type of market outlet.

Selling in a Different Way

Eric Stenzel started selling dental products to dentists right after college. He has become successful selling panoramic (full mouth) X-ray machines directly to dentists. He finds his customers at trade shows and through magazine ads and direct mail brochures. Stenzel is all alone in his market channel; his competitors sell through a network of dental dealers and distributors. Because he sells direct, Stenzel's costs are lower, and he has been able to gain market share by offering a lower price.

Selling to a Customer in a Different Market

S.I.T. Co. is a small manufacturer of guitar strings. Sales through U.S. music stores are competitive. So S.I.T. looked around for a market with less competition and found it overseas, which now accounts for 40 percent of S.I.T.'s sales.

Fingerhut, the big mail-order catalog house, did the same thing when it targeted low- to middle-income consumers, who had been ignored by other catalog houses. Another example is a Little Caesar's outlet located in a Kmart store.

Singling Out a Small Market Segment

The maker of Nautilus exercise equipment is a major player in sales to health clubs. Nordic Track has built a huge company primarily from direct sales to consumers through magazine ads. Other manufacturers sell to physical therapists, have exclusive sales agreements with major retailers like Sears, or sell through manufacturers' representatives that supply small chains and individual sporting goods stores. Each of these companies singles out one market channel to sell through.

Adjusting Your Professional Association

Doctors can have a small neighborhood office, be a member of a large clinic, be associated with a hospital, or work at an emergency medical clinic. People can't see what they buy from a doctor, dentist, lawyer, or service company. So they buy because they trust someone, not because they know what results they'll end up getting. Your professional association is a part of your market channel, and changing it can limit your competition. Doctors can be associated with hospitals, teaching universities, or medical societies. An auto mechanic can be associated with a training program or a quality care network, a real estate agency can be associated with Century 21, and a lawyer could be tied to a prominent ex-judge.

Creating a New Type of Market Outlet

GM is trying to develop a different market channel for its Saturn car by redefining what a dealer should be like. Quick service, one nonnegotiable price, and smaller, stand-alone locations are just part of what GM is trying to do.

Little Caesar's pushed carry-out-only pizza stores. A new airline catalog service lets you order products while traveling and have the product delivered to your arrival gate. Large "category killer" stores such as Toys "R" Us, Best Buy, and Office Max are another example of a new type of market outlet.

ACTION STEPS

1. Go back to the market channels you identified in the last section and list the competitors in each channel.

2. Circle markets where either competition is light or the competition is primarily small companies.

MATCHING YOUR RESOURCES TO THE MARKET

Both Eddie Bauer and L.L. Bean produce upscale clothing for people who like to spend time outdoors. L.L. Bean's market is primarily mail-order catalog sales, while Eddie Bauer sells through both mail-order and its own retail stores. Selling through retailers around the country would be a much bigger market for both companies. But both of them reject that strategy, as it would detract from their exclusive image and would cost more in promotional money than they have to spend.

Marketers need to worry about three types of costs when they look at a market: the cost to stimulate customers; the cost to stimulate the market channel, if necessary; and the cost of providing the product or service to the market. Marketers need to calculate these costs and then prepare a start-up budget, either for starting a business or for introducing a new product or service.

Most marketers underestimate the amount of money they will need to cover these three costs. I read over and over again that the biggest mistake new entrepreneurs make is that they are undercapitalized. Yet *Inc.* magazine reports that 26 percent of 1992's top growth companies were started with seed capital of less than $5,000. The problem is not not having enough money, it is selecting a market in which the money the entrepreneur has is enough.

Cost to Stimulate the Market Channel

When you are considering the cost of a market channel, you need to realize that the people in the channel are also customers. For example, your final customer may be teenage girls. However, if you want to sell to them through specialty retail stores, you will also have to convince these stores to carry your product, and that might call for promotional spending on your part.

Earlier I wrote about Eric Stenzel and his panoramic X-ray sales. Eric sold his product directly to dentists, and he was able to build his company into a market leader. At first glance this might seem like a poor strategy. Eric is selling a $10,000 piece of technical equipment without installation or nearby follow-up service.

But Eric started out small. If he had chosen to go through dealers, he would have had to provide training to both sales and service people, and he would have needed an intensive sales effort to get dealers to support his product rather than those of their existing vendors. Eric didn't have the resources to break into the dealer network, so he chose the only channel open to him.

Some of the factors that contribute to costs in a distribution system are:

1. Samples, consignment units, and demo equipment
2. Rent
3. Advertising requirements
4. Expenses for salespeople or manufacturers' representatives
5. Displays
6. Trade show expenses
7. Catalog and mailing expenses
8. Service and follow-up requirements
9. Co-op advertising and other promotional expenses.

Low-Cost Markets

Always look first at market channels where the costs are low. When Horst Rechelbacher started Aveda, he went out and spoke to hair care professionals. At the end of his talk, he asked them to try his new products. Estée Lauder started the same way years earlier; she went door to door with a bag full of products. Costs were low, and these early sales allowed the two to build their companies to the point where they could afford to go after the retail market.

Other companies start by promoting their products on computer bulletin boards, by calling on local companies, or by attending small trade shows. Selling your product through another company, signing a few key distributors to exclusive agreements, and selling to mail-order catalogs are other low-cost market entry tactics.

Multifoods International has sales of over $2 billion per year, but I'm not sure any reader can name any of its products. Multifoods sells to consumers through vending machines, restaurants, and bakeries. It doesn't compete in supermarkets or other markets where you would notice its name. Yet Multifoods still does very well.

Start-up Budgeting

In later chapters I'll suggest low-cost tactics for creating stimulus and motivating customers. But those tactics don't change the fact that each market has a different set of costs. You need to know what those costs are, and whether you can afford them, before you start any program. The costs to consider are:

1. The product itself. For a manufacturer this includes inventory and equipment costs. For a service provider it includes any new equipment or employees. For a retailer it includes the cost of new goods and additional rent, plus the cost of remodeling, new displays, and new employees.

2. Sales collateral. This includes new brochures, consignment units, attendance at trade shows (if you are selling to other companies), or new selling sheets.

3. Sales promotion. This includes advertising, printing a catalog, running a direct mail campaign, creating more signs and banners, or offering co-op advertising discounts or slotting allowances.

4. Training. You may need to pay for sales meetings, dealer or retailer training, or training of customers and technical service personnel.

As you go through your programs, you will find wide differences in the costs of different market channels. You want your resources to cover the costs for at least four to six months until your new program starts to produce sales.

Examples of Choosing a Market Channel

Mothers Work

Rebecca Mathias started Mothers Work, a chain of retail stores that sells upscale maternity clothes to working women who are expecting. She tested a mail-order catalog, but she had trouble locating potential customers. She knew she needed to be in retail malls where women would notice her stores, then return when they were expecting. But normal retail-size stores were too expensive, because only a small percentage of women are expecting at any given time. She didn't want to limit her selection, because expectant mothers buy a lot of clothes at once. So Mathias had her stores stock just one of each size for every item in her inventory and replaced items daily as they were sold. She could afford daily deliveries; she couldn't afford expensive retail space.

Let me review Mathias's strategy. First, she decided on a target customer, middle- to upper-income expectant mothers. Next she selected her product, stylish maternity clothes. Her third step was to select as her market channel retail stores in high-traffic malls. She determined that she needed both mall locations and a wide selection in order to stimulate customers to buy. Finally, she figured out how to restock stores daily, so that she could afford to execute her strategy.

Commodore Computer

Commodore was one of the first manufacturers of personal computers. It faltered in that market because of the intense competition, but it has created instead a personal computer system with excellent video editing capabilities. The computer provides an inexpensive alternative to a traditional video production studio.

Commodore Computer has done a great job finding an underserved customer group and creating the right product for it. However, Commodore faces several problems in finding the right market channel. First, people are predisposed to use traditional video production houses for their editing. Second, potential customers need to see and try out the equipment before they buy it. Third, the people who normally use video are not using computers for editing, and they will require training.

Commodore markets its products through a limited number of highly specialized computer dealers, then supports those dealers with reviews, publicity, and advertising in video magazines. Commodore has to limit its number of dealers because of the amount of support it gives each one.

I've listed below the features advertised by Commodore's Minneapolis dealer to give you a better idea of how closely Commodore has worked with its dealers:

- Complete Amiga demonstration facilities
- Edit suites with Amiga graphics
- Animation and graphic services
- Installation and repair services
- Interactive training
- Rental services and lease-to-own plans
- Video production capabilities.

ACTION STEP

1. Look at Figure 4.1 (page 60), a market channel analysis for Griffin Employee Leasing. You need to prepare a similar analysis for your business to help you decide what market is right for you. I've given the market channels and an analysis next. Read the description of the distribution options first, then review the chart, and finally read the analysis.

Distribution Channel Options Listed in Figure 4.1 for Griffin Employee Leasing Services:

- Sell over a large geographic area with a direct mail/telemarketing distribution strategy aimed at small businesses with ten to thirty employees.

The company would run a direct mail campaign designed to get people to call the company.

- Sell its services through a staff of four to five employees who would call on businesses with twenty-five to forty-five employees in the Philadelphia metro market. Salespeople would generate their own leads or use leads from magazine and newspaper ads.

- Sell only to manufacturing companies with 75 to 125 employees in the Philadelphia area. The company would focus its product line for those customers and would sell products through networking contacts by its president at key association meetings, and through seminars, publicity, and direct mailings to targeted customers.

- Sell to manufacturing companies over a large regional area through seminars, trade show attendance, publicity, direct mailings, and a follow-up telemarketing sales force.

- Sell to companies with 15 to 150 employees over an eight-state area through business brokers, insurance salespeople, management consultants, or other sales agents.

- Offer the employee leasing service through a statewide association of manufacturers or a small-business association. Griffin Employee Leasing Services would provide the service. The association would mail information and set up seminars for its members. The association would get a better price break for its members, plus take a small percentage.

Distribution Strategy Analysis for Figure 4.1:

- CUSTOMER NEEDS KNOWLEDGE. Customer needs knowledge is lowest with a small sales force and selling through agents because the company is trying to sell its services to every possible company. The other four methods involve putting out information and then having interested customers respond. The people who respond will realize that they may have a need.

- STIMULUS NEEDED. Strategies 1 and 4 call for selling to the best customers over a wide geographic area. So a great deal of stimulus is not required, as the companies are almost ready to buy the service. The stimulus needed is also low through the association because the association's backing provides the stimulus.

- PREDISPOSITION. Companies will consider a switch to employee leasing a major shift. They will feel best doing that through contact with a company president or through their trade association.

- PRODUCT REQUIREMENTS. If Griffin Employee Leasing restricts its target market, it will reduce its product requirements. Specializing in one market segment is easiest to prepare and requires the smallest product line.

- MOTIVATION NEEDED. In large markets Griffin will be selling only to the easiest customers, who will require the least motivation. The company will need to provide a great deal more motivation if it tries to sell companies who have no initial interest in employee leasing.
- AMOUNT OF COMPETITION. The wider the geographic area and the more diverse the markets that Griffin attacks, the more competition it will encounter.
- MARKET COSTS VERSUS FIRM RESOURCES. Costs will be low for a networking program or for selling through associations. They will be high if the company tries to sell to manufacturers over a wide area because of the cost of travel and the cost of telemarketing.
- PROFIT POTENTIAL. Profit potential is low for a wide-area direct-mail campaign because the company will sell only to people who immediately like the idea of employee leasing. Selling through agents has a lower potential because of the commission paid to the agents. Profit potential is highest selling to manufacturers over a wide area just because it would be possible to sell to more people.

What channel is best? Selling through an association would be my first choice. If my resources were limited and I had a fairly new company, I'd also choose Option 4, selling to manufacturing companies through networking contacts. If I'd been in business with success for three or four years, I'd select selling to manufacturers over a wider geographic area.

Section 1 — Conclusion

It can Be Easy—Or It can Be Hard

Irving Taggart is the owner of Traders Village in Grand Prairie, Texas. Irving attracts 2.5 million visitors to his Texas-size flea market every year, although he is open only on weekends. Irving started out in 1973 on a dusty two-lane highway. Today his company is Texas' third largest tourist attraction, with 50,000 visitors per weekend.

Irving had the right customers, people looking for a fun time without spending a lot of money; the right product, a flea market with 1,600 vendors; and the right market, a stand-alone flea market between Dallas and Fort Worth. Irving built his business the easy way, by discovering where the money is.

Then, of course, there's the hard way: going after the same target customers as everyone else with the same product in the same market. Children's Palace went out of business last year. Children's Palace tried to stake its claim to a market share by duplicating Toys "R" Us strategy of large stand-alone toy stores. But target customers were flooded with promotions from other similar stores, and Children's Palace didn't have the resources or products to succeed.

The choice is yours. You can try to be like all the other companies in your market, or you can find a niche where you can make money. I recommend that you discover the right customer, product, and market. That's your best chance for success.

Figure 4.1

MARKET CHANNEL	CUSTOMER NEEDS KNOWLEDGE	STIMULUS NEEDED	CUSTOMERS' PREDISPOSITION TOWARDS CHANNEL	PRODUCT REQUIREMENTS	MOTIVATION NEED	AMOUNT OF COMPETITION	MARKET COST vs. FIRM RESOURCES	PROFIT POTENTIAL
Mail/telephone channel to a large area	MEDIUM	LOW	LOW	MEDIUM TO HIGH	LOW	HIGH	MEDIUM	LOW TO MEDIUM
Through small sales force in a small market	LOW	HIGH	MEDIUM	MEDIUM TO HIGH	HIGH	MEDIUM	MEDIUM	MEDIUM
Manufacturing companies only in small area with networking contacts	MEDIUM	MEDIUM	HIGH	LOW TO MEDIUM	MEDIUM	LOW	LOW	MEDIUM
Manufacturing companies in large area through seminars and telemarketing sales	MEDIUM	LOW	LOW	LOW TO MEDIUM	LOW	MEDIUM	HIGH	HIGH
Selling through agents	LOW	MEDIUM	MEDIUM	MEDIUM	HIGH	HIGH	MEDIUM	LOW TO MEDIUM
Selling through association contacts	MEDIUM	LOW	HIGH	LOW TO MEDIUM	MEDIUM	LOW	LOW	MEDIUM

Section 2

Being Better than Everyone Else

Once you have decided which customers and markets you want to target, you need to figure out a way for your business to gain a sustainable advantage. In Section 1 you might have found an underserved customer group, and you might be the first company to serve them. But you won't stay on top long unless you can create reasons for people to buy from you that competitors can't copy.

You can find that elusive sustainable advantage by evaluating your customers, product, and distribution options. ConAgra is a market leader with its Healthy Choice line of frozen entrees. ConAgra evaluated all its options and determined that the way it could get an advantage was to have its entrees taste good. Customers want healthy food choices, but they want them only if they taste good. When ConAgra decides to enter this market, it directed most of its research toward developing food that people liked. Other competitors have entered the market and provide similar products, in similar stores, to the same target customers. But ConAgra recognized early the key element that would let it keep its leading market share, and it devoted the time and energy necessary to keep its food tasting better than anyone else's.

The key to being better than everyone else is to find, as ConAgra did, some detail of your customer, product, or distribution strategy that you can deliver better than any competitor can.

WHAT THIS SECTION IS LIKE

The chapters in this section cover a wide variety of areas in which you may be able to find a way to gain a market advantage. The chapters do not provide a step-by-step approach for you to follow to find your answer. Instead, they are designed to show you as many ways as possible to look at your customer, product, or distribution channel. I hope to open up your mind so that you can look at your business in ways you may never have thought of before.

As you read these chapters, you may find that some of the points mentioned don't apply to your business. Just skip those points and read on until you find five to ten points that do apply and that can give you a way to be better than everyone else.

Chapter 5

Customers: Learning the Keys That Make Customers Buy

ConAgra discovered that taste was the true customer hot button for a healthy frozen entree. Most customer groups have one or two characteristics that generate a terrific response. If you can find them, you're on your way to creating a sustainable edge.

The difference between knowing and not knowing what customers really want can determine whether or not you'll succeed. For example, British Airways gives passengers cotton pajamas on long flights, and Virgin Airways now offers free massages on flights from England to America. These programs are floundering because they miss what air travelers want, which is low prices, convenient schedules, and frequent flier programs.

In sharp contrast, Pitney Bowes successfully introduced the Paragon, a mailing machine that weighs and meters mail at the same time. Pitney Bowes has been successful because it saved two to three hours of work per day for a medium-sized company. Saving employee hours was exactly the benefit small companies were looking for.

This chapter explains questions you can ask to discover keys to customer buying, helpful models that help pinpoint what customers really want, and different methods you can use to find customer hot buttons.

QUESTIONS TO ASK ABOUT CUSTOMERS

The better you know your customers, the better your chances of creating a sustainable advantage. Park Tool Company sells about $5 million of bicycle repair tools each year. The founders were bicycle repairmen who started out by making tools that they needed themselves. Park Tool created its sustainable advantage by having a broad product line of tools that are ideally suited for its targeted customers. Park got this advantage because its owners know, inside and out, what types of tools solve the problems of bicycle repair.

I use five questions to find out what customers really want:

1. What kind of relationship do customers want?
2. Why do customers buy?
3. Why don't customers buy?

4. What features and benefits do customers want?

5. How do customers actually buy?

As you read the discussion of each question, think of the phrase "how come?" When you see the ways customers act, ask yourself why they act that way, and then see if that reason could be a key customer characteristic.

What Kind of Relationship Do Customers Want?

People like to buy products and services from people and companies they like. You want to find out what kinds of things customers would like you to do for them. I guarantee that this is more than just providing a product, and it isn't just service. Customers want you to create some type of relationship with them.

The coach or expert relationship

A few years ago, Nestlé ran a program in which it prominently displayed a toll-free number on its baby food packaging. Calling the number put parents in touch with a licensed dietitian who could answer questions about baby nutrition. The dietitians didn't push Nestlé products; they just offered friendly advice. This toll-free number was a key component of a program that raised Nestlé's market share from 20 to 30 percent.

When people are buying a product that is important to them, they want the company they are buying from to be an expert. And they want to be reassured that they are buying the right product. Nestlé was establishing itself as an expert with its phone number, and that gave people the assurance they wanted when they bought Nestlé's baby food.

The friendly, caring relationship

When Nintendo first introduced its games, it set up a Nintendo fun club that sent out a newsletter discussing tricks for moving from one game level to the next. Nintendo also gave members a toll-free number where they could talk to game counselors, who gave out free game advice. Nintendo was telling its customers that it wanted them to have fun. That attitude tied right back into its products, and it helped Nintendo generate retail sales of $2 billion in just four years. Before you dismiss Nintendo as just a "red hot product," remember that it entered the video market after that market had fallen from $3.2 billion, mostly from Atari games, to just over $100 million per year.

Having the same goals as the customer

Customers like to believe that your goal is to help them. They don't want to believe that your goal is to take their money. This is why fishing stores run by well-known fishermen usually do well. Customers know that the store owners are interested in catching fish. This is one of the advantages of such tactics as classes, seminars, sponsoring events, and store demonstration areas. They help customers believe that you have the same goals that they do.

This principle also applies to industrial companies. Nucor is a fast-rising steel manufacturer. Its sales have increased from $83 million in 1972 to $1.5 billion in the early 1990s—in an industry that is supposedly dying. Ken Iverson, Nucor's president, states that "our efforts are to project a character or personality to make the customer comfortable doing business with us." Ken doesn't have a corporate marketing staff. Instead, his marketers are located at each plant so that they can be close to the customer.

Relationship marketing

Establishing a sense of being related is one of the new frontiers of marketing. Customers want you to be helpful, to care about their welfare, and to truly go out of your way to meet their objectives. If you are a management consultant, this could mean holding key positions in industry associations or community groups like the Chambers of Commerce, holding seminars and classes, sponsoring companies in Junior Achievement, and possibly cosponsoring contests for local businesses such as the year's best entrepreneur. For a tax attorney, this could be having monthly luncheons with key speakers, attending important client events, and holding special training seminars for clients' employees.

Why Do Customers Buy?

An advertising study recently looked at why people buy a particular brand of athletic shoes. It found that people who are motivated by winning or status liked Nike's shoes. Those interested in comfort and stability bought Reeboks. People who liked to pamper themselves bought L.A. Gear shoes. And those that liked simplicity and family values chose Keds.

I had similar results when I looked at reasons for buying equipment for inserting components into PC boards. Some companies wanted speed; others were concerned about quality, training, durability, set-up time, or price.

People buy products for dozens of reasons. You can find a point to specialize on by finding a reason for people to buy that no one else is providing. Some of the reasons people might purchase are listed below:

1. A solution. The product solves a problem that no other product solves.
2. Features/benefits. The customer considers one feature or benefit particularly important.
3. Performance. Some people will buy the product that they feel works best.
4. Comfort. This is especially important for middle-aged and older consumers.
5. Image. The product can reinforce the image customers have of themselves. This can apply equally for a high-status product, such as a Jaguar, or a product with practical simplicity, such as Keds shoes.
6. Quality. This relates to how well the product is built.
7. Price. Some customers will buy the lowest-priced product; others will buy the product they feel has the best value.
8. Relationship. Some people just buy from certain businesses, either because they like the people or because they like the way the company does business.
9. Service/warranty. Return policies, backup service, warranty period, and exchange procedures can all affect a customer's buying decision.

10. Selection. This relates to the number of products stocked in a store or the breadth of the product line of a manufacturer or service company.

11. Location. Certain stores or businesses may be more convenient.

12. Tradition. Some people will continue to buy from the same businesses until they close.

13. Innovation. New, innovative products attract a certain number of customers in virtually any market.

14. Emotion. People will buy a product because it makes them feel good, allows them to impress other people, or is a way to show love or appreciation.

Look at your business and your competitors, and list the reasons people buy from each. Then look at the reasons that no one is addressing, and see whether they would apply for your business.

Why Don't Customers Buy?

Beach Patrol makes and sells swimming suits for high school and college girls. It knows that its suits won't sell if they squash girls' breasts or ride up in the back. No matter how fantastic a suit looks, girls don't want to be uncomfortable.

If you can correct a major reason that people won't buy and make that correction obvious, you will have a point where you can be better than competitors. Some of the reasons people won't buy are:

1. Fear of loss. This affects industrial accounts more than consumers. Buyers don't like to make a purchase for which they could be criticized.

2. Lack of trust. People have to trust your business before they will be willing to buy from you.

3. Lack of comfort. People have feelings that they don't always understand. If they don't feel "right" about your business, they won't buy from you.

4. Lack of quality. Customers won't buy a product if they don't think it looks well made.

5. Not really a solution to the problem. People may not think a product will do what they want it to. This doesn't mean that the product is poorly made, just that it doesn't address the real problem.

6. Lack of need. People don't think they will need the product.

7. Clash with people's lifestyle. Customers all have an image of themselves that they want to project to others.

8. Not that important.

9. Has a defect. Prospects might see something about the product that they feel will cause it to either fail or work poorly.

10. Bad past experiences.

11. Preference for another product.

Surveying people and asking why they don't buy is probably the best way to find a good way to differentiate your product, primarily because it is an area that most people don't look into. You will be able to discover products and benefits you need to include, psychological factors you may need to overcome, and key selling points that you may have but are not communicating.

What Features Do Customers Really Want?

Another area to consider is people's motivation, what they are trying to accomplish when they purchase a product.

Goal-oriented motivation

I mentioned earlier a dynamite new product introduced by Pitney Bowes. After surveying 4,000 people, Pitney Bowes put together a mailing focusing on customer's desire to reduce employee time in the mail room.

That may not be the motivation of every possible customer group. Another company might want a mailing machine that can add a message to every envelope, or one that can either stamp or meter the mail. That company's goal might be to increase sales from its direct mailings. And the machine that best fits this customers' needs will be very different from this Pitney Bowes product.

Image-oriented motivation

A desire to be practical, to have the biggest and best product, or to be on the cutting edge of technology is an image-oriented motivation. The image people have of themselves plays an enormous part in their buying decisions. If you list the last ten purchases you made and honestly state why you made them, you'll find that the image you want to create dominated eight or nine of your purchase decisions.

Cars are a good example. Most cars are good for eight to ten years if all you care about is transportation. But we all care about a lot more than that. A car is a very visible product that we own, and we use it to project an image. Some people want to project an image that they put their children first; they will drive a van. Other people want to show that they are successful; they will always have a new, fancier car. Still others want to show that they are independent; they will drive an older car.

Usage-oriented motivation

Once you have distinguished a customer group based on a broad category, you can segment it still further into usage groups. Consider status-conscious bikers who buy mountain bikes because they are more comfortable. Some of them may just want to take casual rides, others want to ride to work, and still others ride for exercise. Each one of those groups might want slightly different features, and this could give you an opening.

Companies often buy products based on their usage applications, such as a production machine for stuffing forty-two components into a PC board. The purchase decision will be based on what product is best for a very specific use.

Entertainment motivation

Some products are for entertainment, fun, or adventure. Each of these motivations calls for a slightly different product or service.

Phillip Wade and Huib Geerlings created a mail-order wine catalog for people who wanted more variety than they could get at a local liquor store. When looking at customers' motivations, they found that some customers bought wine for dinner parties, others because they enjoyed more variety, and still others for a sense of adventure. Phillip and Huib aimed their catalog at the last group, people looking for a sense of adventure, and now have a mailing list of over 20,000. They include stories about a wine's origin and other interesting data that people exploring new wines would be interested in.

Tracking the Buying Decision

Most buying decisions are not spontaneous. Instead, they involve a whole series of steps. For example, a company buying a new copier might appoint one person or a group of people to decide which copier to buy. Those people will quickly look at ten to twenty models, then choose three or four to evaluate more closely. The study group might then bring in other people and get their comments, and finally submit a purchase recommendation, which has to go into a yearly budget that has to be approved by management.

The key to the buying process is often not the actual purchase but the initial screening period. A copier company won't get any sales if it isn't one of the three or four copiers a purchaser will evaluate. A company will have a tremendous advantage if it can find a place in the buying process where no other company is promoting its product or service.

Action Steps

1. List the key customer characteristics you noted while evaluating your customer with the five questions:
   - How do customers want to relate to you?
   - Why do customers buy from you?
   - Why don't customers buy from you?
   - What features and benefits do customers want?
   - How do customers buy?

2. From your list, pull out the characteristics that are not being met or being met poorly. These are opportunities for you to be better than everyone else.

3. Take an 11- by 17-inch piece of paper and label it "Customer Needs/Possible Strategies." On the right side, make a list of customer needs. List the five or ten characteristics that you pulled out on the left side. Spread them out as much as possible over the top two-thirds of the page. This is the start of the most important chart you'll put together to determine your market strategy. You will add to the chart throughout the next two chapters.

HELPFUL MODELS

The models covered here are meant to help you find different ways to look at customers' needs. I recommend models because they open up your thinking so that you can discover customer characteristics you may have never thought of before.

Don't over rely on models. They are a tool, but they are not as effective as actually testing your ideas in the market and seeing if they work. Owners of bed and breakfasts, those small, quaint mini-hotels, had trouble finding customers in 1992. Those owners studied their customers and then introduced new features. Jacuzzis, in-hotel fax machines, bus tour packages, honeymoon suites, free sports club visits, and one-night getaway packages were just a few of the enticements offered. These programs either worked or didn't work. There was no doubt in any owner's mind. You never get that type of certainty from models, surveys, or focus groups.

Compromise Model

This model gives you an idea of how important certain features are to customers. It is useful in markets where no one can provide every feature customers want at a price they are willing to pay. As a result, every supplier needs to supply a different mix of features for the customer to choose from.

The steps involved in this model are:

1. List all of a customer's buying concerns.
2. Separate the list into three categories:
   a. Must have.
   b. Important to have.
   c. Nice to have.
3. Estimate the relative value, on a scale of from one to ten, of each feature.

As an example, I'll use a company constructing a new photo studio for shooting large products such as furniture, cars, or industrial equipment. Its chart is shown in Figure 5.1.

Figure 5.1
Compromise Model for a Commercial Photographer

Feature	Relative Rating
Must Have	
Staging area to handle large products	10
Sets a minimum of 20 by 30 feet	10
Ability to take elevated shots, at least 15 feet in the air	10
Head photographer with extensive experience	10
Important to Have	
Big studio with curved wall for pullout photographs	7
Location convenient to large number of potential customers	6
Low rates for labor to move products around	4
More than five large sets to handle large shoots for catalogs	5
Nice to Have	
Quick turnaround photo development	3
Spare office space for clients to use while shots are being set up	3
Client ombudsman to handle problems	2

Burger King introduced a fancier dinner service in 1993, with tablecloths, free popcorn, an expanded entrée menu, and limited service. Obviously Burger King couldn't supply all the ambiance of a fancy restaurant and still charge a price customers were willing to pay. So it had to use a compromise model to evaluate what features it should offer. The must-have feature was low prices. Important-to-have features were entrée variety, a relaxed atmosphere, restaurant ambiance, and friendly, courteous service. Nice-to-have features included time to sit and relax before eating, a few appetizers, and music or entertainment. A compromise model helps marketers decide which blend of features works best, and which blend will have the best perceived value.

Reason for Purchase

I've discussed finding customer characteristics by looking at the reasons people buy. I mention this model because it gives you a graph you can put on a wall to help you as you mull over your marketing options.

Minneapolis Sheet Metal is a custom manufacturer of sheet metal products. It provides sheet metal housings for industrial equipment, large computers, and other products as well as display cases for supermarkets and convenience stores. Minneapolis Sheet Metal might have a reason for purchase model that looks like Figure 5.2.

Figure 5.2
Sheet Metal Custom Manufacturing Reason for Purchase Model

29%	10%	8%	13%	32%
Dependable delivery	Quality	Price	Design help	Past purchase history

A reason for purchase model helps you pick an important area to focus on to discover features you can use to promote both current and new products.

Zoll Medical Company manufacturers cardiac resuscitation gear. Its largest competitor is Eli Lilly, a well-known company in the medical field. Zoll's reason for purchase model showed that the two biggest reasons for purchase were brand loyalty and purchasing from an established supplier, both of which gave Eli Lilly an enormous advantage. But Zoll's model also showed that two other reasons were also important: the equipment was easy to use and the gear was lightweight. The last two reasons were important so that the product could be kept closer to patients for immediate use. Zoll concentrated on promoting those two features, and its sales are projected to increase 41 percent in 1993.

The Ultimate Goal Model

I've already discussed evaluating customers' goals as a way to find marketing opportunities. This model just makes it easier to see how products and features fit into customers' goals. To use this model, first state what the customer's real goal is, then list everything you can think of that helps the customer meet that goal. Everything you do to bring the customer closer to his or her ultimate goal will increase your sales.

Ergodyne is a $30 million manufacturer of equipment to prevent repetitive stress disorders like carpal tunnel syndrome. Its customers are companies whose ultimate goal is injury-free workers. Figure 5.3 shows the ultimate goal model for Ergodyne.

Figure 5.3
Ultimate Goal Model for Ergonomic Safety Equipment

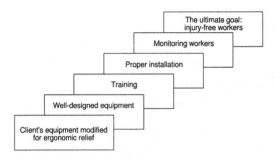

Pep Boys is an auto parts store chain in the Philadelphia area. It knows its customers' true goal is to have their cars running. To help meet that goal, Pep Boys has installed its own service bays, a feature that few other auto parts stores have. Pep Boys also meets customers' second goal, to save money, by not following the typical policy of having the auto repair service mark up the price a second time. That saves customers up to 25 percent on their total repair cost.

Using the Models

These models are meant to help you find customer needs that aren't being met. You have to take the information from one of them and use it to determine a need.

Compromise model

If you were the owner of the photography studio in the example, you would look for features that no one else was providing. For example, the studio owner might find that no one had enough sets, or enough big sets. In that case, customers who photograph a large number of products in one session would be the clients the owner would want to concentrate on. The owner might have to sacrifice convenience to be able to afford a big studio, but an underserved customer segment clearly exists.

Reason for purchase

You have to look at the reasons why people purchase and see if there are any that are either not covered or poorly covered by companies in the market. Zoll Medical discovered that customers need resuscitation units that can be placed close to patients. That was a need that Zoll could address.

The ultimate goal model

With this model you look for steps toward the ultimate goal that customers have trouble attacking. For example, Ergodyne's potential customers might have trouble properly training and monitoring employees. This would be a need you could address. Chapter 6 will talk about how to address that need in a way that will give you a sustainable advantage.

ACTION STEPS

Go back to the list of customer needs, or characteristics, you created. Add to it any new needs or characteristics that you come up with when you use these three models.

CUSTOMER HOT BUTTONS

Every marketer looks for a solution to a customer need that hits the elusive customer hot button that will secure the product's, service's, or store's place in the market. Hot buttons can vary greatly from product to product, but there are certain things that customers always want to see from a company, including making it clear that your claims are true, showing customers you really understand their problems, and giving customers some drama in their lives.

Tell the Truth

In 1987, Campbell ran an aggressive $204 million ad campaign for its soups that failed to increase its market share. At the same time, Campbell's much smaller ad campaign for Prego spaghetti sauce increased Prego's market share 5 percent. There are many reasons for the differing results, but one reason was that Campbell Soup used a vague, unsupported claim ("Soup is good food"), whereas Prego's claim ("a thicker, spicier sauce"), was one that consumers could verify simply by looking in Prego's glass jars.

Customers want proof

A customer survey of 1,500 people found that 75 percent of them believed that advertising for cosmetics was either dishonest or not very honest. That doesn't mean that customers ignore advertising and marketing messages, it just means that they are selective in what, if any, claims they believe. For example, when Macy's advertises a "Once a year gigantic inventory clearance," customers might believe that Macy's is just having another sale. Marketers must do more than offer a message that is targeted and compelling. They also need to prove that their claims are true.

Visual demonstrations

Nike increased its market share from 19 percent in 1987 to 33 percent in 1988. This spurt was significantly helped by a cutaway display shoe that allowed customers to see the exclusive "Nike Air" technology that was featured in Nike's ads. Toyota became a leading car company by having every little component of its cars look like it had a quality design. Toyota also had strong quality reviews and a good service record. But the visual proof in the actual car was an important part of Toyota's image.

Get Real

Cannondale Corporation, a producer of mountain bikes, has, against every piece of conventional wisdom, managed to successfully introduce its products in Japan. It did so, in part, because it stopped being a faceless company and started to seem real to its customers. Cannondale's managers entered bike races every weekend. They generated a lot of publicity, and they had a chance to talk to their Japanese customers to see what they really wanted.

Image is what really counts

Don Schultz and Stanley Tannebaun from Northwestern University have carefully studied customers' buying behavior. They have found that buyers don't take in all the facts about a buying decision. Instead, they take in just enough information to muddle through. In essence, people are buying based on quick impressions. That's why you need to tell the truth and get real. Those are the impressions that get through to customers.

Drama

The unbelievable offer

Glen Johnson owns a plumbing supply company. He was in a competitive business, but he got customers' attention by guaranteeing that they would receive any part free if it wasn't available when they ordered it. That guarantee increased his business 20 percent in the first year.

The dramatic product

Sony's Walkman started out as a simple little recorder, no different from many other available products. Then Sony decided to add tiny headphones. It wasn't the look of the headphones themselves that added drama, it was their look on people's heads. They were very small, and they gave kids a look of detachment that they really liked.

Chem Lawn is another example of adding drama to the product. Chem Lawn was the first major lawn care company. Before Chem Lawn, people either put down dry fertilizer or hired some scruffy-looking guys in an old truck to treat their lawns. Chem Lawn came out with shiny new trucks and employees in clean uniforms. The result was that Chem Lawn had sales of over $1 million in its second year of operation.

ACTION STEPS

1. List all of your claims and your competitors' claims that need to be substantiated. Choose the ones that are most important and list them as a customer need. For example, customers want to buy thick spaghetti sauce, and they want it proven which brand is thickest. Or customers need proof that you are a good dentist.

2. List different ways you could show customers that you really understand their business. Customers have a need to see that you are doing more than just selling products.

3. Customers all have a need to see drama in the following ways:

   • The product itself
   • The way the product is used
   • Product support guarantees.

4. Go back to your list and add these customer needs to it. The next chapter will help you find ways to capitalize on these customer needs and characteristics.

Chapter 6
Creating a Product Advantage

In Chapter 3 I discussed how to find a product that both met a customer need and allowed you to make money. But other companies will copy your efforts. To really cash in on your product, you need a sustainable advantage, something that will let you maintain your position as competitors try to enter the market.

You don't have to be a big company to have a product edge. In fact, often a smaller company can develop and keep an advantage because its target customer group isn't big enough to justify a large competitor's entering the market.

Mello Smello makes scratch-and-sniff stickers with scents of peanut butter, lemonade, and other treats. The stickers come with motivational messages on them that help teachers and parents reward children for positive behavior. Mello Smello has $10 million annual sales of stickers and related products. It also has a array of sustainable features that should keep it profitable for years.

The first of these is size. Sales of $10 million per year is certainly nice, but it is not enough to induce a bigger company to take on an entrenched supplier. Second, Mello Smello has the value-added feature of the sticker's motivational messages. Jon and Leah Miner, the company's founders, are both former teachers, and they knew the types of messages parents wanted. Another value-added feature is Mello Smello's licensing arrangements with both Disney and Nintendo.

Mello Smello also has several cost advantages. It has its own printing and stationery companies, and it has manufacturing and sales outlets in the United States, Korea, Taiwan, and Hong Kong, which cuts costs.

These are the types of advantages you should build into your product. This chapter discusses how to sustain an advantage by adding value, using service as a marketing tool, and creating proprietary advantages, such as patented technology, low costs, or unique manufacturing capabilities.

ADDING VALUE

The two key ways to add value are (1) to include special product features and (2) to provide an unusual level of product support. Byerly's supermarket is adding value with product features when it offers gourmet food sections, cooking classes, and a large deli counter. Amana added value with product support when it introduced its first microwave ovens. It hired home economists who were specially trained in microwave cooking. When a customer purchased an Amana microwave, the home economist would visit his or her home, set up the microwave, and show the customer how to use it.

Customer knowledge is what makes value-added marketing work. You have to know what the customer wants, and then deliver it. Nike and Reebok were unheard of twenty-five years ago. Adidas and Puma were the sports shoes that everyone was wearing. But those shoes didn't really give runners what they were looking for, and the two companies weren't interested in the feedback they received from a runner in Oregon, Bill Bowerman. So Bill went out and started his own company, which he named Nike. He knew which features to include because he knew what runners wanted.

Product Features

As you read the information on product features and product support, you are again just looking for a few ways in which you can specialize your product to give it a competitive edge. Some of the tactics discussed won't apply to your product, or will be tactics that your competitors are using. Skip those tactics, and read on until you find areas that apply to you. I've listed a number of tactics to help you look at your product in as many different ways as possible.

Appearance

Frank Perdue owned a chicken plant and was anxious to expand his sales base. He started surveying customers and found out that they thought chickens in a store looked fresher when they were yellow. So Frank changed his chicken feed so that chickens would have a yellow look. He even decided to pluck out chicken hair so that the chickens would look even more appetizing. Now Perdue is the dominant chicken producer on the East Coast.

Perdue's new features actually provided two benefits: his chickens sold better, and he was able to charge a higher price. His features added value. His advantage was sustainable because he bought from a small number of chicken farms and he could control his product's quality.

Performance

West Publishing publishes books and provides information services for lawyers. All of its product changes and product improvements are performance-related: they offer more or easier-to-find information. Production or testing equipment manufacturers are always offering faster, more versatile, or more accurate products.

Nike's $140 Air Jordan shoes contain all of these added performance features and benefits: a cross-pull strapping system to lock down heels for a customized fit, an external molded upper support for stability, an inner boot to support the midfoot and heel, a polyurethane midsole that offers enhanced flexibility, and an outsole with a cutaway section for reduced weight and enhanced flexibility.

Image

Car manufacturers differentiate their cars through image features such as leather upholstery, engine size, actual car size, automatic car locks and window controls, and the number of gauges on the dashboard. Restaurants add image features through their ambiance and the type of items on their menus. Service providers add image value through the way their offices look, the cars they drive and the type of clothes they wear.

Predispositions

When Pepsi decided to introduce a lemon-lime drink to compete with 7-Up and Sprite, it discovered that people thought those drinks tasted better because they had fruit juice in them. Actually, neither 7-Up nor Sprite has any fruit juice in it. But Pepsi took advantage of customers' predisposition towards fruit juice and included about 10 percent fruit juice in each of its Slice drinks.

Safety

Chrysler has spent a great deal of money promoting its use of auto air bags as a safety feature. Tire companies and makers of children's toys and baby products also frequently promote safety features.

Market shifts

You can gain an edge by being the first company to capitalize on a new market trend. Toro had a big year in 1992 because it was one of the first companies out with a mulching mower after consumers started to become aware of the problems associated with putting grass and leaf clippings in landfills.

Hawaiian Sun Tan Oil was a small sideline of Ron Rice when people suddenly became aware of the dangers of sun exposure. Ron's product had blocking agents that were ideal for what people were looking for, and his sales took off.

Product Support Tactics

You create a competitive edge every time you do something that makes it difficult for someone else to compete with you. Product support tactics are often an inexpensive and effective way to gain a product advantage.

Follow-up support

I have a lifetime wheel alignment guarantee from Sears. I've lived in six states, and the only reason I purchased this guarantee from Sears was that it has stores around the country. That's product support that most other auto service stores can't match.

Computer programming firms often promise to return immediately to help out if a problem develops with their program. Engineers will guarantee their work, and will commit to redesigning products in order to eliminate any last minute foul-ups. Some medical claims processing companies will follow up and correct any payment delays.

Training

We had a competitor in the dental business that offered extensive training classes for dealer service people at its headquarters. We thought the training was a waste of money until the service people started en masse to recommend that competitor's equipment. The competitor capitalized on this further by having the service people redesign certain problem areas in its equipment.

Repair service

AT&T uses support as its primary marketing tool. One commercial has a manager from J.C. Penney's mail-order catalog explaining how AT&T was able to reroute calls to another location after a big storm. Another of AT&T's support tactic is to guarantee that your phone system won't be down for more than two hours. No other competitor can match that guarantee.

Brand-name recognition

This can be especially important in markets that aren't quite big enough to justify a big advertising budget. Walk into your neighborhood drugstore and take a look at the shelf with dental floss. Johnson & Johnson's floss is typically the most expensive, yet it consistently outsells other brands simply because Johnson & Johnson has the best-known name.

Brand recognition is also a big factor in business-to-business marketing. When a big company hires a consultant, it will often hire a well-known firm just because it feels that a big, well-known company must know what it's doing. I've seen several companies hire a well-known advertising agency because it gives them prestige with their investors.

Confidence

Businesses such as law firms, consultants, specialists in engineering and quality control, and advertising agencies all depend on credibility. People buy the service before they can evaluate performance, and so these businesses' ability to inspire confidence will determine their success.

People establish credibility by writing books or articles; being associated with a major institution such as a hospital or university; having prominent people, like an ex-federal court judge, on staff; giving speeches; becoming members of prestigious organizations; or having experience with well-known major firms.

Advertising and promotion

This may seem like a strange way to add value to your product. But it's important because people tend to buy the product they're most familiar with any time they are confused.

For the foreseeable future, Budweiser will always be the King of Beer simply because it has a tremendous promotional advantage. Little businesses can achieve the same effect. Cheap Skates is a roller rink that passes out two-for-one coupons every time someone has a party. Those coupons get used as people start to become regular customers, and that gives Cheap Skates an edge over any potential new competitor.

You can also get an edge through advertising. A quality control testing firm will have a big advantage if it is the only such firm that is listed in industry buyers' guides. An auto repair business will have an edge if it has a billboard at a key location. An auto dealer will generate extra business if it is a long-time sponsor of a popular radio show.

Expertise

Will Sykes is the president of Jer-Neen Spring Co., a $3 million business that specializes in small springs for difficult applications. Seventy percent of Jer-

CREATING A PRODUCT ADVANTAGE

Neen's business comes from medical products such as pacemaker leads, defibrillator coils, defibrillator electrodes, and angioplasty leads and coil wires. Jer-Neen
Spring Co. doesn't just build the springs; in most cases it designed the spring
specifications so that the end product would work.

Action Steps

1. Take out your "Customer Needs/Possible Strategies" chart.

2. Put a new heading, Potential Product Strategies, about four inches over
   from your first column.

3. Look through the product features and product support tactics below, and
   choose the tactics that will help address each need or characteristic. List
   as many tactics as you can for each need.

Product Features	Product Support
Appearance	Follow-up support
Performance	Training
Image	Repair services
Predisposition	Brand-name recognition
Safety	Confidence
Market trends	Advertising and promotion expertise

Figure 6.1 gives an example of this for two characteristics of customers
who are buying new living room furniture.

4. Go through your list and eliminate strategies that you can't afford to execute, that are being used by competitors, or that cost more than you can
   charge for them.

Gaining a Service Advantage

Bugs Burger Bug Killers of Miami offers an incredible four-part service guarantee that gives it a clear-cut advantage:

1. Customers don't pay a penny until every bug is killed.

2. Customers who are unhappy can receive a full refund. Bugs Burger will
   also pay for the services of another exterminator.

3. Any guest spotting a pest gets a free meal or room on both this and their
   next stay at Bugs Burger's expense.

4. If a hotel or motel is closed because of the presence of roaches or rodents,
   Bugs Burger guarantees to pay for all lost profits, *and* kick in another
   $5,000.

Service is really another value-added feature. I discuss it separately because
there are so many ways to use it to gain a competitive edge, and because so much
attention has been given to it over the last few years.

FIGURE 6.1
Customer Needs/Possible Strategies

FURNITURE STORE
LIVING ROOM FURNITURE

1. Wants a room that looks like it's out of a designer catalog
    a. Have furniture laid out in sample rooms, with complete room decorations.
    b. Have a designer on staff to suggest wallpaper, paint, and accessories.
    c. Carry a top-end designer line with the latest furniture fashions. Include posters on the line, and display the line's awards and other honors.
    d. Offer to send a designer to a customer's home for up to one year after purchase for a $25 fee to help coordinate a room's look.
    e. Offer free room decorating classes.

2. Concerned about quality of furniture
    a. Offer a thirty-day, no questions asked return policy.
    b. Have model cutaways of major furniture brands, demonstrating quality.
    c. Offer an extended warranty for any material or construction defects.
    d. Get testimonials from neighborhood craftsmen, such as carpenters and upholsterers.
    e. Put together a display of reviews of furniture lines by trade magazines.
    f. Get a series of photos from factories showing how the products are built.

Service as Part of the Marketing Strategy

Wal-Mart and Nordstrom are two retailing powerhouses that have continued to increase sales in the 1990s. Their success is often attributed to their high level of service, which they certainly have. But service is just one part of Wal-Mart's and Nordstrom's strategy. They also have the right products, at the right price, in the right locations.

A study done by Impact Resources, a market research firm, found that customers' main buying motivations were price, selection, quality, location, and finally service. Service should certainly be part of your marketing strategy, but it can't make up for problems in your product or distribution strategy. I believe it is much more important to have the right product than it is to have the right service.

Service: Management or Marketing?

Service as a marketing tactic succeeds only with management support. For example, Glen Johnson decided to offer his millwork customers any back-ordered part free. Deciding to offer that guarantee was a marketing decision. Executing the strategy before the company goes broke is a management problem. Glen Johnson quickly realized that his employees needed to be highly motivated for the guarantee to work. He offered workers and their spouses a free trip to Hawaii if back orders were low. He also installed a new computerized tracking system to help employees get the job done.

The key to good customer service is a company culture that believes in service. This is difficult to achieve, and it comes about only after an intensive management effort.

Service During the Entire Buying Decision

You can provide service from the first moment a customer thinks about buying to five years or more after the sale is made. Most people concentrate on providing service at the time of the sale and during the first few months after the sale. Pharmacia Health Care Group offers a drug infusion system for patients staying at their own or a relative's home. Pharmacia has a twenty-four-hour-a-day, seven-days-a-week answering service for people who have just purchased a system. This is a traditional service strategy. Pharmacia also offers a variety of services that come into play throughout the entire buying process. It has financial services to help people pay their bills. It aligns itself as a service provider for new treatments to make it easier for clients to get insurance reimbursements. And it works with drug companies to pioneer new treatments for patients' needs.

Service During the Four Steps of a Buying Decision

These steps may be a little different for your business, but as a rule they apply in some way to every sale:

1. The scouting-around period
2. The educational phase
3. The actual sale
4. After-sale service.

The scouting-around period

During this period you need to do things that show that you are related to customers and that you are an expert in your field. You can promote community events; sponsor contests; give speeches; advertise; issue publicity; hold fairs, classes, and seminars; and join key organizations. What you want to do is find a way to make your company's name more visible than your competitors'. Some service steps to consider are:

- Network through industry standard groups like ASTM or industry trade groups.
- Attend key trade shows and list your company in key buyers' guides or the Yellow Pages.
- Write for or appear in magazines or other companies' newsletters.
- Look into sponsoring existing events or fairs.
- Check clubs, radio shows, other stores, or any other connection that will get people to notice your name.
- Run classes or seminars, or pass out free information about your type of product.

The educational phase

Once customers get a feel for what is going on, they start in on a more intentional educational process. Classes, pamphlets, informational brochures, magazine articles, trade show attendance, and effective displays are all ways to give customers service. Here are some service aspects to check for first:

- See if anyone has a good brochure or pamphlet that explains what products work best for each application. Customers really like information in a *Consumer Reports* type of format.

- Check with universities or technical colleges and your industry's trade groups to see if they offer any courses related to your product or service. If they do, consider teaching one.

- Look at your store or business and your competitors' stores or businesses and see which one has the most, and best, educational material for someone who is looking for information on a product or service.

The actual sale

Courtesy and friendliness are the two traditional types of service. But you can do more than that. Best Buy has a chain of consumer electronics superstores. Best Buy did a survey and found that people didn't like being pressured by commissioned salespeople. Best Buy decided it wanted to provide service, so it took out its commissioned sales force and replaced it with a large customer service counter. The customer service people answered questions and explained how customers could get the best product for their needs. The result: sales increased.

Look at the following points to see if you are providing customers with the information they want:

- Are customers comfortable while buying?
- Do customers understand their choices when they are buying?
- Do people have a chance to see, feel, and try out the product as much as they would like?
- Is there any information people would like that they don't get?
- Are customers satisfied with the technical support of your sales force?
- Would customers like to have contact with more people than the sales force? (This is important for large industrial accounts.)
- Is your company calling on enough of the people involved in the buying decision?
- Are you providing requisitioners with enough support to help them push their requests through?

After-sale service

Superior technical service, offering lifetime replacement parts, and free warranty repairs are all ways to create a service advantage. Here are some questions to ask to develop a service-related advantage:

- What problems do customers experience after they purchase?
- What type of follow-up service would customers like to have?
- What type of service do customers feel is valuable?

Examples of Service Marketing
Before-sale service

H.B. Fuller is an adhesives manufacturer. Chemical products can't always be counted on to act in predictable ways. For example, if a customer changes a backing material, the new backing might interact in a new way with an adhesive. Most companies look at this as a problem. Fuller looks at it as a service opportunity.

Fuller makes its technically trained sales force and service department available to customers and potential customers. If a customer has a problem with one of its products, H.B. Fuller will send its people to the scene to try and solve it, even if the problem is not caused by a Fuller adhesive. Fuller wants its customers to keep their production running. This commitment is noticeable, and it helps make Fuller look better than its competitors.

Service at the sale

As I'm writing this book, Compaq Computer is mounting an attack, based on service, against Dell Computer, which has been a superstar in the low-cost computer market. Compaq offers installation for only $135, free installation of software, and forty-eight-hour delivery. Dell Computer hasn't yet been able to match these service features.

Service after the sale

Deluxe Corporation, a leading printer of bank checks, promises forty-eight-hour delivery, not just on the first order, but any time the customer orders checks after that. People who need checks need them fast and without mistakes. Deluxe has sixty-two plants set up throughout the country to meet this service commitment.

Service and Expectations

Your reaction to any company's service depends on two things: how good the service actually was, and what your expectations were. It is important that you manage customers' expectations or you won't be able to keep them happy no matter what you do.

Don't be afraid to be honest with customers. They don't expect any company to be able to do everything. They just want to know if you can do what they want. Customers admire honesty, and they will keep coming back to you if you use it.

ACTION STEPS

1. Take your list "Customer Needs/Possible Strategies." You have already listed value-added features and product support tactics that could address each need.

2. Go through your list and add to it any service tactics that will address each need:

- List your service guarantees, and compare them with competitors'. Whose has the most drama, and if it is not yours, how can you add drama?
- What services would customers like to see during the scouting-around period? during the educational phase? at the time of the sale? after the sale has been made?

3. What information, display, or service can you offer that will give people the proper expectations? This tactic works especially well for building confidence.

PROPRIETARY FEATURES

Another way to generate a sustainable product edge is to have a proprietary feature of some sort that competitors can't match. This could be a patent, trademark, or copyright, or other lesser-known features such as manufacturing processes, trade secrets, a fast-acting management system, or a superior cost position.

Patents

Polaroid has the sales of instant cameras wrapped up because of its patent position. Nobody can compete with it. Patents are probably the best-known proprietary tactic, but I feel they are the weakest. If a competitor can figure out another way to make your product, it can probably introduce a competing product without infringing on your patent. For most consumer products, a patent will do very little to keep other companies from bringing out competing products. Patents are worthwhile on some technology products, but only if you can afford to spend the $5,000 to $15,000 that they cost.

Patent pending status can be beneficial on industrial products, where it might take 9 to 24 months to introduce a product. Once a patent is issued, a competitor can get a copy of it and see how to get around your claims. But your patent application is confidential, and competitors won't know your claims when your patent is pending. It is usually to your advantage to wait as long as possible to apply for a patent.

Trade Dress

Next time you are in your kitchen, take a look at cans of spices. They have a distinctive look, with red across the top and bottom. There is no mistaking a spice can. You might be able to trademark that look for $175, or you can copyright the design for $20, or you can just rely on trade dress protection.

Trade dress is a term that describes the way your product or package looks. Nobody can steal your look if it is distinctive, or if you promote it sufficiently that people recognize it. You can't introduce your own spices in cans that look like those already on the market. This is why you should develop a common packaging look with a distinctive style. You have an advantage when people can walk into a store or a mall and instantly recognize your product or business.

Trademarks

Scotch tape is a name that is known by everyone in America. Scotch tape is in a big market, and it is expensive compared to other products. Yet people continue to make it the market leader because of its name. Kleenex and Band-Aids are two other products with powerful trademarks.

Small companies with clever names can also enjoy trademark protection. Devee Philpot's trademarked name, The Junk Drawer Organizer, is perfectly suited to her product. No other name would work as well, and she has a powerful asset.

Manufacturing Processes

Virtually everyone has heard how rigorously Coke guards its secret formula. Having a proprietary manufacturing process is a fairly common tactic. 3M has dominated the market for Post-it notes, those little semi-sticky note pads, because it created a proprietary (or secret) manufacturing process. 3M solved many production problems, including how to apply the adhesive to a continuous roll of paper, how to get glue to stick to the pads, and not to the memo a Post-it is attached to, and how to cut the paper into small pads. 3M developed each machine it uses, and it has kept its technology secret. Only recently has any other company been able to come out with a competing product.

Management Strategies

Management can make a tremendous difference in a company's performance. A fast-moving management team will consistently arrive at a target first, giving the company a favorable marketing position.

In 1992 *Inc.* magazine rated Kingston Technology the fastest-growing small company in America. Kingston manufacturers memory, storage, and processor upgrades for personal computers. In a business where products constantly change, Kingston stays on top by putting its products on the market before anyone else.

Kingston management has set up its organization for speed. It uses small teams that can create, design, and build products in a fraction of the time its competitors need. Its manufacturing operations are set up to build and ship an order the same day it is received.

ACTION STEPS

1. Make a list of all the proprietary features you currently have. Keep this list separate, as it is one of the three informational sheets you will use to finalize your market strategy.

2. Review your packaging, new products, trademarks, trade dress, and manufacturing processes to see if you are overlooking something that could give you proprietary protection. If you find something, take the steps needed to make it proprietary and add it to the list you put together in Step 1.

3. Institute a policy regarding items that could become proprietary. Some of the policies could be:

- Sign a confidentiality agreement any time equipment is ordered with changes specified by your company.

- Include on all purchase orders for advertising and packaging that the trade dress appearance of the materials belongs to your company and is not to be used again for any other company.

- Have marketing, sales, and engineering managers closely monitor their personnel for any "buzzwords" they create for the product. Consider trade marking any terms that appropriately describe a product in a unique way.

4. Have all appropriate employees attend classes on keeping company property proprietary. For example, engineers know that they should not discuss manufacturing process secrets. But this information can also leak out through salespeople, buyers, and production line workers.

Chapter 7
Dominating with Distribution

The customer, the product, and the market are the three keys to a successful marketing strategy. Finding a way to secure your place in the distribution channel is the final way to become better than everyone else.

Distribution, or placement, is how a product moves and is then bought by the final user. Any business can dominate with distribution. A retailer might have a specialized location strategy, like F.A.O. Schwarz's exclusive, downtown toy stores or Toys "R" Us' stand-alone suburban distribution outlets. A manufacturer might lock up the hardware store market channel. An environmental engineering firm might dominate because of its network of contacts with key state agencies. A medical doctor might meet all of a neighborhood's needs with a strategy of long hours and two convenient locations. A restaurant might control sales with an aggressive delivery program.

Chapter 4, "Locating the Right Market," discussed how to find a market that was open to you. This chapter explains how to lock in your market channel so that you will have a sustainable advantage. This chapter covers the importance of distribution, matching strategy to a product's needs, ways to lock in a market channel, promotion and advertising control, and sales strategy.

IMPORTANCE OF DISTRIBUTION

Distribution is one of the best ways to generate a competitive advantage, first because it is one of a company's major costs, and second because it is so difficult to set up. IBM, for example, ruled the computer world for decades with a distribution policy of direct sales through an extensive sales and technical service network. That network was so large that not only couldn't competitors afford to duplicate it, they probably couldn't find enough qualified people to hire. The actual nature of computers had to change before IBM was dislodged.

Distribution can be just as powerful a tool for small companies. A restaurant might have a location on the busiest corner in a college town. A small company might receive orders from over 2,000 different hardware stores through a network of manufacturers' representatives. A software development firm might have a key contract with a major retailer. A physician might be the chief of surgery at a town's only hospital. All of these distribution strategies are difficult to dislodge.

Distribution as Part of the Marketing Strategy

L'eggs revolutionized pantyhose sales when it introduced its first egg-shaped containers. Part of L'eggs' success was due to its product—pantyhose were much more practical with short skirts than stockings. Part of its success was due to its package, which was far different from the undistinguished flat packages of stockings' and other pantyhose brands. But what gave L'eggs its biggest advantage was its distribution plan. It moved pantyhose out of women's lingerie departments into mass merchandiser outlets. Today L'eggs still accounts for over 50 percent of pantyhose sales, with its nearest competitor, No-Nonsense pantyhose, way back at 12 percent.

L'eggs found a target customer group, women who wore short skirts. It found the right product, and it found a market that was open to it. L'eggs then found that a key customer characteristic was showmanship, and L'eggs delivered that with its egg-shaped container. Then L'eggs worked on locking up its distribution outlets, which it did with its innovative package, its strong advertising support, and its numerous dedicated point-of-purchase displays.

Distribution versus Product Support

In some cases the line between distribution strategy and product support is blurry. For example, having an installation technician explain how to install a new water softener is both a distribution tactic and product support. Your goal in this section of the book is to find several ways to create a unique strategy. These chapters are designed to help you develop a new way to look at your product. So don't worry if some areas overlap; instead, just keep looking for a product aspect you can capitalize on.

DEGREE OF SPECIALIZATION

Specialization is a term I use to describe how much effort is required to sell a product or service. If very little effort is involved, as in selling gas or selling a cheap portable radio, little specialization is involved, and the best distribution strategy is to put the product where people can find it. If it takes a major effort to sell your product, as with an expensive copier, a high-tech stereo system, or life insurance, you need a specialized distribution strategy that will generate the support people need before they buy.

Specialization in the distribution strategy is the area where new business-to-business markets consistently fall short. This includes manufacturers, repair services, engineering and management consultants, and service companies such as environmental waste removal.

A typical example is a new manufacturer of a manual assembly device for surface-mounted electronic components. The machine is designed for low-volume (less than 3,000 pieces) production of PC boards with fewer than seventy components. It is intended for producers of test equipment, monitoring or process control equipment, medical devices, or other low-volume applications. The manufacturer's price was $4,800, versus a cost of $60,000 and up for an automated machine.

The company sent out press releases, attended trade shows, sent out literature, and had manufacturers' representatives call on customers. However, the company did not make many sales because its distribution policy (which includes sales strategy) wasn't nearly specialized enough. The company thought spending $4,800 rather than $60,000 would be an easy choice. But customers didn't just think in terms of money; they were worried about keeping up quality production, and they needed a lot of support before buying.

How Much Specialization Is Needed?

The four factors involved in determining how specialized a strategy needs to be are how important the product is, how necessary it is, how technical it is, and how frequently it is purchased.

How important is the product?

When a product is important, people are more concerned about making the right choice. If you are buying insurance, a cabin at the lake, or a new snowmobile, you are making an important purchase, and you will want to take your time deciding what to buy.

A purchase doesn't have to be expensive to be important. Many golfers buy golf clubs from a golf pro at their local golf shop. Often, these clubs are more expensive than they would be at a golf store. But to some golfers, a golf club is an important purchase, and they want the extra confidence they get from buying a club recommended by a pro.

When you sell to companies, often the important element of the sale is not your product, it is what the customer is trying to do. Often the company will look at a purchase in terms of what could go wrong. For example, one company I worked with spent months of study before replacing a part on its most important product. At the same time, it bought a new office partitioning system for 220 people in less than two weeks.

Companies follow the same rules when they buy services. If a company needs an environmental impact statement, it will hire any firm as long as its reports will be accepted by the state and it has several positive references from other companies. There isn't a lot that could go wrong with that purchase. If a company wants to hire an advertising agency, it is going to want a lot more information. If an ad program goes wrong, the company might not be able to recover. Ad agencies use a specialized strategy, with contact by account managers, the agencies' principals, and creative directors. They will often prepare a sample piece of work for a possible client in order to get the business.

If a purchase isn't important, like a pint of oil, a box for shipping, or office supplies like copy paper, customers will probably buy from the most convenient or least expensive company.

How necessary is the purchase?

People know they need auto insurance. Auto insurance agencies just need to keep their names visible so that people will call them when they need to buy. That's a nonspecialized purchase. Other purchases, like life insurance, may not be necessary and require a more intensive distribution strategy, such as sending sales representatives out to people's homes, conducting special seminars to find prospects, or joining community groups in order to meet new clients.

If you sell to companies, the reverse is true. If a company's purchasing methods for a necessary purchase are set, the company is not likely to change without a very strong reason. I represented a chemical company that was one of the original suppliers of an important chemical component of the antiulcer drug Tagamet. Our plant manager, quality control supervisor, and shipping manager were all involved in making the sale. Smith Kline's factory people visited our plant, and we had to buy special equipment to ship our product. We needed a specialized distribution strategy, with plenty of support, to land the business.

How technical is the purchase?

When I purchased my first microwave and VCR, I read *Consumer Reports*, looked at magazine and newspaper articles, and went to a store that had a large product selection. I went to all this trouble because the products were new to me, I thought they were complicated, and I wanted to be sure I purchased a good product. Today when I buy these products, I just go where prices are low. The products are no longer technical to me.

How frequent is the purchase?

The more often you make a purchase, the more you learn about the product and the less specialization you need. When customers purchase infrequently, they need the support of distribution specialization. Trees and shrubs, for example, are infrequent purchases, and many people need the specialized support they get from a nursery. If an insurance company only rarely uses the services of a computer programmer, it will be careful in making a selection, and several people will probably be involved in the final decision. If the purchase is more frequent, the company will analyze much less, and probably only one or two people will make the decision on which programmer to use.

How to Use This Information

1. Look at your and your competitors' distribution strategies and decide whether each company's strategy has high, medium, or low specialization.

2. Using the four factors just discussed, decide what degree of specialization your product calls for. If your competitors aren't providing the needed support, you can gain an edge by adding features to deliver the specialization needed.

3. You can also use specialization to find customer segments that are not having all their needs met. Go back to your "Customer Needs/Possible Strategies" chart. Go to the second half of the page and start two more headings. Specialization Required and Specialization Present Now.

4. Look at each characteristic and decide if it calls for a specialized strategy. As an example, I've listed some customer concerns below and rated each as requiring high, medium, or low specialization.

Rating	Concerns
Medium	Concerned that a shrub won't survive in the climate.
High	Worried that a new inventory control system will be difficult to implement.
Low	Not sure supplier can deliver copy paper in three days.
High	Doesn't believe life insurance is a good investment.
Low	Doesn't want to pay too high a price.
Medium	Wants to be sure a physician is competent.
High	Isn't sure a lawyer is capable of handling the complexities of a case.
Low	Concerned about getting an extended warranty to cover motor failure.

5. Look for concerns that require more specialization than either you or any other competitor is providing. Customers with that concern can have it met either by product support or by your distribution strategy.

Example of finding a market niche

Consider customers who are about to purchase a home. This is an important, infrequent, and technical purchase. A specialized distribution strategy is clearly called for.

The real estate business has been adding more support by providing short videos on homes, but basically it still relies on small, numerous real estate offices staffed by real estate agents and their MLS books. Here are just are a few of the important questions you have to rely on an agent for:

- How good is the school system?
- Is this a fair price?
- How busy is this street?
- How often does that train go by?

Real estate agents answer most of these questions based on what they have heard from other people, which is not the kind of answer people want on an important decision. Real estate companies should have large central offices with much more technical and informational backup.

You can also go over customers' concerns and see which ones aren't being met from a specialization point of view. I've listed some possible home buyer concerns below:

1. Concerned that all the paperwork will go through smoothly.

2. Want to be sure of purchasing a home in a good neighborhood with good schools.

3. Want to buy in a neighborhood considered prestigious.

4. Would like to buy at a good price.

5. Don't want to have any unexpected home repairs.

6. Want to be able to afford payments.

7. Concerned about seeing enough houses to be sure the house selected is the best choice.

8. Worried about the reliability of the real estate agency.

These are obviously important concerns, and they call for a specialized strategy. Concerns 1, 5, and 7 are fairly well covered by current real estate offices, so a marketer could address the remaining points. To handle points 4 and 7, he or she could set up a large office that could instantly access photos, videos, price sheets, and specifications for a wide range of homes. Points 2 and 3 could be covered by entering all the pertinent factors—average income, crime rate, medium home price, and so on—for various neighborhoods into a computer database so that people would have a more accurate basis for deciding if that was where they wanted to live. And point 8 can be handled by testimonials, membership in the Better Business Bureau, and a comprehensive training course for all agents.

Now, how should a real estate office be set up? Should it be a small office (or maybe even someone's home) with an agent who shows you a three-ring binder? Or should it be a large, high-tech office with large TV screens playing videos of homes and interactive computer screens that can answer people's questions about taxes, neighborhood composition, and school systems? A small real estate business can't afford that type of support. But a larger company using a new strategy of fewer, but larger and electronically equipped, offices can. The two customer groups this strategy would appeal to are people who are nervous and apprehensive about making any purchase and people who are very concerned about the neighborhood they move into.

Examples of Setting Up the Right Distribution System

Every business is stuck with certain costs, either to rent a prime location or to provide showrooms, technical service, and other product support. Companies usually can't afford to have the best of both worlds, so they need to determine how to allocate their resources. How well you do that will often determine your success.

Copier system

Select Copy Systems sells $20,000 and up copiers to businesses. This is a major purchase, and calls for a specialized distribution strategy. Select Copy uses four custom-made mobile showrooms to exhibit its copiers to potential customers. The mobile showrooms go to the customer's location so that everyone involved in the buying decision can see the product. Select Copy's competitors all use a distribution strategy of having a centralized showroom. That strategy doesn't provide quite enough support, as only a few people actually see the equipment, and this lowers everyone's confidence.

Car repair service

There are two car repair services that I've used. One is a Goodyear Service Center on a busy road; it has invested in location. The other is an individual business in an out-of-the way location. This garage has diagnostic equipment that tells the mechanics, and me, what is wrong with the car.

The independent garage has a better distribution strategy. It expends a great deal of effort to convince people that they are getting the repairs their car really needs. Goodyear doesn't do anything to build your confidence; after all, its money is in its location. Repairing your car is an important, and hopefully infrequent, purchase that calls for a specialized strategy.

Restaurant

Wee Bag It is a lunchtime catering business that delivers lunches to businesses, both for individuals and for meetings or conferences. This chain of restaurants has grown rapidly, and has been successful. Wee Bag It also made several key distribution decisions that allowed it to spend its money on support. First, it has no walk-in location. Eliminating this expense allowed it to offer more food and service for the money. Then Wee Bag It decided to serve only lunch. Again, this reduced expenses. Wee Bag It used that money to improve its product.

ACTION STEPS

1. Calculate what percentage of your monthly expenses goes toward visibility and what percentage goes toward customer support.

2. Do the same for each of your competitors.

3. Look at your product, store, or service and decide how important specialization is. List the percentage you feel should go toward customer support based on the specialization the product needs.

4. See whether you or a competitor comes closest to matching that percentage. Often, the company with closest to the optimum split between visibility and support will be the most successful.

5. If your mix is out of balance, either figure out how to balance it or consider changing your product so that you have the right mix.

LOCKING IN YOUR DISTRIBUTION CHANNEL

American Greetings developed the CreataCard, a little booth that lets people make their own greeting card, for just $3.50. Morry Weiss, American Greetings' president, states that he is dedicated to his retailers making money. CreataCard is a product that will give American Greetings' retailers an edge on their Hallmark competitors. That type of support shows that American Greetings wants to be a partner with its distribution channel, and this is the type of support that keeps the customer base.

You want to have a degree of control over your distribution channel. Otherwise you are subject to the whims of your channel, and you could lose your market position fast. There are four ways to lock in control of your market that work for any type of business. They are becoming the key supplier, entering into partnership agreements, developing a low-cost position, and creating a product line that people want.

Becoming a Key Supplier

Gale Publishing puts together large directories, primarily for use in libraries. Gale's reputation is well established. Its books are large and difficult to put together, and it comes out with new directories, such as *Gale's Source of Videos*, whenever libraries see a need for additional information. Gale has a degree of control, and no one is going to take away its market share.

Business-to-business service companies can become key suppliers by developing close contacts with certain customers. A common strategy is for electrical, heating and air conditioning, and other construction contractors to align themselves as key suppliers to certain big contractors. They know all the people at the larger company, and they provide several extra services to maintain a good relationship.

Manufacturers of production equipment often lock in customers through compatibility. Once a client buys one piece of equipment, it is easier to buy additional equipment from the same supplier because the equipment fits together more easily. Manufacturers might also have their equipment written into the specifications for a critical process, or as a key product component, or as an approved supplier.

Partnership Arrangements

Intel and Microsoft products were used in IBM's initial personal computer. These products are also used in IBM-compatible computers. Not surprisingly, this partnership arrangement, along with the growth in the personal computer markets, has made Intel and Microsoft giants in American industry.

Today, every marketer faces stiff competition. Any company's market share can be easily stolen if all it does is sell a product. What marketers have to do first is to add value to the product through product features, support, and service so that it has a unique position in the market. Once you have that, you need a well-entrenched network to sell through. If you can't afford that, one of your options is to set up a partnership agreement with companies in your distribution channel or with other similar, but noncompeting companies.

With the distribution channel

L'eggs made several moves to partner up with its distribution network. It provided specialized shelf displays that helped sell the product. It also provided retailers with a computer that helped customers pick the right type of pantyhose.

When I was in the dental business, one of our distributors wanted to put out a catalog for dentists that had a complete listing of available dental equipment. Dentists preferred this type of catalog because it was the only way they could get a look at all the available products, since dealers couldn't carry everyone's products in their showrooms. This dealer had a good plan, but it couldn't afford to print the catalog on its own, so it asked its suppliers for help. The catalog was successful, and the dealer was loyal to the companies that helped it get the catalog started.

Here are some other ways to partner up with a distribution channel. Be creative when you look at ways to create a partnership, as there are literally dozens of ways to formulate a mutually beneficial arrangement:

1. Exclusive agreements. A manufacturer might give a distributor an exclusive sales agreement provided the distributor sells a required volume of goods. Often exclusive arrangements are proposed by the distributor.

2. Special sales support. A retailer or distributor might agree to have a salesperson or two specially trained on a manufacturer's product, or a manufacturer might furnish salespeople, at no charge, to the store for sales or other busy days. Service suppliers and business-to-business marketers will often supply similar support at key trade shows.

3. Cosponsoring of events, such as seminars, classes, contests, demonstrations, and so on.

4. Co-op advertising programs, where the manufacturer pays 50 percent of the cost of retailer ad space when its products are mentioned.

5. Private label agreements. Here a manufacturer will make a product that is sold under the retailer's name. Sears lawnmowers, which are made by another company, are an example of private labeling. This is also a common practice among service companies, who sell another company's service as their own, and equipment manufacturers, who contract work out to custom manufacturers.

6. Franchise arrangements. This doesn't necessarily have to be an actual franchise, like a McDonald's franchise. It could be a loan, or some other form of financial support, or operating help and advice. For example, some bike shops are associated in a loose franchise arrangement with manufacturers like Schwinn.

With other companies

Adec is currently a leading dental equipment supplier. When it started, the company was small, and it didn't have the financial muscle it needed to get its product line into the distribution network. So it signed a sales agreement with a noncompeting supplier and used that company's sales force, and financial strength, to enter the market. This arrangement benefited both companies. Adec was able to enter the market, and the company it used picked up a 25 percent sales commission when it sold Adec's products.

Here are some other ways to work out a partnership arrangement with another company:

1. Combine efforts with a similar, but noncompeting business. For example, office supply distributors may combine with computer suppliers, with each company's sales force selling the other's products.

2. Sell through another, larger store. Rather than setting up a separate jewelry store, a company might rent space from another retailer.

3. Exchange mailing lists or send out combined mailings with another similar but noncompeting business.

4. Combine efforts on events and seminars.

5. Take in service work for another company. For example, a shoe repair shop and a dry cleaning store might each take in service work for the other. Service firms serving other businesses can also benefit from this tactic. The firm positions itself as a total supplier with customers, and it can increase its sales with little sales effort.

6. Give referral commissions. A fence company and an aluminum siding firm might offer each other's salespeople a referral commission for any lead that results in a purchase of the company's products. Two material testing companies with noncompeting lines could also offer each other referral commissions.

Cost Position

Having an edge in distribution cost is one of the most powerful advantages a company can have. Wal-Mart has excellent customer service, the right products, and a well-known name. But Wal-Mart grew to be the nation's number one retailer by establishing a strong distribution cost position. Wal-Mart's strategy was to set up a ring of stores around a city that could serve as a warehouse hub. This wheel of stores allowed Wal-Mart to set up a distribution system that could offer low prices.

To understand the importance of Wal-Mart's strategy, you need to realize that freight costs on a retail product can often be over 5 percent of the product's cost, and that quantity discounts can range from 5 to 25 percent. Those two costs hurt retailers in small towns. Wal-Mart overcame these cost disadvantages with its warehousing concept.

Industrial companies can also use a low-cost technique. Air Products and Chemicals sells gases like oxygen and nitrogen. It got its start by building plants right next to steel factories. It sent a pipeline into the factory and had a cost advantage that no one could touch. Air Products then shipped to smaller customers by truck. Competitors couldn't afford to put plants in areas where they competed with Air Products.

Product Line Features

Distribution success depends on control. When a product is in demand, the manufacturer has control. When a product is one of many, the distribution channel has control. Rubbermaid has distribution control because of its broad product line. Lego toys has control because Lego sets are a popular, and asked-for, toy.

Marketing tactics are all interrelated. If you know customers well and can give them the value-added features they need, you will be able to have the distribution channel coming to you.

ACTION STEPS

1. The last chart you need to prepare is a Distribution Strategies chart that lists possible strategies for locking out competition. Figure 7.1 is a distribution strategies chart for Kerdoodles Industrial Design, a firm that does initial design, prototype design, and product testing for consumer products such as toys, in-line skates, housewares, and other consumer products.

Figure 7.1
Distribution Strategies

KERDOODLES INDUSTRIAL DESIGN

1. Become a key supplier:
   - Target a small niche market. Kerdoodles could concentrate its efforts on small plastics manufacturers, while other designers targeted large consumer products companies.

2. Partnership agreements:
   - Key customers: Sign a year-long monthly retainer agreement with one or two key customers. These customers would pay a fixed amount per month to Kerdoodles, in return for a lower hourly rate.
   - Manufacturers' associations: Agree to do seminars or classes for a local manufacturing group, or contribute a monthly article to a newsletter.
   - Plastics manufacturers: Join any member groups, volunteer for relevant committees, and offer free service to members.
   - Plastic production equipment distributors: Offer a referral commission, or use salespeople as representatives.

3. Modify product line:
   - Add hardware and industrial products to provide more comprehensive services to plastics manufacturers.

2. Determine which of the tactics listed in this section apply to your business. I've listed the broad tactics discussed for your reference:

   A. Become a key supplier:
   - Target a small niche market.
   - Get involved with the community.
   - Have the most important location.

   B. Set up a partnership arrangement:
   - With the distribution channel.
   - With key vendors.
   - With other companies.

C. List various ways to cut distribution costs.

D. Look for ways to add to or modify your product line to maintain some control of distribution.

E. Keep a file of articles about distribution tactics from trade or business magazines. Add to your list any of these tactics that fit your business.

PROMOTION AND ADVERTISING CONTROL

Customer Promotion Control

Rykä is a small manufacturer with a specialized product, athletic shoes for women. Why should a retailer carry this product? Will it substantially increase sales? Maybe. But it also might just take away from sales of another brand—which doesn't help the retailer. In fact, carrying a small brand without increasing sales hurts the retailer because of the need to carry more stock, the expense of paying additional vendors, and the extra shelf space required.

Rykä has an effective marketing strategy. It drives the business through its retailers. Rykä has as a promotional tool the "Rykä Training Body," a group of 40,000 women fitness instructors who both endorse and use Rykä's products. Members of this group receive newsletters and announcements about six times per year, as well as getting discounts on shoes. They recommend Rykä's shoes, and those recommendations make customers search for a store carrying the product. Retailers are willing to carry Rykä shoes just to have access to this group.

Retail Customer Promotions

The Mind Construction Company is a toy store. It organized a space awareness promotion in conjunction with the Crestwood Mall, the St. Louis Science Museum, and a local radio station. The Science Center brought out a Soviet Space Exhibit, the toy store had a hands-on play area where kids could make space-age bookmarks and color in solar system maps, and the radio station gave away free tickets and gave the event extensive on-air publicity. The promotion not only increased sales for that week, it indelibly impressed the name of the store on the minds of most of its potential customers.

Pizza Hut has one of the best tie-in promotions currently available. Schools run a Book-It program that encourages kids to read a certain number of books each month. Their reward for meeting that goal is a free mini-pizza from Pizza Hut. We have the Book-It goal, with Pizza Hut's name prominently displayed, sitting on our refrigerator.

Advertising

Ninja Turtles were introduced with an ad campaign and a series of cartoons that were distributed across the country. Such support almost guarantees that retailers will at least try the product. They don't want to lose out on the customer demand that the advertising created.

Advertising can work for retailers too. When people travel, they are more likely to eat at a Big Boy or Perkins than at an unknown local restaurant.

Distribution Channel Promotions

Estes Toy Company manufactures and sells toy rockets, primarily to hobby stores. Estes ran a distribution promotion that offered the retail stores with the best Estes rocket displays a trip for two to Hawaii. Estes offered ten free trips. This was a popular program because it was aimed at retail floor salespeople, who normally don't get much vendor attention. Merchants Wests, one of the winning stores, helped its salespeople by making up several 22- by 28-posters and by offering a 33 percent discount on all rockets.

This promotion did several things for Estes: It provided some excitement for its hobby store customers, and it led stores to put up big displays promoting its products, and it created a spirit of cooperation between Estes and its dealers. This is the type of momentum that keeps retailers and manufacturers happy. Estes is a small manufacturer, but it was still able to have an effective promotion.

Manufacturers and service firms often have trip awards or sales contests for distributors and manufacturers' representatives. Other times they offer new sales tools for top performance, such as a TV/VCR combination for distributors that hit a certain sales level.

Back-End Promotions

When I was at the dental company, we ran a program that offered a dealer big discounts once it passed a certain sales level. For example, after a dealer passed $20,000 in purchases, it could get a discount of 10 percent on every purchase made during the promotion period, including the initial $20,000 in sales. If a dealer didn't hit $20,000, it didn't receive any discount.

We introduced the program because we were having trouble getting dealers to support our full product line. We had a dental chair that was a standard in the industry, and that was sold by every dealer. But sales were slow on other products where we didn't have a competitive edge. We set our sales goals so that a dealer's past sales of our leading product would account for about 70 percent of its sales goal. We felt that if dealers got that close to their goals, they would sell our other products rather than give up the discount. We were right, and the program worked. Once dealer salespeople got used to selling our products, it was easy for them to keep doing it.

ACTION STEPS

1. Take out your Distribution Strategies chart.
2. Add to it any of the tactics discussed in this section that might work in your business. The areas that were discussed are:

- Clubs, events, classes, and other customer promotions
- Joint programs with retailers that raise credibility and exposure
- Ongoing customer promotions
- Using an advertising strategy that drives customers through the distribution network

- Distribution promotions that are aimed at salespeople or store managers, rather than offering straight discounts.

3. Also add to the chart any other types of programs that you've seen other companies run or that you've come across in trade magazines.

DOMINATING WITH SALES STRATEGY

The actual sale is a point in the marketing cycle where the right strategy can double or triple your volume. It is an area where you should be constantly trying to create a marketing edge. You can gain an advantage by having the best sales force, having a unique way or place to sell, and shifting your sales influence.

Having the Best Sales Force

Remax, the real estate agency, has agents with twice the normal industry sales experience. Remax claims that because of this experience, its sales per agent are much higher than the industry average, and its customer satisfaction is one of the highest in the industry. Remax keeps its sales force because it offers its sales agents 100 percent commissions. Most real estate companies pay their salespeople 50 percent commission, with the rest of the money going to the agency owner. Remax gives agents 100 percent commission but then charges them an overhead fee. Good agents do better under Remax's structure, and so it is able to keep the industry's top producers.

Other tactics for having the best sales force, besides paying more, are:

1. Having a good training program.

2. Providing superior sales aids.

3. Providing promotional opportunities with the sales force (see Chapter 21).

Having a Unique Way or Place to Sell

Pasta Mama's is a small food supplier making "gourmet" flavored pastas. Pasta Mama's wanted to sell to upscale customers, but supermarkets and other food outlets didn't want to take on a supplier as small as Pasta Mama's. So it decided to start selling its products through gift shops, furniture stores, and other locations where people weren't used to buying food. Pasta Mama's was the only company trying to sell food through those locations, and it was able to slowly build a sales base.

Olan Mills is a large national chain of local photography studios. Most of its competitors sell through outlets in stores like Sears, Kmart, or J.C. Penney. Those competitors rely on newspaper advertising. Olan Mills sells its products differently. It has a telemarketing sales force that calls people up and tries to set up an appointment at the local studio. Olan Mills' strategy is different, and this has helped it grow twice as fast as its competition.

Changing the Sales Emphasis

The Estes toy rocket promotion I discussed earlier is an example of shifting the sales emphasis. Most manufacturers direct all their efforts toward the buyer.

Estes targeted the store manager or floor salesperson. If those people want to promote a product, then the buyers will buy it for them.

Ergodyne is one of the largest producers of safety equipment to prevent repetitive stress disorders such as carpal tunnel syndrome. In 1986, Ergodyne was on the verge of bankruptcy. In 1992, it had sales of over $30 million. Ergodyne succeeded because it changed who it thought its customers were. At first it tried to sell to insurance companies, believing that they would recommend its products in order to lower their medical claims. After two years Ergodyne still didn't have a customer. So it switched its sales strategy and promoted its products to companies that had employees at risk. Those customers were easy to sell because of the high cost of a lost work day.

Looking at all the buying influences: industrial suppliers
When I took over a territory for a chemical products company, I was up against a well-entrenched competitor. I switched my sales efforts from buyers, who liked their current supplier, to the chemists who were involved in producing or improving products. I talked to them to find out what problems they were having. Every now and then, I'd solve someone's problem and get my product designed into a product specification. Then the buyers bought.

There can be a lot of people involved in any purchase decision. Companies often focus on only one of them. For example, one industrial supplier might just call on buyers. Another company might have a more comprehensive approach, calling on marketing, engineering, quality control, and management as well as on the buyers.

Looking at all the buying influences: retail companies
Hansen's Drug Store is in a little strip mall and takes whatever business happens to come to its door. A big Walgreen store has recently entered the market, and Hansen's has looked at its customer base and decided to concentrate on older customers. Some of the buying influences Hansen's might find are senior citizen centers, local physicians, and nursing homes.

Hansen's might decide to concentrate on local doctors and offer these new services: free delivery; a hot line physicians can call to order a prescription while the patient is still in their office; and coupons offering a doctor's patients free aspirin, or some other drug, for every prescription purchased at Hansen's.

ACTION STEPS

1. Add to your distribution strategy chart any sales strategies you might be able to implement. Here are some questions you might want to ask to find such strategies:

   • Are there any ways that you could improve the quality of your sales force?

   • Are there any unique ways, or places, you could use to more effectively sell your product?

   • Are there other buying influences that you should be contacting to get an advantage?

Chapter 8

Finalizing Your Market Strategy

Some readers may have already have a clear idea of the strategy they want to introduce. If that statement applies to you, you can go to the end of the chapter and fill out the Marketing Strategy Form. For the rest of the readers, this chapter will show you how to take your Customer Needs/Possible Strategies, Proprietary Features, and Distribution Strategies charts and turn them into a coherent, easy-to-follow marketing strategy.

Chapters 2 through 7 covered the various aspects of building your marketing strategy. Most of you probably uncovered more potential strategies than you had ever thought possible. At the moment all this information may seem confusing, but this chapter will help you put it into a manageable form. These six chapters have hopefully also done something else for you: given you a feel for what your customers are like. That information will help you see small nuances you can add to your strategy to make it as effective as possible.

This chapter will help you take the information you've put together, see how it fits with other marketing elements, rate each possible strategy, and finally select the best one.

DISCOVERING WHERE THE MONEY IS

Some readers may be starting a company or developing a new product. They should go through this chapter and fill out the form for their main target customer. Other readers will already have established companies, with a customer base. They should fill out the information for their new marketing thrust. For example, you might sell automotive aftermarket products through an auto parts catalog. This year you want to add to that sales base by targeting people who do custom body modifications on trucks. That's the customer group you should address in this chapter.

Who Is Your Target Customer?

Chapter 2 discussed how to segment customers in order to find a target group that is underserved, profitable, and big enough to support your profit goals. Some examples are:

- Sports enthusiasts who want to measure their performance
- People in multinational companies who are responsible for Hispanic advertising

- Manufacturers with hazardous waste disposal problems
- Golf shops looking for premium-priced merchandise
- Older bike riders looking for more comfort
- High-income parents looking for quality day care.

List your target groups. If you have decided on one clearly defined group, just list that one. If you have two possible customer groups and you aren't sure which one to focus on, list both choices.

Choosing the Right Product

Once you have a customer group, you need a product to sell to them. Chapter 3 covered how to determine what product aspects are important to your target customer group. The intent of this chapter wasn't to fully define the product, just to find what type of product customers wanted. Here are some examples:

- A travel agent discovered that corporations wanted controls to keep employees within travel guidelines.
- A sports shoe manufacturer found out that women wanted shoes that were specifically designed for their feet.
- A manufacturer learned that teachers liked the idea of scratch-and-sniff stickers as a motivational tool.

List product characteristic(s) that you have decided that your target customers want.

Finding the Right Market

Chapter 4 covered how to find a distribution channel to sell through. You need to find a channel where you can afford to stimulate the customer, competition is light, and you can meet your sales and profit goals. Some examples are:

- Famous Amos chocolate chip cookies selling to the vending machine market
- Bed Bath and Beyond's strategy of very large, stand-alone bed and bath shops
- Commodore Computer electing to sell its video editing computer systems through full-service, specially trained computer outlets.

List the distribution channel that you have decided on (including location if you're a retailer).

Evaluation

Before you move onto the next section, you really need to double check and make sure that the distribution channel you've chosen will actually handle your product. For example, Commodore Computer might decide to sell through specially trained video dealers. But then it has to either find those dealers and see if they will handle Commodore products or find people willing to be trained as dealers. Famous Amos needed to talk to vending machine companies to be sure they would carry its product. In some cases you may need to go back and modify your product or your target customer group to get a distribution channel to take the product.

List three reasons why you feel certain that your product will work in the channel you have decided on. Some reasons could be other companies' success or a shortage of products in the channel. But at least one of the reasons should be a response from someone in the channel who would buy your product. For instance, a physician might have a survey of twenty potential patients who preferred a personal physician associated with a hospital.

BEING BETTER THAN EVERYONE ELSE

In Section 2 you prepared three charts, Customer Needs/Possible Strategies, Proprietary Features, and Distribution Strategies. Your goal in marketing any product, service, or retail concept is to become a force in the market, with a clear-cut difference from competitors' products. To do that, you need to find a special customer characteristic that you can focus on with both product and distribution strategy.

This does not necessarily mean that your discoveries are going to be complex or difficult to execute. For example, a Sam's Club in a St. Paul suburb discovered that 25 percent of its customers were Asians. This store decided that it was going to focus its marketing strategy for the next year on this customer group. This doesn't mean that Sam's Club was going to ignore other customers, only that it would make a special effort for Asian customers. The store manager surveyed Asian customers and found that they wanted food products similar to what they could buy in Asia. These products were not readily available, but the manager worked out an arrangement with a Sam's Club store in Hawaii to get the products he needed.

This strategy was not complicated. All it called for was the manager to keep his eyes open to what was happening in his store, so that he could see where his opportunities were.

The next four sections of the book cover tactics you can use to support your strategy. Tactics work best when they are all based on a central marketing strategy. That way you develop a consistency that ties your tactics together.

Learning the Keys that Make Customers Buy

Chapter 5 discussed a wide variety of ways to look at the people or companies that are your target customers so that you could find one characteristic that few if any other companies were properly addressing. The goal was to find several characteristics you could focus on to create a sustainable product advantage.

Pull out the three charts you prepared, Customer Needs/Possible Strategies, Proprietary Features, and Distribution Strategies. In Chapters 6 and 7 you added product features and distribution strategies for each customer need. You now want to pick out one or two customer needs to focus on.

You have three considerations: (1) how important the need is to the customer, (2) how many strategies you've developed to attack that need, and (3) how effectively you can execute those strategies. Obviously, you would like to have several strategies you can easily execute for the customer's most important need, but that doesn't always happen.

You want to make the largest possible impact on your customer. This might mean that you execute only one strategy, or it might mean that you execute three or four smaller ones. Evaluate the impact of a strategy versus the strategy's cost using the same criteria you used in Chapter 4 to evaluate whether or not you can afford to stimulate a market. These criteria included:

- Product requirements
- Motivation needed
- Needs awareness
- Location
- Predisposition
- Advertising required.

You should also factor in the importance of a customer need. If a customer need is twice as important, your marketing strategies need to be only half as effective to have the same impact. If you have a choice of two needs, one that is more important but that you have fewer strategies for and another less important need that you have more ways to address, always go with the top customer need.

Some examples of customer characteristics attacked in a marketing strategy are the following:

- Nestlé discovered that customers wanted to buy baby food from a company with nutritional expertise.
- The Jaguar marketing approach is aimed at people who want to make a statement about themselves.
- Prego found that people wanted to know who really had the thickest sauce.
- Park Tool Co. learned that bicycle mechanics wanted specially-made tools for their needs.

List the one, two, or three customer needs or characteristics that you have decided to capitalize on.

Creating a Product Advantage

Chapter 6 covered adding value to a product through features and product support tactics, gaining a service advantage, and the use of proprietary features. Features, support, and service were three ways you could gain an edge because of your ability to meet customer needs. Proprietary features take advantage of U.S. laws to prevent competition.

Needs-related product features

When you prepared your Customer Needs/Possible Strategies chart, you listed tactics next to the customer needs they helped address. Look at the customer needs you have just chosen to focus on and list the possible strategies you identified previously that could meet each need. Here are some examples:

- Pepsi added 10 percent fruit juice to its Slice line of soft drinks to capitalize on peoples' belief that fruit juice makes soft drinks taste better.
- Mello Smello met the motivational needs of parents and teachers by adding motivational messages to its scratch-and-sniff stickers and by aligning itself with Disney and Nintendo through licensing agreements.
- Nike keeps its market share by continuing to upgrade its shoes with performance-related features.
- Target department stores found that people want assurance that they can always return products. So Target set up a return policy that allows people to return products without a receipt, as long as Target sells the product.

List the product strategies you've identified for each customer characteristic your strategy addresses.

Proprietary features

At the end of Chapter 6, I mentioned steps you could take to give yourself an advantage based on U.S. laws. Some of these proprietary features are:

- Trademarks
- Patents
- Trade dress
- Copyrights
- Manufacturing processes
- Management strategy.

List any proprietary features you can include in your product.

Dominating with Distribution

Chapter 7 discussed distribution strategies that you could use to address the customer characteristic you've identified. Don't overlook this area; in fact, I recommend that you try one or two distribution strategies each year, because distribution tactics are hard to duplicate effectively. You should have written down distribution strategies that address your customer characteristic on your Customer Needs/Possible Strategies chart. Some of those strategies were:

- Matching your distribution strategy to your customer needs
- Locking in your distribution channel by being a key supplier, signing partnership agreements, developing a low-cost distribution system, or creating an in-demand product line
- Controlling the distribution channel through promotion and advertising.

Examples of distribution strategies are:

- L'eggs' strategy of selling through mass merchandisers rather than women's clothing stores or women's departments of large department stores. L'eggs' policy of providing point-of-purchase displays and shelf racks was also a distribution strategy.

- Select Copier's decision to equip four mobile showrooms that could show its product line to potential customers.
- Wee Bag It's strategy of not having a sit-down restaurant and only delivering food at lunch time.

List the distribution strategies you could implement to meet each customer need or characteristic you are focusing on.

Budgeting

As I mentioned earlier, you need to pick a strategy that addresses a major customer characteristic in a major way. You also need to be able to afford to execute your strategy.

Look at the strategies you've listed and estimate their costs and their ability to increase sales. You need enough money to execute your strategy and still preserve operating capital, in order to be successful. Before you finalize your strategy, put together a budget. List your introduction timetable, your projected cash flow, and your expenses for each tactic then list how you plan to fund each tactic. For example, Figure 8.1 shows a budget chart for a special-interest video production company. This chart only covers extra expenses. Your normal marketing expenses are not listed. Another point to note is that some strategies are implemented in several steps.

This chart lets you see how much you will need to invest in your strategy and when. If this amount is more than you can afford, you need to go back and experiment with other strategies and other customer needs until you find an affordable strategy that will work for you.

ACTION STEPS

1. Prepare a marketing strategy chart to refer to when you are getting ready to execute a tactic. Figure 8.2 is a layout for this chart. It simply lists the six key steps you looked at when you were formulating a marketing strategy.

2. Prepare a marketing budgeting chart similar to Figure 8.1 for your chosen strategy.

SECTION 2 — CONCLUSION

You Have to Find a Way to Be Better

Every year thousands of companies go out of business. Most of those companies have a totally unfocused strategy. If you were to ask their owners what their advantage was, most of them would not be able to answer. The companies that succeed do so by focusing on specialized niche markets, where they can be a force and where they can develop a competitive advantage.

MacTemps is a temporary help agency with $13 million per year in revenues from providing temporary operators for Macintosh computers. Glitterwrap sells

Figure 8.1
Marketing Strategy Introduction

BUDGET CHART
VIDEO PRODUCTION COMPANY

Target customer group:	Working people who don't feel they can introduce their own product.
Product:	Videotape series explaining how to introduce a product.
Distribution channel:	Direct response radio and TV advertising.
Key customer characteristics:	People are afraid, and need a step-by-step, easy-to-follow format.
Product strategies:	Provide a video kit with relevant forms and workbooks, and offer a follow-up phone consultation service. Also need testimonials and favorable reviews.
Distribution Strategies:	Run radio and TV advertising in Southwestern United States.

Fiscal Year: July 1, 1993 to June 30, 1994

Month	Action	Cost	Funding Source
July-October	Prepare workbooks, forms and other additional data	$12,000	Partners' investment
October	Send out press kits for reviews and testimonials. Follow up as needed	1,000	Operating capital
January	Prepare press kits for radio talk show hosts	4,000	Operating capital
January	Send out press kits, and then follow-up for radio publicity	1,000	Operating capital
October-December	Prepare mailing packages for radio respondents	4,500	Partners' investment
January-March	Test radio ads in five test markets	3,000	Partners' investment
April-June	Continue to run radio ads in select markets as finances allow	15,000	$5,000 Operating capital $10,000 Partners' investment

over $10 million of metallic and iridescent gift wrap each year. Select Ticketing Systems has annual sales of over $8 million from its computerized box-office and outlet ticketing systems. All these companies are specializing, finding the right customer, product, and market. They aren't going to disappear. They will continue to grow and prosper.

You need the same strategy as these three companies. Find a place where you can be a major market force. Discover how you can control your destiny, and you'll make profits year in and year out.

Figure 8.2
Marketing Strategy

Fiscal Year 19___
Company Name

Target customer group: _____

Product: _____

Distribution channel: _____

Key customer characteristic: _____

Product strategies: _____

Distribution Strategies: _____

Section 3
Finding Customers

Not too long ago companies found their customers through media advertising, direct mail campaigns, telephone selling, trade show attendance, and face-to-face contacts. In today's competitive world, these techniques are often not enough. Even if you do use them, you need to fine-tune them if they are to work properly. Your best bet for an effective program is to understand all the techniques for finding customers, then implement the ones that make sense for your particular business.

Failure to find customers sinks more small- to medium-size companies than any other marketing problem. In most cases, the phrase "we were undercapitalized" is just a euphemism for "we couldn't find enough customers." For some reason, finding customers, or making it easy for customers to find you, is an overlooked part of marketing. Everyone assumes that all they need to do is run an ad program and customers will find them. Unfortunately, it never works like that. Finding customers is difficult, but it can still be done, even when a company has a limited promotional budget.

This section covers how to discover the right way for a specific business to find customers, how to find them for very little money, how to use moderately priced techniques, and finally, how to implement some emerging tactics.

Chapter 9

The Right Way for Your Business

Over the last several weeks, I've heard dozens of commercials for the Yellow Pages. Every one of these ads has a testimonial success story about how business has skyrocketed since a company started to advertise. Now Yellow Pages, or product directories, or listings of clubs or associations are an effective way for some companies to find customers, but they are a totally wrong approach for others. It depends on the business and the buying mode of the customer.

As you read through the tactics in this section, try any that might work. Customers and markets are always full of surprises, no matter how well you evaluate them. Testing several tactics gives you a better chance to find the tactic that will work best for you.

Some tactics for finding customers are selective and can be directed at specific groups of customers. Other tactics are broad-based, and can be used to find a few prospects in a large group of people or companies. Some tactics are virtually free, and others are expensive. To decide how to find customers, you need to know how many prospects are in the market, how much each of those prospects might buy, and how easy they will be to find. Once you have a basic strategy set, you can fine-tune it by understanding the customer's buying mode, knowing how to get a prospect's name, and leaving a positive impression with every prospect.

HOW MANY, HOW MUCH, HOW EASY TO FIND

The ideal situation is to have a large number of potential customers who will purchase a great many products and are easy to find. Unfortunately, that is rarely the case. Typically you'll be missing at least one of these favorable factors, and sometimes all three, which means you will have to be careful in selecting a strategy.

How Many Customers?

How many prospects you have determines how selective you need to be in finding them. If 40 percent of people or companies are prospects, you can use more expensive techniques such as a field sales force, billboard advertising, trade show attendance, advertising, and "high-impact" (three dimensional) direct mailings. If only a small percentage of people or companies are likely to be prospects, then you need to watch how you spend your money. Low-cost methods like Yellow Pages advertising, directory listings, seminars or free classes, and membership in community groups such as Chambers of Commerce are often effective.

How Much Will Customers Buy?

If customers will make a large purchase from you, you can afford to spend more money to find them. For example, an advertising agency, a waste disposal company, or a large accounting firm will probably have extensive billings from any one customer. These companies can afford to spend time and money to find accounts. On the other hand, if a purchase amount is small, you need low-cost methods. For example, an industrial vacuum pump repair service might have an average billing of $800 to $1,200. It will need to rely on directory listings, mailings to maintenance engineers, or an agreement with a pump company to find customers. A plumber would have to rely on truck signs, Yellow Pages advertising, or advertisements on local football schedules.

How Easy Are Customers to Find?

Child Care Management Inc. runs employer-sponsored child care centers. Every company with employees is technically a prospect. But in fact, the vast majority of companies aren't interested in sponsoring a child care center, either because they think it is too expensive or because they think it is too much trouble. There are only a few potential customers, and Child Care Management has to find them in a broad-based way. Its best options are to network closely with associations of personnel managers, to offer seminars and classes at key trade shows, or to run ads in trade magazines.

Chemical Waste Management Inc. handles acid wastes, such as hydrofluoric acid, sulfuric acid, and nitric acid, for semiconductor manufacturers. Chemical Waste Management has no trouble finding a list of companies to contact: It just needs to look up semiconductor production plants in an industrial directory. The company can afford to spend money to establish relationships with those prospects through high-impact direct mailings or a field sales force because it knows these companies could buy.

Many small- to medium-sized companies compete in markets where conditions aren't favorable for finding customers. That may be to their advantage. Low-cost tactics for finding customers are easier to execute, and will usually produce plenty of customers.

ACTION STEP

Using the how many, how much, and how easy to find guidelines, decide if your company needs to be careful about how it spends its money finding customers, or if it can spend more freely to determine which potential customers are true prospects.

Need Low-Cost Spending Methods	Can Afford to Spend More
Low percentage of people or companies are prospects.	High percentage are prospects.
Relatively low order value per customer.	High order value per customer.
Customers are difficult to find.	Customers are easy to find.

THE CUSTOMER'S BUYING MODE

When you buy auto insurance, a gasket for a plumbing leak, food for your family, mandatory employee training classes, environmental impact reports, or printing for a new brochure, you are going to buy it. These purchases aren't that important, but they have to be made. You may look in the Yellow Pages or a product directory, call another person for a recommendation, or call a company you saw advertised on a billboard or in a magazine ad. The point is that you are going to find someone to buy from. Often you'll buy from whatever company or firm looks good to you after a cursory look.

Other times you have to buy a product, but it is an important purchase, such as new production-line equipment, a new room addition, or a physician to help deliver a baby. Here people have to buy, but they will buy only after they are confident that they have made the right choice.

People make purchase decisions in many different ways for many different products. Sometimes you have to be sure prospects can find you. Other times you have to be sure to go out and find customers before they decide to buy. The three key factors in determining customers' buying mode are how soon they will buy, how necessary the purchase is, and where prospects look for information.

How Soon Will They Buy?

Buying right away

When people have to buy a product right away, they often will buy it from whatever source comes to their mind first. This could be a printer that just happens to send a direct mailing, a business that's right down the street, or a company that advertises on a nearby billboard. Or they might look up companies' names in the Yellow Pages or in product or industrial directories.

When potential customers are going to want to buy right away, you need to be sure your name is easy to find. Some tactics you can use are the following:

- Yellow Pages or directory advertising.
- Billboard ads.
- Advertising specialties (these can be especially effective in business-to-business advertising).
- Visible signs on buildings or trucks. This works for every type of business. I once worked with a testing company whose building was visible from a busy freeway. It used to get several leads a month from those signs.
- Stickers. Service companies should leave their name and phone number on equipment they work on.
- Order forms. A box company sends me order forms every two or three weeks. Whenever I need to order, I just order from them because it's easy.
- Telemarketing calls. This is similar to the order form tactic in that a call is made to potential customers every two to four weeks.
- Trade magazine ads. Some companies will always have an ad on the back cover of key magazines.

- Store or business locations. Clothing stores are in malls because that's where people go when they want to buy clothes. For the same reason, many companies that provide services to businesses are located in industrial parks.

Making a future purchase decision

People are more thorough in their buying decision when they are making an important decision and they have time to decide. For example, people take their time making decisions such as where to go on vacation, buying equipment for a plant currently under construction, or buying engineering design services for a product being introduced in two years.

When customers are thinking of making a decision in the future, they will watch for ads and publicity releases, look for products at trade shows or at other people's homes or businesses, and try to get input from other people well in advance of when they will actually buy. People will usually narrow their choices down to three or four before they actually contact a company's salesperson. For example, I worked with a manufacturing engineer to select a new type of switching mechanism for a product. The engineer sent away for brochures and information from twenty-two companies. We then went through the brochures and pulled out the four manufacturers we wanted to talk further with.

The key to selling to customers making a longer-time-span purchase decision is to find them in the contemplation stage; then you can keep contacting them to resolve any perceived problems before they rule you out during the screening period. Some ways to find prospects early in their decision process are:

- Trade show attendance.
- Publicity release programs.
- Card pack advertising.
- Magazine advertising.
- Having a newsletter to send out monthly or bimonthly.
- Classes or free seminars.
- Contests or events.
- Tracking programs. For example, one company that sold products to new metallurgical laboratories tracked publicity releases and construction permits to find companies that were considering building laboratories.
- Offering free buying information in company ads.

How Necessary, How Important?

These two questions help you decide whether to spend your money on the product or on finding customers. If customers feel that a purchase is important, marketers need to spend money on the product, as customers will typically search for what they believe to be the best product. Customers won't research an unimportant purchase, and so marketers need to concentrate on spending money to find customers.

Industrial examples

Sentry Security Systems sells security systems for businesses that cost from $4,000 to $20,000. Is this an important purchase? Probably not. I've been involved in a security system purchase, and the general attitude was that a security system will stop kids and amateur burglars, but it won't stop a dedicated thief. We didn't think it mattered which system we bought. However, production equipment decisions and advertising space buys were important decisions because they affected our bottom line.

Sentry Security needs to slant its spending towards finding customers. Direct mail programs, a telemarketing campaign, direct sales calls, magazine advertising, and billboards are all ways to keeps Sentry's name in front of potential customers.

Kurka Consulting specializes in designing and implementing new order entry systems. Kurka Consulting's target customers are companies that are expanding and outgrowing a manual or lightly computerized order entry system.

This is an extremely important purchase. Order entry is a company's lifeblood, and choosing a consultant group is a decision the company will closely watch. Companies will also worry about the turnaround time needed to implement a new system. Kurka Consulting needs to focus its spending on the product. Technical backup, well-qualified programmers, twenty-four-hour service, and guaranteed turnaround are a few of the features Kurka might need to add.

Some guidelines for knowing whether an industrial purchase is important are:

- Past trouble. Companies will spend more time looking into a product or service that has given them problems in the past. Copiers are often an important purchase for this reason.

- Dollar amount. The larger the purchase, the more likely it is to be important.

- Affects something important. When a purchase affects an important company operation, it is important.

- What could be lost. A product is important if it affects sales or production.

- Trouble it could cause. A company will have a lot of misery if its payroll service can't handle the work.

Consumer products examples

When people buy a car, they like to see a big showroom, an efficient service department, a large inventory, and a somewhat convenient location. That's because it is an important purchase. This doesn't leave dealers with a lot of money for finding customers. But the product is crucial here. People do check several dealers before buying. Dealers need to advertise and to have a visible location, but most of their money needs to go into their product.

Chem Lawn provides lawn care services. This is not that important to most people. They can always fertilize the lawn themselves, or they can even skip fertilizing altogether. Chem Lawn can't wait for customers to come to it; it needs to go out and find them through direct mail, circulars, signs on its trucks, signs on the lawns it treats, and telemarketing.

Sometimes your target customer group determines whether a purchase is important. Musicland targets casual music buyers; it puts its stores in malls, stocks them with top-selling hits, and tries to pick up impulse purchases. Title Wave has large stand-alone stores that appeal to heavy music buyers, to whom music purchases are important.

Some guidelines for deciding if a consumer products purchase is important are:

- How much the item costs.
- Whether or not it affects a person's lifestyle. A person who spends a lot of time entertaining outdoors will look carefully at any outdoor barbecue product.
- Hobbies. Dedicated golfers will worry about any putter they purchase.
- Image. People consider clothes, cars, homes, and anything else that affects their image of themselves as important.
- Past trouble. People will pay more attention to products that have failed them in the past.
- Children. Many parents consider purchases for their children to be more important than those they make for themselves.

Where Do Customers Look for Information?

When you decide to buy furniture, what's the first thing you do? Probably look in the Saturday or Sunday newspaper to see who is having a sale. If you need a consultant or a service business, you look in the Yellow Pages or a trade directory, or maybe you look through a file of information you've received in the past.

For many products there is a certain place possible customers will look for information. If that's the case for your business, be sure you are listed wherever prospects are going to look. The Thomas Registry, newspaper ads, discount mall locations, directories, and trade shows are all places where you may need to advertise your business. When you hear a testimonial ad for the Yellow Pages, people looked for that business in the Yellow Pages.

ACTION STEPS

1. Decide whether you need to concentrate your resources on high visibility, or on product features.

   - Be sure customers can find you—have high visibility or take your messages to prospects.
   - Need to spend to make the product as strong as possible to prospects.

   Characteristics:

   - Purchasing right away, or companies are prospects.
   - Making a purchase decision over a period of time.
   - Purchase not considered important.
   - Purchase is important or necessary.

2. Write down the three major places where people look for information on your type of product.

3. List three successful companies in your market. Then give a weighting to how much effort they give to finding customers and how much to product support. You should consider a weighting similar to that of the top-ranking companies.

GETTING THE CUSTOMER'S NAME

Buick has started a radio campaign in which it gives an 800 number that people can call to receive more information. I strongly support this type of campaign. If your ad generates a reaction in someone, you want to get his or her name.

As I mentioned earlier, customers have a contemplation period, during which they consider what to do. In this period they order or pick up information. If you want to maximize your sales, you have to keep contacting people after the initial contact, and you can't contact them unless you know their names.

Importance of Getting a Name

One of the hot marketing tactics of the 1990s is *database marketing*. This is a strategy in which companies first find prospects' names, and then have marketers contact those prospects repeatedly to encourage them to buy. The John Deere mailing mentioned in Chapter 2 is an example of database marketing. Using a variety of methods, John Deere had compiled a mailing list of 20,000 farmers who owned competitors' equipment. Then it made repeated mailings to those farmers, and attracted 25 percent of them into showrooms.

Your Own List of Prospects

Database marketing works best when you develop a list of prospects from people who have contacted you. Some of the ways you can get names are:

1. Include 800 numbers on all your ads, and offer a free newsletter, information pamphlet, or other source of information.

2. Get the names of people who buy something from you. Radio Shack does this, and so can other retailers and restaurants.

3. Have a contest, or offer a free sample evaluation or free information kit to people who contact you at a trade show.

4. Create a phone call-in form on which employees note the name and address of anyone who calls in for future mailings.

5. Take people's names from the checks they give you.

6. For a restaurant, have a business card drawing for a free lunch.

7. Keep the names of attendees at classes or seminars that you hold or attend.

8. Have people join a club or association related to your business.

The Value of Collecting Names

I was once in charge of a large advertising campaign for a new set of dental equipment. When I took over, all the company did was ask customers to circle a number on a magazine's business reply card if they wanted more information. The first thing I did was switch to an 800 number so that people could call immediately. That tripled our response rate.

The sales force wouldn't follow up on these leads because they were "just lookers." I knew that wasn't the case; the people were in their contemplative stage. We put in place a simple database program that contacted 800-number prospects every sixty days and offered a free in-office demonstration. Our sales went up 18 percent.

When I was in an auto parts store waiting for a repair to be finished, the service counter received nine calls while I was waiting. The employees did not take down even one of the callers' names. That's just bad business; those callers are prospects, and they should be receiving mailings.

Companies that sell to other businesses are usually even worse at getting names. A call comes in to a receptionist, who sometimes will answer a question without getting a name. The same thing can happen in customer service, and even with salespeople. Often companies will just let a lead stay with a salesperson. This is an extremely bad strategy. The salesperson might toss a lead after three or four weeks if the person doesn't buy. But that person is still a prospect you should keep contacting. Make sure your system enters every salesperson lead for follow-up.

ACTION STEP

Review the various ways of getting a customer's name that were given in this section. Implement at least three or four of them in your business.

YOUR FIRST CONTACT—MAKING THE RIGHT IMPRESSION

Your first contact is important. Retail businesses usually do a good job here, but service companies, professional offices, and companies selling to other companies often do a poor job. Two areas you should work on are the initial phone contact and a reception area.

Initial Phone Contact

The main reason initial phone calls are handled poorly is that companies look at them as an expense. They are happy if one overworked receptionist can handle every call. I did a little survey once trying to relate the length of an incoming phone call and our sales results. We made a concerted effort to talk longer. We increased the length of our initial calls from about two to three minutes to about eight minutes. Our appointment rate went from about 10 percent to over 30 percent. All we really did to lengthen the calls was to ask more questions.

Some of the questions you can use are:

- What action have you taken so far?
- What are you hoping we can do for you?
- What is your application?

- Have you seen our equipment demonstrated?
- How did you hear about us?
- May I make a couple of suggestions?

Receptionists can't ask these types of questions and sound natural. You need to have a knowledgeable person available.

The Reception Area

I'm not sure this is the best term, but I use it to mean the area where a person waits to see you. I believe it is important for a company's waiting area to show that the company really understands its customers. One law firm I visited had me wait in a law library. It was much larger than I expected, and it was impressive. We used to have dentists wait in a demonstration room where they could try out our products. They were really impressed with the fact that we would leave experimental products out for them to see. In my invention business I like to have people wait in our staging area, where we prepare products for shipping. All of these waiting room strategies help show customers that you know what you're doing.

ACTION STEPS

1. Set up a policy for incoming phone calls. Decide how they should be handled by the receptionist and what type of knowledgeable person should be available. Don't leave phones uncovered.
2. If quite a few customers visit you, look over your waiting room area. You'll get considerable benefit if you can make it reflect your business.

Chapter 10

Personal Contacts, Referrals, Speeches, and Publicity

This chapter explains ten low-cost tactics for finding customers. For a small- to medium-size company, these tactics are more than just low-cost; they are also very effective. They will provide you with a steady flow of incoming business year after year. This chapter covers personal contacts (or networking), face-to-face contacts, classes, free speeches, publicity, circulars, signs, and small ads.

These tactics work for manufacturers, engineering firms, day-care centers, retailers, and every other type of business. Sometimes when I give speeches, people will tell me that they are handling marketing for a manufacturer, so they have to stick to advertising. This type of thinking is shortsighted. One manufacturer I worked with picked up an order worth over $3 million (10 percent of the company's yearly volume) from a networking contact a manager met at an industry standards meeting.

PERSONAL CONTACTS

Networking

Scott Turner received $200,000 to $300,000 in overseas orders for his $750,000-per-year business. He didn't run any promotions, he rarely advertised, and he had only a tiny marketing budget. Turner's overseas business was all the result of networking. When he started his business, he made contact with key industry experts and explained his product, which measured diffusion depths for semiconductors (diffusion is an active electronic layer in memory chips). Turner showed how his product worked and why it was important. His payoff came when these experts wrote semiconductor operating specifications for overseas plants and designed his product into the approved testing methods.

Networking includes all the proactive steps you take to contact and follow up with people who can help your business. Insurance agents who join the Lions Club, the Chamber of Commerce, or the school board are networking. But there are many other ways that aren't so obvious.

1. Contact members of clubs or associations that could be interested in your product or service. For example, a hobby shop should network with Cub masters about its products for the Pinewood derby. A computer products

or software manufacturer should network with computer clubs, or with associations of accountants if it sells an accounting product.

2. Contact people at key state agencies. For example, at one time I sold a tire cutter for cutting up waste tires. I had a contact at a state agency that kept me advised of hearings, conventions, and other key events. The contact also suggested improvements I could make to better meet state and federal guidelines.

3. Network with potential customers that can't visit you. A clothing store might network with a nursing home to pick up extra business.

4. Serve on standards committees or other key industry groups, such as advisory boards or association committees for addressing industry changes. This is a good way to meet key industry people.

5. Develop contacts in complementary businesses that can help you. For example, new stockbrokers often set up professional contacts with estate planners or CPA's. An engineering company or consulting firm might want contacts with manufacturers' representatives in related businesses who might know of companies that need its products or services.

6. Develop helpful customer contacts. A key customer contact can give you a lot of information. When I started selling videos to libraries, I did most of my market research with the help of three librarian buyers. Those librarians still help me out.

Personal Letters and Telephone Solicitation

I look at marketing as an effort to establish a link or relationship with customers. Personal letters and telephone calls, when done properly, help establish a better relationship and improve your business. The most effective way to use personal letters and phone calls is to put them into a campaign with the following steps:

1. Find names of people you would like to connect to your business:

- Networking contacts.
- Key people's names that you have seen in newsletters, magazine articles, and newspapers.
- Trade show organizers and members of relevant associations.
- People who have contacted you in the past that you feel could be important customers.

2. Have a compelling reason for writing. You could be:

- Looking for members for an advisory board.
- Hosting a large open house.
- Conducting a special seminar with known industry speakers.
- Conducting a first-time showing of a new product.
- Sponsoring an industry roundtable on a key topic.

- Explaining a new, key feature of your business.

3. Prepare and mail a short letter. The letter should:

- Be short and clear.
- Ask people to call.
- Tell people you will call if you don't hear from them.
- Include a photograph or other interesting visual.
- Include a sample or any other item that's appropriate.

4. Follow up with a phone call.

- Call people if they don't call you.
- Explain briefly who you are.
- Refer to your letter.
- State why you feel the prospect is important to you, and why you hope that he or she will attend your event.
- If the prospect can't come, ask if you can keep him or her on your list for future mailings.

You want mailings and phone calls to key prospects or key potential contacts to be done by a person with an important title, like president or vice president of marketing. Don't trust these contacts to salespeople. Prospects are flattered when they receive a contact from a key person, and this will help you generate marketing momentum.

Face-to-Face Contacts

I prefer to follow up a phone call with a face-to-face contact. A key contact might produce business for you over many years, and direct contact will give you valuable customer input and produce an increased level of sales.

One of my favorite tactics with industrial companies is to send a personal letter before a major trade show, association meeting, or some other event that the person is likely to attend. I would then follow up the letter with a phone call, and state that I hoped to connect with the person at the meeting.

REFERRAL PROGRAMS

Once you have a customer, there is a good chance that he or she knows other people who are also prospects. The trick is to get these names without alienating the customer. It is usually easy to get an industrial referral, especially if your business is specialized. Many consumers, on the other hand, don't like to give out referrals, and you don't want to upset someone who is already your customer.

Some of the many ways you can generate referrals are to:

1. Ask people if they discussed their purchase with anyone else.

2. Ask people if they know someone else who would want to receive information on your product or service.

3. Give customers something about your product to pass on, such as stickers, fliers, or circulars.

4. Offer customers an award or certificate that they can put up in their homes—for example, a lifetime waterproofing guarantee, an interior design award, and a certificate for approved chemical waste removal are all ways to make your name visible to new customers.

5. Give away a free or low-cost product to a key industry person. For example, a sign or plaque manufacturer could give a plaque to a major contractor who is visited by architects or corporation building committees.

6. Offer customers advertising specialties like pens, magnets, or calendars.

7. Send customers business reply cards offering free subscriptions to your newsletter.

8. Send customers free tickets to seminars or classes to give to their friends.

9. Offer a free one-hour demonstration at a customer's home. A beauty consultant might do this for a good client's friends.

10. Offer a free product for a referral. A restaurant sent my secretary a free lunch coupon every time she booked a party of six or more.

11. Sell a coupon book. For example, a car wash near my home sells a coupon book of ten coupons for only $3.

12. Place your product name prominently on the product. On the gate of my fence is a plaque that prominently displays the installing company's name.

13. Offer a little gift that is closely related to your business. I like to give a little invention to people who visit me. Usually the items are cute, but more important, they are products an inventor has actually sold to a company.

GIVING CLASSES AND SPEECHES

Nighttime Classes

Neighborhood community centers, technical colleges, and local junior colleges offer adult education courses. They typically include such courses as:

- Starting a Day-Care Business
- Micro Enterprises—Home-Based Businesses
- Advertising and Public Relations for High-Tech Companies
- Estate Planning: Making Your Dollars Work Harder
- Botany for the Gardener
- Introduction to the Macintosh Personal Computer.

These classes are an ideal way to find customers. Go to the community education centers and junior and technical colleges in your area and get a copy of their adult education schedules. See what types of classes they offer, and prepare a class related to your business. Then approach the person in charge and ask to teach the course. Many of the courses offered have been suggested by area businesspeople, and there is a good chance that you can teach one and meet new customers.

Be sure to post the description and location of any class you teach in a visible location in your business. It helps your credibility, and it lets customers see that you are looking out for their interests.

Classes for Associations or Trade Shows

At a recent technology licensing convention in Minneapolis, booths were set up by companies that were looking for companies to network with, companies to license products to, or sources of funding. The convention also had a list of classes that people could attend throughout the day.

These classes are ideal ways for consultants, design firms, manufacturers, or other service businesses to find customers. You just need to contact the trade show, find out who is in charge of the convention program, and then propose a class you would like to offer.

A dental company was offering a new endodontics product that was used for cleaning and preparing root canals. To find customers, the company hired a leading dentist and had him run seminars at leading shows that explained how the product worked. The dentist was able to get on the seminar program because of his reputation, and 100 to 400 dentists attended each seminar.

Free Speeches

You can get opportunities to speak to relevant groups for virtually every type of business. The steps you should take to create an effective speaking program are listed below:

1. Find groups interested in hearing you.
   - Check your local newspapers for community group meetings. Note the groups that you would like to speak to and each group's contact person.
   - Check trade magazines and other industry publications for groups and associations you could speak to.
   - Ask your networking contacts if they know of possible places to speak. Sometimes there are hidden locations where you could speak. For instance, a stock brokerage house might want an accountant to explain new IRS rulings at a local seminar. I've given several one-hour lectures on measuring coating thickness in the middle of another company's two-day seminar on coating process technologies. Those short lectures resulted in over 100 leads.

2. Select an interesting topic. Look at trade magazines or relevant consumer magazines, and make a list of ten to twenty topics that catch your interest. From those articles and your past experience, choose two or three topics people would like to know more about.

3. Contact the appropriate people.
   - Offer your services at no charge.

- Promise free samples or other information to people who hear your speech.
- Have back-up testimonials from your past speeches.
- Include a hands-on activity. I usually have a group act as a focus group for market research. It makes the speech much more informative and interesting.

4. Have a method in place to get people's names.

- Have sign-up sheets for free samples, newsletters, or an advertising specialty item.
- Have a sign-up sheet for people to fill out.
- Offer a coupon for a free seminar.
- Bring a small, inexpensive item to sell. Then get people's names when you give them a receipt.

PUBLICITY AND FLIERS

Publicity

I believe that everyone can get some publicity. Before I wrote this chapter, I wanted to release some publicity about a new educational video to video magazines and library journals. As a little test, I had Lisa Rusinko, my secretary, do her first publicity campaign.

She took the following steps:

1. Obtained the names of magazines editors by looking in back issues and from *Gale's Source of Publications* (available at your local library).
2. Contacted the editors, gave them about two minutes of information about the video, and asked if they wanted to receive more information.
3. Prepared a simple press kit with a short publicity release and some back-up material consisting of a photograph, some testimonial letters, and previous reviews of the book the video was based on.
4. Followed up with the editors and received a commitment from several to run at least some of the information.

Figure 10.1 shows the press release that Lisa sent out.

The Two Rules of Publicity

Have events that are worthy of publicity

You need to develop an eye for publicity. Editors of newspapers and magazines or radio producers won't carry everything you send them. New products and new store openings are traditional ways of getting publicity. You can also use classes, seminars, demonstrations, contests, or store or business visits by celebrities. A Schwinn dealer near my home recently started to sponsor bike rodeos for local Cub Scout and Boy Scout troops. This tactic did a great job of generating publicity.

One often ignored publicity channel is the community bulletin boards in your local newspaper or on a local radio station. They will run publicity for seminars, classes, or any other event you run. I've run seminars where 50 percent of those attending came as a result of a community bulletin board announcement.

Figure 10.1
Sample Press Release (Sent to Library Reviewers)

CONTACT: FOR IMMEDIATE RELEASE

Lisa Rusinko
Product to Market Seminars
888 W. County Rd. #104
New Brighton, MN 55112
612-555-1212

New Video for Inventors Shows How to Take an Idea to Market without Spending a Fortune.

Taking a product to market has become a popular topic with students in high school and college with the rise in Young Inventor's Fairs and Entrepreneur Classes. Libraries have responded by buying more books on the subject, but up until now there haven't been any videotapes on the subject available.

Don Debelak's video, EIGHT PROVEN TACTICS FOR TAKING AN IDEA TO MARKET, explains how anyone, from a high school student to a retired housewife, can introduce a new product. Based on the critically acclaimed HOW TO BRING A PRODUCT TO MARKET FOR LESS THAN $5,000 (John Wiley & Sons, 1991, $14.95), it covers these eight proven tactics for success:

- Evening up the odds against big corporations
- Avoiding patent expense
- Obtaining cheap market research
- Getting free help from the experts
- Making models and prototypes for the lowest possible cost
- Finding investors the easy way
- Manufacturing the product with no up-front money
- Selling products without a big promotional budget.

The library price, which includes public performance rights, is $119.95. Running time 62 minutes. Color cover.

Get your announcement out in time
It often takes two to four months to get a magazine to run a publicity release, and newspapers take two to three weeks. Even community bulletin boards require ten days to two weeks notice. You should post in your office a list of every newspaper or magazine you plan on using, the name of the key contact at each one, and how far in advance you need to send information. Editors will usually gladly give you this information.

One of the reasons I like to call editors in advance is that sometimes they will run a bigger story than just a short press release. They might send a writer to cover the event, or they might ask you for a short report. Either way, the extra publicity will help.

Fliers or Circulars

Consumer fliers

A flier or circular is a simple one-page sales brochure that states what you do and offers something free to potential customers, such as a discount, a free estimate, or a free consultation. You can hand-deliver fliers, post small versions of them on community bulletin boards at shopping malls or banks, and have them delivered at another business. For example, a shoe repair business might distribute fliers for a dry cleaning shop.

Business-to-business fliers

The most common industrial use of fliers is as an insert to a trade magazine, an insert in a monthly billing or other communication, or an insert in another company's mailing.

For a fee, trade magazines will include a piece of promotional literature. Depending on its size, a trade magazine might also insert a flier for a small geographic area. You can also make up fliers to go out with routine correspondence during a particular period. If much of your correspondence goes to buyers or marketers (rather than accounting or customer service), you can also exchange fliers with another company that serves the same market.

Dated announcements

Have your flier centered around a dated announcement. For example, fliers work well if you are announcing a seminar or class, a one-week sale, or a week when people can come and use your equipment in a production setting. Dated coupons are another common tactic.

You can also offer something free to the first respondents. When I run Saturday morning seminars, I offer a free book to the first ten registrants. I actually give the book to anyone who registers during the first week. That tactic usually almost doubles attendance.

SIGNS AND CLASSIFIED ADS

Signs

A sign is a good way to alert people to your business and a good way to remind them of your company. You should put signs in as many places as possible—on your store or business, on every product, on advertising specialty items, at locations where you are working, and in any other crucial spot. You should also use banners whenever possible, as they are something different that people will notice. I use banners all the time at trade shows, especially when I have a new product. They don't cost much, and they do make people take notice.

Keep your signs simple. All you are trying to do is have people remember your name and what you do. Everson's Environmental Engineering is all the sign needs to say. That's also all a person is going to read.

Classified Advertising

For many businesses, classified advertising is an effective tool for finding customers. You might run a classified ad in a newspaper, a consumer magazine, or a relevant trade magazine. The three key points are to have the right type of product for classified advertising, have the right type of heading in the magazine or newspaper, and follow the five rules of classified advertising.

Right type of product

The types of products that work best are those that people can't find anywhere else, such as used copy machines or unusual industrial products or services, and easy-to-understand products that are hard to find. For instance, I ran an ad for a plastic prototype kit in *Popular Mechanics* and received about twenty-five responses per insertion.

Other products that work well are those that call for an immediate action, such as an auction or some other event that is coming up. For example, an industrial supplier might run classified ads if it was running some special event attached to an upcoming trade show.

Right heading for your product

I used to run a classified ad for an invention marketing business in the Business Personals section of the *Minneapolis Star and Tribune*. It pulled thirty to fifty responses per month. Then the paper eliminated the heading and put the ad in Business Information. My responses dropped to less than ten with the heading change. Before you advertise, watch the heading for a few weeks and see how many ads keep repeating. You can also call up advertisers who might tell you how many responses to expect. Don't advertise under a heading unless some companies advertise there every issue.

Five steps to successful classified ads

1. Find a newspaper or magazine that would be appropriate for your business.
2. Find a heading that makes sense.
3. Offer free information or a low-cost product that will motivate people to contact you.
4. Design your ad to be different from others around it.
5. Have follow-up products to sell people, especially if you are offering a low-cost product.

Commit to running a magazine ad at least three times and a newspaper ad for at least five days. Ads rarely pull that well the first time they are run.

ACTION STEPS

Listed next are the nine tactics discussed in this section and the action steps you need to take for each one. Pick out at least three or four low-cost tactics to use to find customers.

Networking
- Decide which organizations can be beneficial to your business, then join them.
- Keep an active watch for people who are speakers, who are quoted often, or who write articles about your type of business. Put them on your list of people to contact.
- Be active in any industry groups relating to standards or industry trends.

Personal Letters and Telephone Solicitations
- Create a mailing list of key customers and contacts that you want to devote extra attention to.
- Plan at least two to three events or activities per year for which you can run a personal letter campaign.
- Incorporate at least one follow-up telephone campaign from key company executives to important contacts and key customers.

Face-to-Face Contacts
- Make it a company policy to try to arrange yearly meetings between key contacts and customers and company executives.

Referral Programs
- Review the list of tactics for getting referrals given in this chapter. Try to implement at least three of them.

Free Speeches and Classes
- Make a list of all the places you could give a speech or offer a class. These can include speeches to industry groups, classes at colleges, seminars at trade shows, and speeches to community organizations. Keep an updated list, including contact names. Then try to at least teach one class or make one speech each year. You may not get many leads, but they will be of extremely high quality.

Publicity
- Keep a publicity file on different stories or events that other companies run. Use this file to help you get ideas for programs you could run. It will also give you samples of what your releases should look like.
- Prepare a publicity schedule that lists all the newspapers and magazines you might run releases in. List the dates prior to publication by which you need to get your stories in. Also include key contacts at each paper or magazine.
- Include publicity releases as a standard part of your marketing program. Not only will you get more leads, you'll also get articles that will improve your credibility.

Fliers
- List possible ways you could use fliers in your business. Include options from door-to-door delivery to using the fliers as inserts in trade magazines

or in other companies' mailings. Try using fliers if you can find an effective way to do so.

Signs

- Look at your business and see if there are any additional places you can put a sign or banner. Consider trucks, your business location, your trade show booth, and delivery boxes.

Classified Ads

- Keep a file on any magazines or newspapers where you might run an ad. Watch the headings, and watch which ads run for a prolonged period. If an ad location looks promising, try your own ad.

- Try to create a low-priced product or a free information packet or sample that can pull well in a classified ad. Make sure your offer will attract people that could buy your other products.

Chapter 11

Advertising, Trade Shows, Seminars, and Direct Mail

Oppenheimer and Co. wanted to promote a corporate investment vehicle to pension fund managers and chief financial officers—a tough crowd to reach. To get past executives' secretaries, Oppenheimer mailed out a gyroscope with every letter. The gyroscope not only helped get the envelope opened, it was also intriguing enough that executives kept it on their desks to play with.

This is the type of reception every company would like to have. And you can, as I'll discuss in upcoming chapters. But this type of marketing approach is expensive, and you can only afford to mail to people you know are viable prospects.

This chapter covers eleven different tactics you can use to get people to identify themselves as prospects. They are broken down into four groups: response-oriented advertising, such as Yellow Pages or magazine advertising; taking-it-to-the-customer tactics like seminars and trade shows; mass media advertising such as radio or billboard ads; and mailing tactics, which include direct mail, warranty cards, and coupons.

I'll discuss some of these tactics further in the sections on motivating and communicating with customers. This chapter shows you how to use these tactics to find customers.

As you consider these tactics, you will have to decide how much money to spend on preparing ads or brochures and how much on buying ad space or mailings to prospects. You want your information to look professional, but you don't want to spend a fortune to get that look. Though there is certainly no hard and fast rule, I recommend that you commit between 10 and 15 percent of your advertising budget to material preparation.

RESPONSE ADVERTISING

A response ad is one where a customer is expected to call, write, or visit you. A person who sees your ad in the Yellow Pages may respond either by calling or by visiting the store. A card pack ad asks you to fill out and return a postcard or call an 800 number. A small magazine ad typically asks people to send in or call in for more information.

Yellow Pages and Directory Advertising

Advertising in the Yellow Pages and trade directories is essential for businesses offering a product or service that is purchased infrequently. For example, if you want to duplicate 100 copies of an audio tape, you'll look for that service in the Yellow Pages. If you need injection-molded foam packaging for a big international order, you'll probably look either in the Yellow Pages or in an industrial directory to find a source.

Business-to-business suppliers often overlook the Yellow Pages or just run a one-line listing. I recommend that every business try a one-inch listing in the Yellow Pages for at least one year. You can get orders from the strangest places. We received an inquiry from an exporter that resulted in an $18,000 order for China off of a Yellow Pages listing. The exporter received an inquiry about a product he knew nothing about, and so he called us.

Important points about directory advertising

1. Your competitors will be advertising on the same or nearby pages. Make sure your ad looks different and offers a unique reason to call you.

2. Many people will call only one ad's number, or at the most three or four. Your ad needs to be powerful. Spend time making sure you have the best possible ad.

3. You may spend $750 to $1,000 per year or more on a Yellow Pages or directory ad. Hire a graphic artist to prepare an eye-catching ad.

4. Your ad should give a reason for people to call you. Some of the reasons you can ask people to call are:
   - To receive a legislative update
   - For an in-home demonstration
   - For a free sample evaluation
   - For a one-hour free consultation
   - For a free repair evaluation and estimate.

5. Your ads should be at least as big as competitors' ads.

Card Pack Advertising

Card packs are groups of postcard-size ads wrapped in plastic that are delivered to your home or business. Typically a card pack is directed at a specific customer group, such as small-business marketers, gardeners, quality control engineers, metallurgical engineers, or independent accountants.

Card packs will help you find customers. I've received anywhere from 70 to 400 responses from an 80,000- to 100,000-piece mailing. I use card packs primarily when only a few people in a group are prospects. The low cost per address makes card packs a cost-effective way of finding those customers.

I've found that card packs work better for companies selling to other companies than for companies selling to consumers. I once ran an ad in a card pack directed at quality control engineers. I wanted to know which companies both purchased nitrided products and were having trouble inspecting them. I received 49 leads from a 40,000-piece mailing. That was a better response than I could have gotten any other way.

Advantages/disadvantages

Card packs cost only about two cents per person, which compares very well to a direct mailing cost of thirty to fifty cents per person. Card packs also work well for small- to medium-size companies because every company's card is the same size. That takes away the disadvantage small companies have when their small magazine ads are placed next to a large competitor's full-page ad.

The big disadvantage of card packs is that you miss many prospects. Only a percentage of prospects receive card packs, and only a percentage of those who do open them up and look at them.

Sources

Trade or specialty magazines often run their own card packs. Check with the advertising departments of key magazines for information. If a magazine doesn't have its own card pack, talk to the person responsible for selling its mailing list. Typically that person will know two or three card packs that buy its list. You can also check at your local library for *SRDS Card Pack Rates & Data Directory* (SRDS, 3004 Glenview Road, Wilmette, IL 60091).

Key points about card packs

1. They work much better for finding customers than for selling products. By offering free information or free samples, I've been able to get four to five times the number of responses I got when I tried to sell something.

2. Keep your postcard simple. Just state what you do and why you're better, then make an offer for people to respond to.

3. Always list an 800 number. You'll lose at least 50 percent of your respondents if you wait for people to get around to sending for information.

4. If possible, run a contest for a free gift. One company had 1,000 people respond to a contest for the most unusual use of its type of product, which was a small industrial spring.

Action Steps

1. Tear out Yellow Pages or directory ads for both your and your competitors' products. See if your ad stands out, and if it is more compelling than the competition.

2. Go through the directories and tear out any ads that you feel stand out. Find at least ten compelling ads, then rework your ad based on those examples.

3. Keep an updated list of card packs you could mail through. If you can't get a list from the sources listed in this chapter, call up the reference section of the main library of a large city and ask for packs listed in the SRDS card pack directory.

GOING OUT AND FINDING CUSTOMERS

Gail Ellison created a tube of material that could be folded in six different ways to become a hood, headband, neck warmer, face mask, earband, or hat. Her company, Maxit Designs, got its big break in February 1987 at a trade show, where she got the San Francisco 49ers to try out her product. That success gave her the leverage she needed to have her product picked up by sporting goods stores.

Most marketing tactics leave the control of the contact to the customer. Marketers can take charge by using tactics that take their product to the customers. Two ways to do that are to attend trade shows that customers attend and to conduct your own seminars and workshops.

Going out and finding customers is especially important when customers have a long contemplation period. Setting up a retirement fund, finding a new business location, buying a new computer system, and deciding on an advertising agency are all decisions that people mull over. If suppliers of these products and services don't contact customers early, they may not get a chance to contact them at all.

Trade Shows

The three key steps to cashing in on trade shows are: (1) finding ones that fit your company, (2) making sure your booth works for you, and (3) making sure you get prospects' names.

Choosing the right show

1. Get a list of shows you might attend.
   - Call your local convention bureau for a list of upcoming shows.
   - Look at past issues of your local paper's community activity calendar.
   - Check past issues of trade magazines for local or national trade shows.
   - Ask relevant associations about trade shows.
   - Check your local library for directories of trade shows. You can also get issues of *Trade Shows and Conventions* (49 Music Square West, Nashville, TN 37203).

2. Decide which shows would work for you.
   - Don't automatically decide to attend big shows. Sometimes small- to medium-size companies do better at a small show where people have time to talk to them. Sometimes prospects will talk to so many people at a big show that they'll forget all about you.
   - Contact the show's sponsor and get a copy of last year's program guide. Look through the guide for companies that look about your size; call them up and talk to the person in charge of shows or the marketing director to see what they thought of the show. Don't attend a show where you don't get positive reviews from past attendees.
   - Try to visit a show before you purchase space. Also, attend a few smaller shows first; then if you are successful, go to a larger one.

Have your booth work for you

1. Make sure your booth looks as good as the ones around you.

   - One reason to avoid national shows at first is that most companies will have expensive booths that may make yours look cheap.
   - Have large graphics with little copy, and have the graphics professionally prepared. Nothing looks worse in a booth than wall graphics that are full of little letters.
   - Have literature stands that hold literature straight up. Try to avoid having your literature lie flat. Literature stands are available at office supplies stores.
   - Give people a reason to talk to you. Have a product to demonstrate, a model, or a contest, or ask a question on your booth graphics.

2. Work your booth properly.

   - Don't sit down.
   - Have an open-ended question or two to ask people when they look at your booth: "What types of acids are you trying to dispose of?" "How did you get your last new product designed?" "What type of deck would you like to have?"
   - Stand in the aisle when you're not talking to someone, then follow people over to your booth.

Get as many names as possible

1. Typical methods:

   - Collect business cards.
   - Have a contest, or have people sign up to receive literature.
   - Have a form you fill out, or rent an imprinter (from show management) to stamp people's badges on a form.

2. Unusual tactics:

   - Walk around the show, look for businesses that are complementary to yours, and exchange lead names.
   - Don't give out brochures. Make people give you their names and then send information later. A lot of people just pick up literature and never buy. That can cost you money. You'll have better success if you have people give you their names.

Seminars and Workshops

I like seminars and workshops because they are an ideal referral tactic, they work well as a sign-up tool at speeches or trade shows, they are an excellent reason to send key prospects an invitation, and they are a good publicity vehicle.

Any business can have a seminar, workshop, or demonstration. Fleet Farm, a large, farm-oriented discount store, has a big department for hunters and fishermen. It recently had a demonstration by one of the country's leading turkey-calling experts. Fleet Farm's campaign included in-store promotions, newspaper ads, and an active publicity program that was picked up by local papers and radio stations.

I used to set up demonstrations in hotel rooms for both dental equipment and metallurgical equipment. I'd set up for two days, have engineering support, and have people come to see the equipment. This demonstration let me see more people in two days, under ideal conditions, than a sales representative could effectively see in two or three weeks.

You don't need a big crowd to have a seminar. Five or so people is just fine. Most of your results from a seminar come from people who don't attend. Your publicity releases, in-business promotion, newsletter announcements, and personal invitations will reach a large number of prospects. That impact will produce sales.

Getting attendees

You can get attendees by giving free tickets to customers as a referral tool, through publicity releases, from your personal invitations to key accounts, and through in-business promotions. I also like to attract at least five to ten people through a direct mailing. I get a list from another company or a list compiler and send out 1,000 direct mail fliers on a seminar. Typically a seminar mailing to a good list will generate a 0.5 to 1 percent response, which is five to ten people.

Key points about seminars

1. Have seminars in hotels whenever possible. That is where big companies hold them, and it will help your image.

2. Two-and-a-half-hour seminars work better than all-day seminars. People won't commit themselves to a whole day, and it's difficult to be interesting for a whole day.

3. Bring posters, copies of publicity releases in stand-up picture frames, and other pertinent information.

4. Try to include a short motivational or humorous video. You can find these at your library or video store, or by looking in the Yellow Pages under Motivational and Self-Improvement Training.

5. Have at least two people present information, one of them an expert on your product.

6. Set up a five- or ten-minute period at the end of the seminar to talk to people individually or in small groups. Don't let people leave without setting up an appointment or another action step.

7. Promote your seminar to clubs or other related groups.

8. Use heavy in-business promotions.

ACTION STEPS

1. Choose one trade show or convention, even if it is just a small local show. Every business can benefit from exposure. If you are a retailer, attend a community event like a festival in the park. If you are an accountant, attend a local small business and entrepreneur show. If you are a

manufacturer, find a show that prospects will attend. If you don't get good results, you don't have to attend again, but the possibilities are too great not to try it out.

2. Look at your business and determine a topic you can use for a demonstration, a workshop, or a seminar; then go ahead and hold one. Remember to include publicity, mailings to key accounts, newsletter announcements before and after the seminar, and mailings to other accounts.

RADIO, MAGAZINE, AND NEWSPAPER ADS

The formula for finding customers through ads is quite simple. First, you need a headline or question that is directed at what the customer wants. "Take the weekend off" is a great headline for Chem Lawn. Second, you have to give people a reason to call you. That's all there is to it. You don't need much copy; after all, your goal is not to educate people, but to get them to call you.

Newspaper Ads

Large ads

Many people look through the Saturday or Sunday paper to see who is having a sale. If people look for your type of product in a newspaper, you had better be there, or customers will never find you. Your competitors will probably also have ads, so be sure your ad is similar in size to theirs. If big newspaper ads are too expensive for you, put ads in small local papers, as it's unlikely that anyone will read your small ad in a major paper.

Little ads

Little newspaper ads might pay off for you if you have an unusual business that people might not otherwise hear of. Before buying space, check the paper for a few weeks to see how many people advertise repeatedly. If it looks as if ads for products like yours are working, try an ad and see what the result is.

My experience is that the best spot to place a newspaper ad is in the weekly TV guide. People keep the guide for a week, and they see the ads when they look at that day's listing.

Magazine Advertising

Magazines are typically more cost effective than newspapers because they go to a more targeted audience. They are a good choice if you can find a magazine where at least 20 to 30 percent of the readers are prospects. You'll see some ads in magazines to sell products, most of which cost less than $10. However, most of the ads in magazines are trying to find customers.

Start by finding magazines you think might be appropriate. Be sure to look in a directory like *Gale's Source of Publications* for possible magazines. If you have a consumer product, you might also look in *Writers Handbook*, which lists quite a few small magazines.

Call the magazine and get three or four back issues and a demographic breakout of its subscribers. If the list looks promising, go through the back issues and pull out the ads that have run in every issue. Only run ads in magazines that have a high percentage of repeat advertisers.

Chapter 15 explains how to prepare the copy and layout for an ad. Another point to consider is to try different size ads. I've found that quarter- and one third-page ads pull almost as many prospects as a full-page ad. This can vary for each product, so try out different sizes.

One last point is that the rate chart a magazine sends you is highly negotiable. Ask for first-time discounts, half-page ads for a quarter-page price, or any other deal that can save you money.

Industrial products

Ads in trade magazines are extremely effective for nonconsumer products. A $4,000 full-page ad in a dental magazine consistently pulled 250 to 400 leads. This is about $10 to $15 a prospect. A successful direct mail campaign might have a 2 or 3 percent response. At a mailing cost of about fifty cents a piece, a mailing to 100 people will cost $50 for 2 or 3 leads.

I was marketing a product for testing coated products. I ran these four campaigns with *Quality Magazine*:

1. Purchased a 5,000-name mailing list of subscribers for a direct mail campaign.

2. Exhibited at a *Quality Magazine*-sponsored trade show.

3. Advertised in a magazine-run card pack.

4. Ran a quarter-page ad in the magazine.

The ad itself produced more leads per dollar than any other tactic. That was surprising because we only purchased names of electro coaters for the mailing list. An added plus was that the ad pulled responses for more than two years.

Billboards

Drive into a resort town and you'll see one billboard after another. Universal Studios has a billboard in Florida that it paid over $100,000 for. In tourist areas, people look at billboards to decide where to go. But billboards are also becoming more popular in cities, where they advertise stores, real estate and insurance agencies, and business services.

Billboards are expensive, but they do a nice job of communicating with a certain part of the market. For example, a Midas store near my home has a billboard ad that everybody who drives by sees. I think billboards are effective for products that virtually everyone needs, but that are needed only infrequently. Insurance agencies, car repair shops, real estate agencies, and tire stores are all businesses that can use billboards to find customers. Billboards are especially cost-effective in small towns where rates are lower.

Radio Advertising

An ad for a new business consulting franchise has recently run many times on the radio. The ad offers a free video that explains the new venture and repeats an

800 number to call. The ad keeps running because it works. It has a strong headline and a free offer with a toll-free number.

I believe many companies, including industrial suppliers, mistakenly overlook radio advertising. It is a low-cost approach that can be directed at a targeted customer group. It also has several other advantages:

1. Production costs are low. Typically radio personalities will read your ad free as part of the cost of radio time.

2. You can change your ad several times to see which version works best.

3. By using small stations, you can experiment and test your ads without spending much money.

4. You can run ads immediately, often in less than three days. No other medium is this immediate.

5. You can establish an immediate rapport and immediate credibility by having radio personalities talk about your product. You can even have a dialogue between you and the radio DJ.

Radio ads are similar to others in having a headline and a free offer, but you need to include two additional things: You have to repeat an 800 number at least three or four times, and you need to establish credibility by listing information about how long you have been in business, how you are associated with a big organization, or some other fact that shows you are a legitimate company— "world's largest company," "in business for twenty-four years," "associated with the University of Pennsylvania hospital."

Industrial companies

You may be successful on the radio if you sell a product that can be used by a fairly large group of companies, and if your town has a radio talk/news show that appeals to businesspeople. Copiers are an example of a product that will do well with a radio ad because every company needs one. But other products can also do well. Business consultants, finance companies that buy receivables, product designers, specialized advertising agencies, and hazardous waste disposal firms can all sell on radio. Suppliers to small- to medium-size companies can reach many more prospects than they can any other way. One advantage of radio is that few industrial suppliers advertise there, so listeners will pay more attention than you might expect.

ACTION STEPS

1. Start a file with all the ads you can find from your competitors or from companies that have similar types of products. Either tape or write down radio ads.

2. When you see an ad that is run repeatedly, decide what makes the ad work. If you're not sure, call up and ask why the company thinks it works. Usually people will be flattered by your attention and tell you what they think.

3. Experiment with a radio, newspaper, or magazine ad at least once every six months. Do this even if another tactic is working. You need to be constantly trying new techniques to stay ahead of your competitors.

MAILING TECHNIQUES

People receive so much of what they call "junk mail" that it is becoming increasingly difficult to successfully find customers through the mail. But this is still a crucial tactic for companies, especially industrial suppliers, that have only a few scattered customers located throughout a wide area. Direct mail is often the only cost-effective option.

To have a cost-effective mailing program for finding new customers, you need to have a good mailing list, have a reason for people to call immediately, have a short, effective message, and hold costs to a minimum.

A Good Mailing List

List compilers

Many small businesses buy names from companies that sell lists of people based on a customer profile that you request, such as income, location, or occupation.

I've never been that happy with those lists because the compilers typically try to get you to take as many names as possible, not just the names that have the best quality. For example, I wanted to buy a list of people who had joined inventors' groups or associations within the last year. I couldn't get a company to give me that list. Instead, they wanted to sell me a complete membership list of inventors' groups. I didn't want that list because many of those inventors had already given up on their ideas. The compilers didn't want to sell the smaller list because it didn't have enough names.

Compile your own list

I compiled my own list of names of inventors by finding the names of people who had just been awarded patents. Every week the U.S. government publishes the names of people awarded a patent in the *U.S. Patent Gazette*. I just went through the *Gazette* and pulled out the names of people who had inventions we were interested in working on.

Some of the other ways you can compile your own list are the following:

1. From public documents

2. From library directories, such as *Directory of Specialty Retailers and Wholesale Representatives* or *Thomas Registry*

3. From state industrial directories

4. From the Yellow Pages and business-to-business directories

5. From trade directories

6. From industrial buying guides.

Purchased lists

You can buy a wide variety of lists from sources other than list compilers:

1. Customers of another company that sells to the same target group
2. Mail-order catalog house buyers
3. Members of relevant associations
4. Subscribers to appropriate magazines
5. Attendees of local or national trade shows.

The effectiveness of any of these tactics depends on your product. If you have a product for runners, you will probably get a good list if you buy a list from a running magazine or an entry list from a local marathon. If you sell laser scanners to enter model and prototype dimensions into a computer, you'll probably get a good list from a design engineering magazine. But if you sell a jewelry product, what type of list can you buy?

There really isn't one. Where will you find a list of companies looking for a graphic design firm? Again, it's much harder to purchase a list.

A Reason to Respond Immediately

I've always received 60 to 80 percent of the responses to a mailing within one or two weeks. On some mailings this has been as high as 90 percent. If people don't respond quickly, they don't respond at all. Here are some options for getting a quick response:

1. Offer a product for $1 or $2 or even free provided people order by a certain date.
2. Offer free pamphlets, books, consultations, or demonstrations.
3. Have a buy-one-get-one-free or some other similar offer.
4. Run a contest or sweepstakes for people who respond by an earlier date.
5. Offer an extended warranty or extra services.

Short, Effective Messages

Most direct mail packages you receive are fat and full of information. Those packages are designed to sell a product. That is not your goal here. You want someone to call you. If you tell prospects everything possible about your company, there will be no reason for them to call. So keep your message to one side of one page, and make sure you are offering a piece of information or a product that is new and intriguing for the reader. One of the reasons I like postcards for finding customers is that you are forced to keep the message brief.

Cost-Saving Measures

Bulk mail

You can save a lot of money by using bulk mail rates. You only need to mail 200 pieces at a time to qualify for a bulk-rate discount. The most you will pay for a bulk-rate letter is 19.8 cents, even if your letters are going all over the country. If you are mailing to a specific Zip code, you can reduce your bulk mail charges to 16.8 or 14.5 cents per letter. You can apply for a bulk mailing permit (which costs only $75 per year) from the main post office in your town.

Bulk mail is an even better deal for industrial manufacturers who mail out 6- by 9- or 9- by 12-inch envelopes. These will go for prices only about a third of first class mail.

The trouble with bulk mail is that you can't be sure when it will arrive. I've found that bulk mail takes about twice as long as regular mail as long as you don't mail in December. Bulk rates give your mailings a much better chance of being cost-effective, and I recommend that you use them.

Other ways to cut costs

1. Mail with other companies. Try to find other companies like yours at conventions or through publicity releases in trade magazines, then suggest sending out a mailing together to cut costs.

2. Use an advertising service or a coupon mailer that combines different companies' mailings.

3. Mail out postcards. They cost only 19 cents to mail first class, cost less to print than a letter, and are easier to prepare than a letter mailing. More people will read a postcard than a letter, so this is a tactic you should try.

ACTION STEPS

1. Start a list of similar companies you can buy mailing lists from or exchange lists with. The two best ways to find these companies are to attend trade shows and to watch for press releases or ads in trade magazines.

2. Respond to ads in magazines, direct-mail pieces, and radio ads. You'll get on more mailing lists than you can possibly imagine. Keep information you get that either motivates you or is on products similar to yours. Keep a file of these pieces to use as examples.

Chapter 12

Bulletin Boards, Computers, and Talk Shows

I overheard the manager of a stock brokerage house complaining about some unique problems presented by engineers: They like to know every detail about a purchase, and they aren't particularly responsive to the personal approach stockbrokers typically use. I told the manager he should set up a computer bulletin board system for engineers so that he could interface with them through a technology they enjoyed.

This chapter discusses two new methods of finding customers that are starting to take hold. One is the use of computer technology, which offers a variety of new techniques, and the other is an aggressive publicity strategy that capitalizes on the new special-interest radio and TV talk shows.

COMPUTER MAGIC—LEADS FROM NOWHERE

In this section I'll explain what computers can do for you. I'm not going to try to explain the technical details of setting up a system. One reason is that I am not totally sure how to do it. I know someone who knows the technical details, and he does it for me. A computer club or a computer store can either help you set up your own system or give you the names of a few people who can help you. If you'd like more technical information, I recommend the book *Bulletin Board Systems for Business*, by Lamont Wood and Dan Blankenhorn (John Wiley & Sons, 1992).

Computer systems are especially useful for business-to-business marketers. They work well when you have technical information, complex ordering possibilities, or a widely scattered customer base. Another advantage is that computers give you access to people when they are available. This makes them an ideal tool for reaching engineers, production managers, distributors, manufacturers' representatives, and other very busy people.

Definitions

Electronic mail

This is a message you write on your computer screen and then send to someone else's computer; that person can either read it on the screen or print it on a piece of paper. You can use the telephone to send this message to another computer if both computers are hooked up to modems (the computer-to-phone-line connection device), or you can send it to a central computer that will store it until the intended recipient retrieves it. This can be done through services such as CompuServe that provide each member with an electronic address and an access code.

Bulletin board systems

A bulletin board is similar to electronic mail except that it allows you to store information on-line for people to access. For example, you might have technical service information on your bulletin board. A customer could call up your bulletin board and go through a menu to find the information he or she wants. People can also leave electronic messages, order products or additional information, or request that someone telephone them on the bulletin board. To access a bulletin board, all you need is its phone number and your own computer and modem.

CD-ROMs

A CD-ROM is a memory disk that can hold an unbelievable amount of information—the equivalent of 100 to 200 books. A CD-ROM system consists of a computer equipped with a CD-ROM drive (available for less than $3,000), one or more CD-ROM discs of information, and software that allows you to access that information. Libraries are starting to buy a few CD-ROM systems to access databases such as newspaper and magazine articles and car repair procedures. The advantages of a CD-ROM system are the large amounts of data it can store and the fact that the data can be accessed instantly, without having to go through a menu.

The Computer Future

I have a huge library of information about marketing inventions, including the names of trade shows, distributors, and manufacturers, and information about patents, market channels, and hundreds of other topics. If I put every piece of information I have on a CD-ROM disc, it probably will take up less than 20 percent of the available capacity. Once I combine a CD-ROM system with a bulletin board, I have an incredible tool for providing information and finding prospects. I can either set up my own system or work through a computer information system like CompuServe or Prodigy.

The reasons these methods are valuable, particularly for nonconsumer suppliers, are the following:

1. A large percentage of customers have access to computers.

2. Few companies have entered the computer marketing era.

3. Customers, customer service departments, salespeople, and technical service departments can use the system to get an immediate response to questions they might not otherwise be able to answer.

4. Customers can quickly get the information they want without contacting salespeople. Many manufacturing and engineering managers prefer to do that.

5. Buyers can place orders at off-peak hours, when they have more available time.

Computer Information Systems

For $8.95 per month you can become a member of CompuServe and access all of its databases. For another fee of less than $50, you can place a small classified ad in the CompuServe information service. If people are looking for information about your type of product, they can type in that category and see your ad. They can then leave an electronic mail message for you, which you can pick up by calling CompuServe and entering your access code.

You can also advertise on Prodigy's or CompuServe's electronic mall. Companies place a few of their products, or in some cases their entire product catalog, in these malls, and those catalogs produce plenty of prospects, and in some cases plenty of sales. Electronic malls are ideal if you have a computer-related product or service, or if you have a technical product for which users might otherwise be hard to find. John Wiley & Sons has its entire book catalog on CompuServe, which is a smart strategy because bookstores will carry some books for only four to six months. On CompuServe, Wiley can keep its books (which include business, engineering, and science books) in front of its target customer group.

Advertisements on computer services are different from magazine ads because:

1. Some people like using their computers and check through systems just to see what's new.

2. Not many companies advertise on these services at the moment, making computer advertising a novelty.

3. All people have to do is enter a category name and the ads will come up on their screen. This is an easier way to find information.

Bulletin Board Systems

Interactive information is what a bulletin board can provide. This makes it an excellent tool for finding prospects in their contemplative stage. For example, a company selling mountain bikes could set up a bulletin board system with information about bike features, which types of features work best for different groups of people, current prices of bikes from major suppliers, a product catalog, and tips on repairing bikes. A person who is interested in mountain bikes, can get the phone number of this system from a computer network database. That person can then call up the bulletin board, find the information, and request whatever extra information he or she would like.

Types of bulletin boards

Many companies setting up their first bulletin board will go through a commercial bulletin board network like Channel 1 (617-864-0741) or The Business Board (212-477-0408). Those companies will help you set up your board and make sure you have a workable system.

You can also set up your own board in your office with either regular, toll-free, or 900 number call-ins. Usually 800 numbers are the method of choice for service-related bulletin boards, and 900 numbers will increasingly be chosen by information-related boards.

Bulletin board costs

You can probably set up a system for $5,000 to $10,000, which is less than the cost of most magazine and TV campaigns. And the bulletin board will last forever. I highly recommend boards for any company with products for which people like to see a lot of information, with many ordering options, geared toward computer owners or accountants and engineers, and for which heavy technical back-up is required.

ACTION STEPS

1. If you have a computer or access to a computer, you should explore electronic mail systems. They cost less than $15 per month to join, and you can advertise on them for less than $50 per month. Try this even if you have a local business; the number of computer users is so high that you can still benefit from the ad.

    Some resources you can contact are:

    CompuServe
    5000 Arlington Centre Blvd.
    Columbus, OH 43220
    1-800-368-3343

    Electronic Mail Assn.
    1555 Wilson Blvd.
    Suite 300
    Arlington, VA 22209
    703-875-0150

    PC Pursuit (U.S. Sprint)
    12490 Sunrise Valley Drive
    Reston, VA 22096

    National Videotex Network
    111 Mulberry Street
    Suite 1A
    Newark, NJ 07102
    201-242-3119

2. Subscribe to *Boardwatch* magazine (303-973-4222). This is a listing of bulletin board activity around the country.

3. If you aren't ready to start your own board, contact The Business Board (213-477-0408), or Channel 1 (617-864-0741) for information. These two companies can set your board up on their larger systems.

4. Go to a local computer store and get the names of the computer-user networks in your town. Call them up to find someone who can set up a system for you. Get a start-up estimate. You'll be surprised at how low the cost is.

5. Investigate a CD-ROM system at a local store. This can be an effective tool if you can store all of your industry, product, and service information on CD-ROM. If your information is extensive, you can buy a scanner to enter information into the computer.

AN AGGRESSIVE MEDIA STRATEGY

Most marketers think of publicity as just sending out news releases and occasionally hosting an event. Over the last few years, however, the proliferation of radio talk shows, new cable TV programs, specialty magazines, newsletters, and seminars has opened up new publicity outlets for shrewd marketers.

Long-Term Benefits

Publicity won't always get immediate results, but it can provide substantial long-term benefits. Recently I received a call from the Minnesota Small Business Development Center. It wanted me to give a speech at upcoming seminars on how to do research on market size. This was an excellent opportunity for me, as I would be addressing medium-size companies that are typical clients.

I got this contact through publicity. Several local papers ran stories on my last book. About nine months after these stories were run, I was contacted by someone who saved the stories to be a judge at an inventor's fair. There I made a contact with a man who worked to develop new business in the state, and it was through that contact that I ended up getting this call.

Radio and TV Talk Shows

The magazine *Radio-TV Interview Report* contains ads for people who want to be talk show guests. Here are some of the people who were promoting their companies:

1. Robin Young, who created a system that turns TV shows and video games into interactive learning tools.

2. Dave Gorman, who has a company that offers Calculated Couples Matching Parties.

3. Nancy Power, owner of Power's Research and Training Institute, which helps people control their future.

Once you are on a show, you need an 800 number so that people can call to either get more information or order a product.

Newsworthy events

I wrote about publicity back in Chapter 10. Newspapers and magazines require a release to have some newsworthy characteristics, but you need a unique or unusual product or story to make it onto a large number of radio talk shows.

You need to learn to watch for publicity possibilities. For example, Zubas, which were wild-looking pants, were created by a couple of Minnesota body builders. They gave a pair of pants to Lawrence Taylor, the New York Giants football star. One week later Taylor was injured, and he was photographed standing on the sidelines wearing his Zubas. A buyer from J.C. Penney saw the picture and started to buy the product.

This is an interesting story. J.C. Penney should have capitalized on it by sending the inventors onto talk shows. Professional wrestlers worked out at the inventors' gym, and the inventors would have been great TV guests if they brought some of their friends along. Getting radio or TV publicity depends more on your ability to spot opportunities when they occur than on preplanning activities.

Herberger's, a small department store chain, decided to add a new line of cosmetics. As part of the distribution deal, the founder of the cosmetic line came out to give product demonstrations. Herberger's had the founder on both radio and TV talk shows to publicize her visit and promote her products.

Another way to generate publicity is to combine with a school, a hospital, another business, or a community group to sponsor relevant events. A manufacturing company could cosponsor an event with a science museum, or an engineering firm could sponsor a quality manufacturing conference.

Contacting the media

1. Listen to local stations to see which ones carry guests. Call up the stations that do and talk to the producer. Ask what it would take to get you on as a guest.

2. If you want to contact talk shows on a national basis, contact Bradlee Media Publications, 135 E. Plumstead Ave., Box 206, Landsdowne, PA 19050. This is the same company that publishes *Radio-TV Interview Report*. *Gale's Source of Publications*, at your local library also has a list of radio stations.

3. When you have a story, call the stations and see if they would like to receive your press kit. If they would, send a kit out and then follow up after a few days.

ACTION STEPS

1. Generate a list of radio and TV contacts in your town. Don't wait until you have an event coming up to get these names, or you'll take too long to put the word out.

2. Start a publicity file. As ideas come to you, write them down and keep them on file. Also tear out publicity pieces you see in the paper or hear on the radio or TV. You'll see many things that you could also do.

3. Make a commitment to try to do something newsworthy in the next six months, then publicize it and see how many customers you might find. Doing publicity is work, but it doesn't cost much, and I believe you will be happy with the results.

SECTION 3 — CONCLUSION

You Don't Have a Business If You Can't Find Customers

If you can't find customers, your business will fail, no matter how well you do everything else. Finding customers is the single most difficult marketing activity for small- to medium size firms. I recommend that you put together a plan for finding customers.

Here is a plan for finding customers for PALS, a business that sells Play and Learn Software for children:

1. Run special activity days on Saturdays, such as Sierra Discovery Days or Comic Book Maker, where kids can come in and, for a small fee, try out certain software.

2. Run publicity in community activity sections of local papers.

3. Network with early childhood departments at local school districts.
4. In conjunction with neighborhood schools, run contests and workshops during school hours. Offer kids who do well coupons for activity days.
5. Set up booths at carnivals and fairs in nearby communities during the summer and fall.
6. Offer courses titled "Pre-Schoolers and Computers" at local community colleges.
7. Write a pamphlet on using computers to teach kids to be creative that you can promote on radio talk shows.
8. Advertise in *Minnesota Parent*, a local free magazine, to promote Saturday activity days and other events.
9. Exchange mailing lists with two stores that sell creative children's toys.
10. Have three joint mailings each year with two manufacturers of creative children's toys and a publisher of a book on low-cost activities for children.

These are the types of programs that will find you customers. Be aggressive, be creative, and be as thrifty as possible.

Section 4

Motivating Customers

Sometimes customers provide their own motivation, as when an industrial company replaces a piece of production equipment that has unexpectedly stopped working. Other times outside sources provide motivation. For instance, the state might require companies to buy a certain type of unemployment compensation insurance or might require certain reports or training. Most of the time, however, motivation has to be provided by the marketer.

Key factors involved in motivation are having the right product, choosing a memorable identity, developing a pertinent message, creating an emotional desire, and giving people a reason to buy now.

In 1992 the hottest new supermarket product was a dog food from Alpo, Prime Cuts (it was a bad year for new products). Prime Cuts had all the key elements of motivation. It was a premium dog food that owners could give their pampered pets. The company's name, Alpo, was well known as that of a premium dog food supplier. Alpo's name and market history gave customers confidence. Alpo created emotion by playing off owners' devotion to their dogs. Prime Cuts is a great name. It states the product's benefit, and it's easy to remember. Dogs need to eat every day, so people need to buy dog food every week. Alpo had all the key elements of motivation, and the product sold.

Chapter 13
Creating an Identity

The first two sections of this book discussed how to create a focused product position that will motivate your target customers. All your efforts to generate influence and to position yourself in a powerful manner come together in your identity. This is a crucial marketing element. You get only two to three seconds to communicate a message. Once you have taken the time to create a winning market position, be sure to take the time to develop a clear, memorable identity that explains who you are and why people should buy from you.

Tom Redmond discovered a black, gunky hair conditioner in the labs of an Australian chemist. He felt the product was a winner, despite its appearance, because it gave hair "great body." Redmond had been in the business for thirty years, he had a distribution network set up, and he had secured financing. But he wasn't ready to go ahead until he had a clear identity.

Redmond decided on the name "The Australian 3 Minute Miracle." He felt that it captured the mystery of Australia, and that the words "3 Minute Miracle" went well with the product's black, gunky appearance as well as playing to customers' desire to have a miracle make them look better.

Redmond wanted to make his product stand out, so he added a little story about the product, along with a photograph of his family, on the package. That not only added to the product's "mysterious" image, it let consumers know that this wasn't a product from a big company.

The important point is that Tom Redmond realized that creating an identity was a critical task. He spent the time and effort necessary to find one that worked. There are four steps in creating an identity:

1. You need to find a clear image that communicates quickly what your product is and why people should buy it.
2. You must discover a relatedness between you and your customers.
3. You need to match the style of your name, logo, and slogans to your customers' self-image.
4. You need to bring all these elements together in a convincing way.

Logos are important for consumer companies, but they are even more important for business-to-business marketers because companies often are not well differentiated. For example, companies providing engineering services don't have visible products. Buyers often blur suppliers' images and the company that wins is often the one with the clearest identity.

Communicating Quickly

In any given week, a typical consumer is exposed to dozens, if not hundreds, of messages. Can you remember the last twenty products or businesses you were exposed to? Can you remember even one? Most consumers deliberately don't listen for more than a second or two. So you need to work hard to communicate quickly and effectively.

Clarity

In seven or eight words, and no more, tell what your business does. Then, in another seven or eight words, state your product's biggest benefit. Finally, list three to five proof statements that back up your product or service claims.

For example, Tierney Brothers is a distributor of portable lettering systems by companies like Kroy, Varitronics, Brother, and Gerber. These machines are used for lettering on products, brochures, booklets, and service manuals. Their biggest users are small companies' engineering departments. These departments use them for labeling drawings, product specifications, manufacturing processes, and quality control instructions.

Tierney Brothers's business statement is "supplies labeling systems for engineering applications." Its feature/benefit statement is "Minnesota's most comprehensive labeling distributor." Its proof statements would be:

1. Carries every major brand of labeling equipment.
2. Guarantees supply shipments within three days.
3. Provides loaner equipment in case of repairs.
4. Has the most experienced sales staff in the state.

The owner of a clothing store for teenagers might have the statements "sells clothes to people under 25" and "has the widest selection of the latest fashions." Its proof statements might be:

1. Carries nine fashion labels.
2. Introduced the top three styles of 1994 to the area.
3. Has 50 percent more stock than the local Gap or The Limited.
4. Has clerks who can help you pick out popular color combinations.

These clear statements are the starting point for creating a message. Some readers may have been surprised to see that I recommend that you document your claims rather than stating your benefits. That goes back to my earlier comments about people being skeptical of unsupported claims.

Visualization

What do people want to accomplish when they buy your product? And what visual image will create that impression in their minds? For example, an engineering department wants the labels on its various drawings to be easy to read. A good visual image for Tierney Brothers would be to have its name, printed by one of its labeling machines, on an engineering drawing. A service that provides temporary secretaries might just have a small photograph of a professional secretary. When I worked with a testing instrument company, our visual image was a diagram of what people would see when they used our product.

Creating a visual

If you have trouble coming up with a visual image, start by listing what people want and situations in which they might really need your product. For example, a manufacturer of Instant Tire Repair knows that people want to eliminate any chance of being stuck on the road. One situation in which this would be important is when a couple is on the way to an important event on a rainy, freezing night. The image needs to take the product away from features and benefits and place it in real situations.

Next, come up with a visual image that conveys either the problem or the solution. Solutions work better. For example, a flat tire on a freeway shows a problem. A can of tire repair and a two-minute clock shows a solution. People prefer a solution image.

Create four or five visual images and ask your family, friends, business associates, and customers which one they prefer and why. For example, people liked the two-minute clock because it was a specific, easy-to-understand claim.

Logic versus emotion

People may give logical reasons for buying a product, but in fact they often, if not always, buy based on emotion. That's why emotion is so important. People can understand that a product will fix a flat tire. But the message is much more important when you translate that feature into a two-minute repair on a dark and stormy night.

Power Phrases

You need to compile a list of words that convey strong positive action. Some high-impact words are "you," "money," "easy," "safety," "solves," "saves," "discovery," "fears," "guaranteed," "proven," "now," "free," "announcing," "undisputed," "proven," "create," "love," "results," "yes," "fast," and "sale."

You also need riveting power phrases that fit your product or service. Some tips on coming up with phrases are:

1. Be clear and specific. "Three minutes" is better than "saves time."

2. Personalize your message. "I'll help you" or "I'll talk to you" is much better than "complete technical service department."

3. Use a series of three words or phrases—snap, crackle, pop; proven, fast, and easy to use. For some reason a series of three words puts emphasis on a point.

4. Write everything from the customer's point of view. "New patented nozzle snaps onto the air valve to cut tire repair time" is written from the

company's point of view. "Easy to use, even when you're cold, wet, and tired" is from a customer's perspective.

5. Address customers' anxieties: "Don't be another face in the crowd" or "don't run out of supplies when your big order is due to ship."

6. Use statements that meet customers' goals. "On time, on spec, and on budget." "You'll be able to ride farther and faster than ever before."

7. Include alliteration. Wild, woolly, and wonderful are three words for an amusement park ride. Develop, diagnose, and direct are three words to describe the activities of a management consultant.

8. Use parallel construction, which means that you use the same sentence structure for each power phrase. "Saves time, promotes accuracy, delivers promptly" is an example of two-word phrases starting with a verb.

9. Don't be judgmental and rule out phrases. Often you'll think of a point later on what will strengthen a power phrase.

ACTION STEPS

1. List one or two clear statements that describe your business and its biggest feature.

2. Add to your list visualizations and power phrases you came up with to enhance those statements.

3. Figures 13.1 and 13.2 show preliminary identity statements for a home remodeling contractor and an Epson printer. You need to put together a similar chart for your product or service.

4. Compare your identity statement to the chart you prepared in Chapter 8. Make sure the image reinforces your competitive advantages.

Figure 13.1
Identity Statements

HOME REMODELING CONTRACTOR

Identifying statement:	Raises roofs to double home living space.
Benefit statement:	A lot more living space without spending a lot of money.
Supporting statements:	Doubled the living space for over 100 families. 50 percent cheaper than the cost of adding a room. "I never thought we could add so much room for so little money." — J.T., Norristown, PA
Power phrases:	Fastest, cleanest, and cheapest way to add a room. The perfect solution when kids come faster than raises. Buy yourself some privacy with an upstairs bedroom.

FIGURE 13.2
Identity Statements

EPSON LASER PRINTER

Identifying statement:	Supplies personal laser printers for less than $1,000.
Benefit statement:	Has more features than any other printer in its price range.
Supporting statements:	Has won scores of industry awards, including *PC World's* "Best Buy" and *Info World's* "Recommended Product."
	Sharpest output of text and graphics.
	Thirteen scalable fonts.
	Prints six pages per minute versus fastest competitor's four pages per minute.
	Has a two-year warranty versus industry standard of one year.
	Includes a 150-sheet paper tray that handles multiple paper sizes, as well as envelopes.
Power phrases:	For the blackest blacks.
	You can't get this much for this little anywhere else.
	Join the experts, and see why Epson is best.
	Fastest printer available for the money.
	Hook up to the Epson Hotline.

RELATEDNESS

Relatedness means creating a bond between you and your customers. A related attitude reflects your desire to work with and help customers. This is a new trend in marketing, and it replaces an attitude that separates the customer and the company into two separate entities. That attitude, which is still common, states a product's features and benefits from the company's point of view.

Advertising

"Behind this smart look is an intelligent idea" is a new slogan from American Express advertising its gold card. Is this slogan from a customer point of view? No, it's American Express patting itself on the back.

Relatedness is a technique, a way to operate. But it is also a style, one in which you act as if you were talking with the customer. Federal Express uses a slogan "I want it on time and cheap." That's relatedness, both in style and in content—the ad is from the customer's point of view.

AT&T has an excellent slogan: "We get to your problems before they get to you." Again, both style and content are related. Compare those slogans with non-related ones such as "If it were just another minivan, it wouldn't be a Mercury" or "Two reasons to choose the Quiet Company. One, it keeps your business in the family, and two, the superior financial strength of Northwestern Mutual Life." Related ads are more interesting and more memorable.

Product Packaging

I surveyed some products at Target to see how manufacturers were using relatedness. I came across two products, a baby walker from Century Products and a nursery monitor from Fisher Price. Here are Century's sales points: play gym keeps baby busy and amused, bounces baby for exercise and fun, adjusts for height, and is made of easy-to-clean vinyl—definitely company-oriented benefits that aren't that interesting. The product didn't even have a picture of a baby on it. Fisher Price does a much better job. One line of copy is "Let's you see and hear your baby's sounds." On the package Fisher Price uses three pictures: one of a sleeping baby, one of a busy baby, and one of a happy baby. These are great images. Fisher Price sells its monitor so that people can enjoy their babies.

Industrial Products

Related messages are slowly creeping into consumer marketing, but they are just as important for industrial companies, although typically business-to-business marketers don't use quite as much personalization. Look at the three slogans below and see which one sounds best for a manufacturer of semiautomatic electronic insertion equipment:

1. Quick setup time for short-run boards.

2. Video overlay keys production sequence and placement for operator.

3. Movable storage tray brings parts to placement location.

Statement 1 is written from the customer's point of view, Statement 2 is only partially from the customer's perspective, and Statement 3 is totally from a company point of view. Statement 1 is more memorable. Statements 2 and 3 are rewritten in a related style below:

2. Video overlay minimizes operator mistakes by keying production sequence and placement.

3. Movable tray improves placement accuracy and cuts production time by bringing parts to placement location.

ACTION STEPS

1. Earlier in the chapter you put together a series of identity statements similar to Figures 13.1 and 13.2. Try to rewrite those statements so that they are related to your customers.

2. Go through all the phrases and identifying statements you use in your literature or advertising and decide whether they are customer- or company-oriented. Rewrite them to be as customer-oriented as possible.

MATCHING THE STYLE TO THE MESSAGE

Marshall McLuhan came out with his classic book, *The Medium is the Message,* in the mid 1960s. McLuhan suggested that the way you present information is the way people respond to it. I've found that this principle is also true in marketing.

Your motif, business cards, brochures, advertising style, and logo all go together to create an image. The style you use—professional, fun-loving, rugged, quality, high-performance—often communicates a message more effectively than the message itself.

The Look

All American Products puts out a bicycle seat for kids called the Kiddie Ryder. The name looks as if it was written with crayons. The product has all kinds of features that make it clear that this is for kids—for example, the spots where kids put their feet are called happy feet foot buckets. The dominant visual on the package is a kid with a big smile. There are cartoon stickers all over the product, and the product looks like fun. That's matching the style of a product to the message. You notice that the product is for kids before you even notice what the product is. That's effective marketing.

Connecting with Customers

A dentist with a children's practice should have business cards and signs that show that his or her customers are kids. People will notice the style long before they notice the words "dentistry for children" or "pediatric dentistry."

Suppliers to businesses need to spend time developing a logo or business card style that connects with customers. This is an area where business-to-business suppliers actually have an advantage because they are more focused than consumer companies. But most industrial suppliers don't capitalize on this advantage.

Earlier I mentioned Tierney Brothers, a distributor of labeling equipment. Having a logo that shows labeling typeset on an engineering drawing is connecting with customers. Tierney Brothers' actual business card just says Tierney Brothers. I once marketed a device that could measure the thickness of layers in a gallium arsenide computer chip quantum well. Gallium arsenide is a replacement for silicon in high-speed applications, and quantum wells have fifteen to twenty active layers about 200 angstroms thick. (This is much thinner than a human hair.) The logo showed a drawing of a quantum well. It meant nothing to most people, but it told our customers exactly what the product did.

Overworking Professionalism

Many small businesspeople, especially in industrial companies, believe that their business cards, logo, and stationery should look "professional." They interpret this to mean that a card should look like a lawyer's card, with the result that most cards are dull and conforming. When people say that your cards should look professional, they really mean that you shouldn't have a card that looks cheap. Your logo and business cards should make it look like you're going to stay in business. But you can still have a visual on your card, use color, and use glossy stock. Your card will look just fine, and it will communicate a message.

ACTION STEPS

1. Look at your target customer group and decide what style you want your identity to convey. Performance-oriented, usage-oriented, fun, rugged, economical, sleek, and scholarly are all possibilities.

2. Put together five to ten options for your logo design. Come up with the initial design yourself, but have the final logo put together by a freelance artist, a graphic designer, or an advertising agency.

EXECUTING YOUR IDENTITY

Now you know what you are trying to convey, what style you want, and how you can relate your business to customers. You just need to put everything together so that this is obvious to customers.

Name

Ideally you want a name that immediately conveys who you are and why you're different. I like names such as Everything but the Kitchen Sink, Environmental Packaging, Musicland, Rubbermaid, E-Z Stop, and Discovery Toys.

Be distinctive

I don't like names such as Theilan Marketing, Peterson Drug Store, Arrow Electronics, or Johnson Brothers Manufacturing. These names are too bland. You can't always get a perfect name, but if you can't you are better off going with a distinctive name that people might remember, like Nerf, Nintendo, Chevrolet, or Apple Computer.

Sometimes you can combine a name with a visual to make the name distinctive. For example, LensCrafters came out with a new product called FeatherWates. The name doesn't mean much by itself, but its meaning is crystal clear when you see it next to a pair of glasses.

Three key points

When you choose a name, consider: (1) what feature or characteristic you want to communicate, (2) what you want the name to accomplish, and (3) who you want to appeal to.

The company name I use when dealing with inventors is Product to Market Seminars. I chose this name with the help of these three points. First, I wanted people to know that I help product creators put their ideas on the market. Second, I wanted people involved with a new product to call me when they get their idea. Since people like to gather information before they start spending money, adding "seminars" to the company name gets people to call me exactly when I want to talk to them. Third, I wanted to appeal to both small companies and inventors. I wanted the name to be straightforward and practical in order to appeal to both groups.

Watts Regulators is a company that sells incoming electric controls for industry. Its products ensure that electric spikes don't throw off production in chemical, medical, and electronic production facilities. The name makes this very clear to its target customer. "Watts" lets customers know that the products are for larger companies with heavy electric usage, and "Regulators" tells customers the product's functions.

Logos

A visual image can support your name and make it easier to remember. The guidelines for an effective logo are: make it distinctive, keep it simple, and have it match the tone of your business.

Make it distinctive

LensCrafters makes glasses and contact lenses. Its big feature is that it can produce a pair of glasses in one hour. Its logo has its name with a clock that is shaded between twelve and one o'clock. The logo is distinctive, and it makes the company's main benefit clear.

Keep it simple

Nike's logo is a swirling-looking check. Nike displays this logo prominently on all of its shoes and supports it with advertising. The logo is athletic-looking. It doesn't have a meaning, but it is simple and easily recognized. You can tell a pair of Nike shoes with just a quick glance.

Match the tone

AT&T's logo is a globe with high-tech lines running through it. The lines give this logo an image of sophistication, and the globe reminds people that AT&T is the worldwide technological leader in telecommunications.

Be sure to ask people what they think of your logo before you make its design final. You may have spent so much time thinking about it that you won't know what a casual observer will think of it after a quick glance.

Slogans

Another method of identifying who you are is to have a slogan that goes with your name and logo. This slogan should either create an emotional response, identify your target customer, or state your best benefit.

Create an emotional response

Toyota has a great slogan: "I love what you do for me, Toyota." This statement works on both relatedness and emotion, and it communicates directly to customers. Other effective slogans are Federal Express's "Our most important package is yours," American Express's "Don't leave home without it," and Mass Mutual's "We help you keep your promise."

Identify your target customer

This is a standard tactic for industrial suppliers. Have a Portion Inc.'s slogan is "customer food packaging." Other examples are Alliant Staffing's "employee leasing services," Northwest Payroll's "payroll services for small businesses," and J.W.S.'s "structural consultants, tubular & shapes."

List your competitive edge

Examples are "double your living space," "287 colors of paint," "world's largest toy store," "everything you need for a metallurgical laboratory," "specializing in short production runs," and "America's largest bookstore."

Routine Business Operations

Your identity is effective only if it applies to the way the company is run. One company I dealt with talked exclusively about its quality, but the first product I received from it came in a box with newspapers used as the packing material. The newspapers didn't hurt the product, but they hurt the company's identity.

Three words should completely describe your marketing strategy: consistency, familiarity, and confidence. Consumers gain confidence when they become familiar with a company because of its consistency. Your identity, throughout your entire operation, is crucial if you want to generate confidence.

ACTION STEPS

1. List at least five or six possible names, slogans, and logos for your company. Do this even if you are already in business. You may want to introduce a new marketing strategy when you finish this book, and if you do, a name change is a dramatic way to alert customers to your marketing efforts.

2. Get a group of customers or prospective customers together and ask them the following questions about combinations of your names, logos, and slogans:

   • What price range does this business serve?
   • Who are the company's target customers?
   • What type of products does the company sell?
   • What is the firm's competitive advantage?

   Then ask them which name, logo, and slogan they like best.

3. Repeat Step 2 every year. You must remember that reality in the marketplace is what customers think, not what you believe. Hopefully people understand what your business is and why they should buy from you. If they don't you will have to work harder to get your point across.

Chapter 14
Inspiring Confidence

Ross Perot did much better than expected in the 1992 election. There were many reasons for this, but one was that he had the right style: natural and likable—a style that inspired confidence. To a lesser degree Bill Clinton was also able to inspire confidence, whereas George Bush was never able to adjust to a world of style over substance, and his likability quotient never matched Perot's or Clinton's.

The last election points out a hidden item on the marketing agenda: Most people won't listen to anything you say until they trust you. This rule applies for any product. No matter how good the product is, you won't be able to succeed until you get the customer to trust you.

Don't look at this chapter as a way to persuade customers to do something that is not in their interests. Instead, look at it as a way to invite customers to learn about your firm. This chapter covers intuition, a customer's first line of defense; why emotion is more important than fact; visuals versus the written word; a style that inspires confidence; and using momentum to motivate customers.

INTUITION—A CUSTOMER'S FIRST LINE OF DEFENSE

People have a natural resistance to someone they don't know, and you have to break through this if you want to motivate them. We all have a world of experiences and our own personal biases, and we draw on them when someone starts talking to us or we see an ad or brochure. People don't consciously think about these factors, but they do subconsciously evaluate every new contact. They may feel comfortable, neutral, or suspicious. People usually call this first defense against making a bad choice intuition. If someone's intuition tells him or her that something is not right, even if he or she has no idea why it's wrong, that person won't listen to you.

Style versus Substance

Information flow in our society has become polarized. On the one hand, people respond to visuals, sound bites, and an intuitive feel for whether or not they should do business with you. On the other hand, we are in an information age, and more and better information is available. A marketer has to be able to combine these two elements effectively.

The two key words are *image* and *support*. You need an image to move people, and you need support to show them that you know what you're doing. I hesitate to use the word "support" because in a way that too is image. Very, very few people actually check out all your background data. They just want to know that you have it.

EMOTION VERSUS FACT

Several years ago a study showed that more people read automotive ads after buying a car than read them before buying. What this study really found out was that people buy on the basis of emotion, not fact. People look for facts after they buy to show what a good choice they made.

My wife and I are a study in contrasts. I like salespeople who close, and close early. My wife considers these salespeople pushy and doesn't like them. I purchased an insurance policy from a salesperson my wife didn't like. He was too pushy for her, and she didn't like or trust him. After he left, we had a discussion. She listed all the reasons I shouldn't have said yes, and I listed all the positive reasons for making the purchase. Our conversation went nowhere. Neither of us was interested in the facts; we were only trying to make a case to support our emotional decisions. That's the way most people buy, and so you need to deal with trust.

Trust

Trust is important in selling to consumers, but it is even more important in selling to businesses. If a consumer makes a wrong choice, it's something he or she will have to live with, but it's not something other people will complain about. But if a person at a company buys something and it's a bad choice, he or she could hear about it for days, months, or even years. I worked at one company where a production manager bought an inventory system that didn't work too well. After about twelve months of trying to fix it, the manager was fired. People requisitioning products for companies have a lot at stake, and they have to trust you.

Demonstrating that what you say is true

People don't believe what you say at first; instead, they check you out to see if it is true. If people can't check your statements out, as a rule, they won't believe you. So you need to make an effort to prove that what you say is true. For industrial suppliers, demonstrations, free loaners, in-plant trial periods, and free installation and setup are a few ways of proving your claims.

Service companies have a much more difficult time demonstrating that their claims are true. They usually use testimonials, offer samples of past work, or take on a small job to prove their competence.

GM's Saturn

When General Motors introduced its new line of Saturn cars, it used a two-pronged strategy. One was to promote the way Saturns are sold, through a network of dealers that sell cars in a new way, and the second was to promote the Saturn as a little car with the style, features, and quality that customers want.

GM is building customer trust by effectively demonstrating both points. It set up new dealers that carry only Saturns. These dealerships are away from the auto malls, in stand-alone locations. GM has also highly publicized the way its dealers list only one nonnegotiable price. Finally, GM has run ads featuring real-life buyers who verify GM's one-price strategy.

GM's other key claim is that Saturn is a great little car with the style, quality, and features that people want. People can see the car's style. To show its quality, the dealer showroom I was in had a car cut in two so that people could see how well built the Saturn is. Most people can't tell if a car has quality by looking at a cutaway, but that is not really important. The cutaway creates the image that GM is proud of its car and is willing to put it up for scrutiny.

ACTION STEPS

1. List your key claims first, then list the support you offer for those claims. Figure 14.1 shows a customer confidence chart for The Summit Company, Inc., a small accounting firm.

2. List all the parts of your company that customers come in contact with. For each, list the image that part of the company creates.

3. Look through your past advertising and brochures for claims and decide how well you document them.

4. List the image you want for your business, then decide what parts of your business support that image.

5. Go through the customer confidence chart (see Figure 14.1) and indicate where you need improvements.

Figure 14.1
Customer Confidence Chart

THE SUMMIT COMPANY, INC.

Key Claims	Support Provided
Affordable monthly accounting	Fee chart comparing its fees to competitors'
High-quality service	Four testimonial letters
	Three references that can be contacted
Personal, caring service	None
No hidden costs	Signed contracts with customers that detail payment data
Financing and cash flow assistance	None
Job cost and profitability analysis	Two samples of past work

Customer Contacts	Impression Made
Office visits	Office somewhat in disarray, looks disorganized
Field visits by accountants	Organized and professional

Improvement Needed	Action Steps
Personal, caring service	Assign account representative
	Develop personal relationships
Financing and cash flow assistance	Obtain testimonials and samples from other clients
Office visits	Organize office, separate client files better, introduce new tracking system

Visuals Versus the Written and Spoken Word

Most people don't like to write anymore. They prefer to call someone on the phone or speak to him or her in person. This is why many marketers concentrate on visuals, no matter what advertising medium they are using. In my paper today, in most ads over 70 percent of the layout was occupied by a visual image, with only 10 to 20 percent containing copy. A visual creates an immediate reaction; if that reaction is positive, people may read the copy.

The Spoken Word

When people listen to the spoken word, all of their "antennas" are up. They listen to how someone sounds, how fast he or she talks, and how authoritarian or friendly the voice sounds. People's antennas determine whether they listen to you or not.

John Madden is a popular celebrity. He is popular not because he was a great coach, and not because he is a better football analyst than anyone else, but because his speaking style immediately makes people feel good about him. He is an animated, lively speaker. He likes to joke around and have fun. People believe Madden because of all the audio cues he sends out. His credibility comes from his style more than from what he says.

The Written Word

People don't have an immediate response to the written word. They don't know if they will enjoy reading a book or an article when they first see it. They don't have any visual or auditory clues. People's natural response to a lack of stimulation is not to read.

Publishers of books and magazines create stimulation with visuals—photographs, creative graphics, and big and bold headlines. People have to be pulled into the written word, and they have to get their clues about what an article or an ad is like from visual images.

What does this mean for marketers? First, you have to set the stage for who you are and what you are like with visuals. Whether it is a picture, or a headline, or a graphic, the visual is all-important. Second, the style and quality of the written word has to be friendly, natural, and conversational.

Action Steps

1. Collect some of your past ads and brochures, some ads you think are effective, and some ads you don't like.

2. Rate the visual of each ad—both the picture and the headline—on both how clear the message is, and how much impact it has. Score each ad on a scale of one to five.

3. Rate the ads on how they build believability. Take into account both the style of their communication (personal, animated, fun, friendly) and their efforts to support their claims.

4. The high-scoring ads will be the ones that are most effective.

STYLE

I've already mentioned tactics that help marketers relate to customers. But these tactics don't stand alone; they call for a change in your style of relating to people. You have to stop being a figure of authority and start being an adviser and a friend.

Authoritarian Style

A stockbroker working in a traditional manner calls people up, tells them about a great new stock, and recommends that they buy it. The broker might make notes about what types of stock people want or what their goals are, but the stockbroker is acting as the authority.

Relationship Style

Stockbrokers operating in the new marketing style will be advisors, helping and guiding people in making investment choices. These stockbrokers might have quarterly reviews with clients. They could see if stocks are performing adequately, explain changes in stocks' performance, and express concern about poor-performing stocks. Once clients are sure of what their options are, the stockbroker could make a recommendation. The key to this process is to have the customer feel that he or she is in charge of the buying process.

Writing Style

I picked up a brochure from McDonald's about its efforts to protect the environment. McDonald's is changing over to a relationship-communication style, as you can see from this paragraph about its Earth Effort.

> We're your neighbors. That's the real reason behind McDonald's Earth Effort. The people who live in your McDonald's restaurant also live in your community. And they're as dedicated as you are to making sure that the neighborhood—as well as the planet—we share is as clean and healthy as possible. For all of us.

McDonald's had this set in type that actually looked like someone's hand printing. McDonald's message is, "Hey, we are people just like you." This is a big turnaround in communication style for McDonald's, which for years emphasized how many burgers it sold. This switch can be seen in all McDonald's materials: it is going away from glossy, slick ads and promotional material toward more natural, almost home-made graphics.

ACTION STEPS

1. Take a look at the ads, fliers, brochures, and circulars that you use. Circle parts of them that should be changed either because of their lack of visual appeal or because of their authoritarian style.

2. Take one piece of this printed material, change it, and use the new version in a mailing or as a handout. You should notice an immediate improvement in the ad's performance.

3. Monitor your voice and your key employees' voices. Decide if they sound relaxed and natural. If not, focus on being more friendly on the phone.

MOMENTUM—BEING A WINNER

Americans may love an underdog in sports, but they don't go for underdogs when buying products. They want to go with winners. Nothing boosts customer confidence like buying from a company everyone else is buying from.

The key to momentum is to keep looking like a winner. Three ways you can do that are to keep your lead product strong, make sure your product is available, and show that you are going to stay in business.

Keep Your Lead Product Strong

The dental company I worked for had a 20 percent market share in high-speed drills, and these accounted for 40 percent of our sales. One year the company decided it could increase profits by concentrating on secondary product lines. Within a year, the sales of all our products were dropping. A competitor had introduced a new feature on its drills that we couldn't match. Customers lost faith in our entire line because we couldn't keep our lead product strong.

Ford used a lead product strategy to create market momentum in the 1980s. In the early 1980s Ford was in real trouble, with sales slumping, lawsuits pending regarding safety problems with the Pinto, and heavy shareholder pressure resulting from several years of financial losses.

Then Ford introduced the Escort, promoting it as a world-class car. This lead product strategy began to convince people that Ford knew what it was doing, and sales started to improve. Ford's efforts really paid off when it switched its lead product to the Taurus and Sable car lines. The products were praised in the media, and customers came to believe that Ford *really* knew what it was doing.

A lead product doesn't have to be the product with the highest demand; it just needs to be interesting or important. A metallurgical supplier had the best cross-sectioning equipment (for measuring coating quality) available. The company promoted that product, which performed a key test, even though it represented only about 10 percent of the company's sales. That key product pulled along the company's entire product line.

Make Sure Your Product Is Available

Distribution, or putting your product where people can buy it, is a key tactic in gaining momentum. If you have more sales outlets, you are likely to have more sales and more market momentum.

Less than fifteen years ago, U-Haul was the largest company renting moving equipment to people moving themselves. One of U-Haul's strengths was its vast distribution network. It seemed as if every town had two or three gas stations that rented U-Haul equipment. As traditional gas stations were replaced by convenience stores, U-Haul lost a big percentage of its distribution outlets. Then Ryder entered the market with stand-alone locations and took a large percentage of U-Haul's business.

Evaluating distribution strategy against momentum

Recently I consulted with a company regarding distribution strategy. The company's product was in about 250 individual or small chain retail outlets, the company was adding 30 to 40 outlets every six months, and the product was gaining momentum with consumers and retailers. Then the company got a call from a large discount chain. The chain wanted to buy a huge quantity of the product, but the price it was willing to pay was 30 percent lower than what the company's current customers were paying.

The company wanted to know whether or not it should accept the order. The order would be profitable, but the company was worried about what its current customers would do if the chain sold the product at a much lower price.

I recommended against taking the chain's order. The order would clearly help out in the short term, but many current customers were upscale stores. They would drop the product if it was available at discount stores at a lower price. What would happen if the chain dropped the product after six to nine months? The company would lose part of its sales base, and the discount image would haunt the product for a long time. That would be a tough position to recover from.

Most companies look only at sales statistics. You should also keep an eye on your number of sales outlets, whether they are distributors, manufacturers' representatives, your own sales force, or retail outlets. You need to take corrective action any time your number of sales outlets stops growing or starts to drop.

Show You Are Going to Stay in Business

Customers are risk-averse when making a purchase, especially a big one. They want to be sure you will still be around if they need to make a return, have service work done, or connect your equipment to someone else's.

Many small manufacturing companies start out by supplying the owner's past employer or firms the owner has worked with previously. Companies often fail if they don't have an initial base of business based on past relationships. Those companies' biggest problem is that they can't show a sales base that will convince people that they will still be in business in several years. A company just can't build momentum if people are worried about its future.

I used to require a 50 percent deposit from small companies that didn't have an extensive background. Those companies didn't mind; they were, in fact, receiving similar requests from other companies. But when I asked a large car manufacturer for a 50 percent deposit, I almost lost the order. The manufacturer thought the deposit requirement meant we were in financial distress. I don't like the word "professional," but make sure everything you do is done in a quality way and that your efforts don't look cheap or amateurish.

ACTION STEPS

1. Ask customers what product or service is your specialty, or lead product. You have a problem if they can't tell you what it is. A lead product strategy makes it much easier for people to remember your firm.
2. If you don't have a clearly identified lead product, choose one that is clearly differentiated from its competition or the one that will be the most important or most interesting to customers.

3. Start emphasizing your lead product in everything you do, including your ads, brochure, store layout, and business logo.

4. Every month, look for ways you can add to your distribution channels. Also, be especially alert to any changes in the number of distribution outlets you already have.

Chapter 15

Copy and Layout — Motivating Through Print, Radio, and TV

You did most of the hard work of preparing an ad in Sections 1 and 2 of this book. You know who your target customers are and why they want your product. You know what customer characteristics you want to capitalize on, and you know what features appeal to those characteristics. You know why you are better than anyone else, and you know what images will sell your products. This is the groundwork that has to be done if you are to have an effective ad program.

You may want to hire an artist, copywriter, or advertising agency to help you put materials together. Before you do that, do the following preliminary work:

1. Decide what you want the piece to say.
2. Prepare a rough layout of the piece using the visuals and power statements you've put together.
3. Write an initial version of the copy you want.

If you do this, you will save money, and you will be sure the material will do what you want it to do. I do recommend that you hire professional help until you have been involved in producing ten to twenty ads or sales promotion pieces.

This chapter covers the general principles of motivation, how to write effective copy, creating an attractive print layout, and preparing successful radio and TV spots.

GENERAL PRINCIPLES FOR MOTIVATING CUSTOMERS

If you are going to motivate people, you have to know how to put information in a form that will attract readers, listeners, or viewers. The four key elements of motivating customers are:

1. Get customers' attention.
2. Have something interesting to see or read.
3. Create desire in the reader or viewer.
4. Generate action.

These elements are easy to understand. You have a second or two to catch people's attention. Once you have someone looking at your material, you have another couple of seconds to involve that person. You create desire by helping people realize that they want or need your product. Some of the actions you can generate are sending for more information or visiting your store. This section discusses several tactics you can use to provide these four elements. "You" advertising is almost always more effective than "me" advertising; visuals need to tell most, if not all, of your message; copy should tell people something they don't already know; and messages sell when they make people smile.

"You" Advertising Is More Effective than "Me" Advertising

Consider these two headlines: "Only one machine equals a balanced workout. Best of all, it's a NordicTrack." "Transform your idea into a powerful business plan." The first headline is from an ad for a total body fitness system, and the second is from an ad for business plan information that includes both a workbook and a computer disc.

Which headline invites you into the ad? "You" ads almost always work better. Even for business-to-business ads, "You can cut your down time by 85 percent" is stronger than "Cuts down time 85 percent." And it is *much* better than "Optoelectric scanning minimizes jamming." You buy products because of what they will do for you. Your customers do the same. They buy for their reasons, not anyone else's. That's why "you" language works.

Visuals Have to Tell Part of the Story

Two crucial parts of any communication are the visual image and the headline. My all-time favorite visual is the one in the Coppertone ads where a small dog tugs on the pants of a little blonde girl, exposing her tan line. The headline was: "tan, don't burn." That's all an ad needs: a strong visual and a clarifying headline. Coppertone is still using that same ad even though it has been running for at least twenty-five years, because it works.

A visual doesn't have to tell the whole story by itself. It only has to tell half the story. But the visual plus the headline needs to communicate the entire message. An ad in a parenting magazine showed a little girl of about seven dressed in outdoor clothes. The headline read, "Ready for camp?" Those two images made it clear what the ad was all about.

I like to prepare at least four or five possible headline/visual combinations for any ad or brochure I'm working on. Then I put them on the wall and ask people which one(s) they like, and why.

Tell People Something They Don't Know

Piquing curiosity is a great technique for gaining interest. Glenlivet, a Scotch whiskey, has this headline: "These hair-trigger pistols once stopped a band of cutthroats." The headline promises that something intriguing might be in the ad's copy. This is an especially effective tactic when it's difficult to differentiate your product from competitive products.

This tactic works well for products sold to businesses. A Panasonic ad had this headline: "If it has Adobe scalable fonts, color, and quiet technology, it can only be from Panasonic." This is pretty dull stuff. The ad would be more effective if it was turned around and had this headline: "You can have your sales letters read by 80 percent more people." How? The text could continue: "By getting a printer that lets you add color and different-size lettering (known as scalable fonts)."

Spring Arbor is a consulting company that helps owners lay out Christian bookstores. Its headline states: "You can look this good, for less than you think." I like this headline because it uses "you" language and it promises to tell people something they might not know.

Writing Down Your Goals

Everyone who does marketing gets ideas at night, while eating, or during some other activity. And often marketers take these ideas and turn them into programs. However, using a clever idea without making sure it communicates the right message can be a mistake. What you need to do first is decide what you want to tell people. Then you can worry about how to tell it.

Six questions to ask yourself

1. Who is my target customer?

2. What is my product?

3. What is my objective?

4. Why should people want to buy?

5. What makes the product special?

6. How can I prove it's special?

Don't be brief in your answers. List everything you can think of that's relevant. You want your final copy to be brief, but now is not the time to cut back. You are looking for as many ideas as possible.

Make People Smile

Cute, clever, witty ads are one way to make people smile. I talked about this tactic in the last chapter. It works effectively if it doesn't detract from the product. Another way to make people smile is showmanship. This is the tactic you should use if your product category is overadvertised, has too many products, or has poor differentiation between products.

Tide has a TV commercial that I like. It starts out with a teenage boy listening to rock music and dancing in his room as he gets dressed. He wears a white tee shirt and long white boxer shorts. He then pulls on jeans with holes in them so that his white underclothes are hanging out all over. The commercial ends by saying that no matter what the kids wear, their whites can still be white. This commercial has drama and showmanship, and it gets your attention.

Industrial companies typically use demonstrations to generate showmanship. A company might show one machine with eight packaging stations around it, all backed up, trying to keep up with a production line. The headline, "I didn't know it was this fast!" adds to the showmanship. Business-to-business marketers can benefit from showmanship just because very few companies use it.

Print ads can also use showmanship. UPS ran an ad of a truck sitting on top of enormous wheels, like you'd see at a monster truck show, to announce its 3 Day Select Program.

Be Sure the Ad Makes Sense

When gel toothpaste first came out, people couldn't understand why they should use it. The manufacturer didn't have a good reason why the gel was better than the traditional type of toothpaste. The product didn't sell. Then the manufacturer started to advertise that the gel could combine toothpaste whitener with breath freshener. Now the product made sense.

I've read hundreds of ads and brochures for industrial products that don't quite make sense. The biggest problem for industrial marketers is that they say far too much. That confuses people. Start by stating your ad's goal, then look at each and every sentence and ask if it helps promote that goal. If it doesn't, take the line out. Industrial marketers like to list every possible product benefit. That only confuses people, and will detract from a piece's effectiveness.

ACTION STEPS

1. Make a chart that lists these six guidelines. Pull it out every time you are ready to prepare an ad.
   - "You" advertising is more effective than "me" advertising.
   - Visuals and headlines have to tell the story.
   - Tell people something they don't know.
   - Write down your goals.
   - Make people smile.
   - Does the piece make sense?

2. Start a "hot button" file. Whenever an idea occurs to you, or whenever someone makes a statement that might work in an ad or brochure, write it down and put it in a file. This way you'll have a running start when you decide to do an ad, brochure, or circular.

3. Start a file on competitors' ads. You want to be sure that your ads, brochures, and other written materials are clearly different from your competitors'.

WRITING EFFECTIVE COPY

Before you start to write copy, headlines, or brochures, answer the product questions below. Figure 15.1 shows how the answers would look for The Fireplace Center, a business that specializes in installing high-end fireplaces in expensive homes. Refer to the charts you prepared in Chapters 8 and 13 for your answers to these questions for your business:

1. Who is your target customer?
2. What product or products are you selling?
3. What unmet need or desire of your customer are you targeting?

4. What are the special customer characteristics that apply to that need or desire?

5. What features or services have you added to appeal to those customer characteristics?

6. Why will the customers want to buy from you?

7. What power phrases have you developed? (See chapter 13.)

8. What types of visuals do you feel will motivate customers?

9. What supporting or proof statements do you have to back up your product claims?

You won't want to put all of this information into your copy, but it does clarify your message. A consistent message is vital to effective communication. Each message about you has to relate to, and build upon, things you've said before. Using the same chart, everything will keep your message consistent.

Figure 15.1
Basic Marketing Thrust

THE FIREPLACE CENTER

1. Target customer: Homeowners living in the affluent west side suburbs of Chicago.
2. Products being sold: High-end fireplace systems designed to be a room's visual focus.
3. Unmet need being filled: Need to turn an ordinary room into an extravagant entertainment area.
4. Special customer characteristic: Wants accessories, such as stone, mantels, and so on, to create an impressive fireplace wall. Also wants skilled craftsmen as installers to ensure a "perfect" look.
5. Features to meet customers' characteristics: Large showroom to display full fireplace walls, guaranteed installation of all fireplaces and accessories by skilled craftsmen, on-staff interior designer to help design fireplace walls in keeping with a room's dimensions, and a large inventory of accessories.
6. Why will the customer buy from you? To create a showcase entertainment room.
7. Power phrases: "Entertain in style." "Create a room you can be really proud of." "After a hard day, sometimes you need a place to go hide."
8. Visuals: Impressive-looking room for either a party or a man and woman alone, relaxing on a couch, watching a fire.
9. Supporting claims: Pictures of actual installations, testimonials from satisfied customers.

Rules for Writing Effective Copy

1. Use short sentences. They are easier to read.

2. Use clear statements. Avoid any clarifying or explanatory sentences. They dilute the original messages.

3. Keep your messages simple. People are exposed to hundreds of messages every day. They can only remember the simple ones.

4. Be specific. You shouldn't say, "low-calorie dessert." Say instead "less than 150 calories."

5. Ask questions. That invites a reader into the piece. Apple Computer asks the question, "Why should every kid have an Apple after school?"

6. Write with flair. A little drama, a little excitement, are tactics that will keep people reading.

7. Use only the present tense. It reads faster, and its intent is clearer.

8. Don't brag. Use testimonials and reinforce your points, but do it without bragging. Words like "biggest," "wonderful," and "most" have lost their punch and can hurt your credibility.

9. Focus on just one objective. Otherwise your message will become garbled.

ACTION STEP

1. Look at Question 6 on your basic marketing thrust chart (see Figure 15.1), "Why will the customers want to buy from you?" Is your answer, by itself, strong enough to convince people to take the action you want? You need to be very critical here. If your reason isn't strong enough, you will be wasting your money on the ad. If your reason is too weak, you need to either rework it or add a promotion or event like the ones discussed in the next chapter.

PRINT LAYOUT

Section 3 explained how to find customers, and Section 5 shows how to communicate with those customers. Most of your communication will be through print—ads, circulars, postcards, brochures, and newsletters. Print layouts are extremely important to your program, and so this is something you must do well. Effective layouts need a consistent look and style, they have to invite readers into the piece, and they need an easy-to-walk-through format.

Create a Consistent Look

If you are a small- to medium-size company, you will probably have a limited amount of contact with customers. To maximize your impact, you need to do everything you can to make your materials look consistent. You might do this with a border, the placement of your logo, a color, a style of type, or your ad layout. The look of your ad or brochure should meet three criteria: it should match the style of your target customers, it should match the medium you are working with, and it should match the nature of your product.

Match the style of your target customers

A manufacturer of ski equipment, whose target customers are young adults, needs a look that says "have some fun, let yourself go, be adventurous." Instead of using formal type, an artist might handwrite the headline, using bright, vibrant colors. In contrast, a prestigious golf resort aimed at business executives might use sedate colors and stylized, prestigious-looking type.

I once worked on a brochure for a product that was aimed at dental schools. The brochure needed a graphic that related the product to schools. A designer had done a rough drawing of the product with an arrow between each product feature and its description. The drawing's original purpose was to show engineers what features to include. But the drawing looked like it came off a professor's blackboard, and we used it with great success.

Another time we were selling a product to help engineers test electronic components. We used the product's actual engineering drawing on the cover, and the engineers loved it.

Match the ad to the medium you're in

Our ski manufacturer would not want to run the same ad in *Time* magazine and in a youth-oriented skiing magazine. *Time* is a serious magazine, and it is read by analytical people. You are likely to match the style of potential customers if you match the style of the magazine.

You can match a magazine's style and still be different. Allen Edmonds, a manufacturer of quality shoes, has an excellent ad that I've seen in several magazines. The visual is the toe of a wing-tip shoe, and it takes up 90 percent of the ad space. The headline, in a framed box in the middle of the page, reads, "To a stockbroker, this is an excellent tip." The ad looks different but still matches the tone.

Match your look to the product

If your product or service is practical, have your ad look practical. If your product is inexpensive, your ad should look economical—simple type, a straightforward layout, and a feature/benefit-oriented message. An expensive product needs a glossier look, stylized type, and a visual that looks expensive, either because of the setting or because of the complexity of the shot. For example, a low-priced kitchen product might be sitting alone on a counter, whereas an expensive product might have people interacting around it or have food next to it.

I attended a course once where it was claimed that only 5 percent of the information exchanged in a conversation comes from what people say. The other 95 percent is derived from the way people look and talk. While 95 percent seems a little high, there is no doubt that the style and tone you communicate with are crucial.

Inviting People In

People have a lot of information to look at and read, and they are very selective about how they spend their time. You need to help them decide to read your material by using tactics that invite them in. You can do that by thinking in terms of two-second bursts; having an action orientation; using the golden rectangle rule; ensuring that your ad has balance, dominance, and unity; and having your material easy to visually walk through.

Two-second bursts

People read ads and brochures in short bursts. They look at an ad for a second or two. If they see something they like, they'll look for another few seconds. At any time, they may lose interest and stop reading.

Try to put three two-second bursts into your piece. One should be the visual; it should show something unusual to catch people's eye. The next burst has to be the headline. Make sure the headline and visual let people know what your product is and why they should buy it. I recommend that you include one more burst that invites people to read the ad. A question or a promise of new information will help encourage readers to look into the piece. You can put this third burst on the bottom of the page.

People often can't understand why I tell them to put the third burst on the bottom of the page. They believe it should be right after the headline. But people don't read an ad or brochure the way they read a book. Instead, they look at the dominating visual images on the page. They will look first at the strongest or most noticeable visual, then at the second image, and so on. When you put your third image next to the headline, you run the risk of blurring the two, destroying the ad's impact.

To be a dominating visual, a picture or headline has to take up space. Have your top visual take up at least a third to half the page.

Action orientation

Ads that show people doing something or equipment in operation are much more likely to be read or watched. A State Farm ad has an excellent image of a woman and a young girl on the beach looking at some seashells. The setting is intriguing, and people give the ad a couple of extra seconds of time.

Golden rectangle rule

This rule states that visuals should have a height-to-width or width-to-height ratio of 2-to-3. It claims that rectangles are just more interesting shapes than squares. I have no idea why this ratio holds up, but it does. Watch the ads you see in print or on TV, and you'll see that 2-to-3 rectangles are commonly used.

Balance, dominance, and unity

Ads have many elements: a headline, a visual, copy, possibly smaller pictures, and a call to some sort of action. *Balance* refers to the way the elements are placed so that they all seem to be in harmony. If one side or the other seems top-heavy, the piece just won't look right. *Dominance* refers to the way one ad element immediately grabs the reader's attention. Every page needs some image, either a headline or a visual, that dominates. *Unity* is the way the entire piece seems to hold together. Color schemes, background colors, boxes, and white space can all give an ad unity. The piece has to look "right" or customers will think something is wrong.

Have a Piece That Is Easy to Walk Through

Any ad or brochure should follow a pattern as you look from one element to the next. The pattern doesn't have to go from top to bottom; it might go in a circle, or up and down, or back and forth. People look at an ad by following the dominant visuals. You need to be sure that there is a smooth flow from one element to the next, or your piece will be choppy and hard to read. For example, I don't like copy on both sides of a visual. It makes reading difficult and your message hard to follow.

ACTION STEPS

1. As you prepare ads or brochures, remember these guidelines for an effective layout:

    A. Create a consistent look.
       - Match the style of your customers.
       - Match the medium your ad runs in.
       - Match your look to the product.

    B. Invite people into your piece.
       - Use visuals or headlines that grab people's interest in less than two seconds.
       - Have an action orientation.
       - Use the golden rectangle rule.
       - Add balance, dominance, and unity.

    C. Make your literature, flier, or ad easy to walk through.

RADIO AND TV ADS

People typically need to see or hear a radio or TV ad anywhere from three to ten times before they actually take action. You have to be prepared to air commercials repeatedly in order to have a chance to succeed. Don't use radio or TV ads unless you are prepared to do this.

Personally, I believe radio is a much better ad medium for a small business just because you can easily match the quality of a large company's ads. It is difficult, and expensive, to duplicate the quality of TV ads from companies like Coke, Toyota, and Procter & Gamble.

Radio Ads

Advantages:
- Production and advertising costs are low.
- By advertising on three or four stations, you can usually reach a targeted customer group.
- People tend to listen to the radio at the same time every day.
- People listen to the radio in their homes or cars, making it potentially a very personal medium.
- It provides excellent follow-up to a TV ad or publicity campaign.

Disadvantages:
- Some people treat radio as background noise.
- You can't get a visual impact.
- An emotional response is hard to generate.

- You need to advertise more often to get a response.

Guidelines

1. You must get people's attention in the first three or four seconds.

2. Consider using a celebrity's voice, especially an on-the-air radio personality's voice. More people will listen to a voice they know.

3. Start your ad with a question: Do you have? Do you need? Are you looking for? A question helps catch people's attention. "Are you looking for a mulching mower?" is a standard type of opening for a radio ad.

4. Be brief and concise. Don't ramble on. Make just one or two points, and make those points clear.

5. Repeat the action you want people to take at least three times so that they have a chance to remember it.

6. Follow the same motivation formula as in print ads: attention, interest, desire, and action.

7. Make sure you have a friendly voice reading your ad. Don't be afraid to try out several announcers to see which one has a natural, friendly voice that will connect with your customers.

8. Space power phrases throughout your ad to keep people listening.

TV Ads

Advantages:

- They have the greatest impact. TV is the way people like to get information, and ads on it are the most effective.

- The increasing number of cable TV channels allows marketers to accurately target certain customer groups.

- TV ads are much more memorable than other ads.

- TV ads can have both fun and drama, which holds viewer attention.

- TV ads provide leverage for obtaining distribution outlets, and they make ads in other media more effective.

Disadvantages:

- TV ads are expensive; in particular, production costs are high.

- It is difficult to run an inexpensive test.

Guidelines

1. TV stations will produce your ads for you. The quality won't be up to Coke's, but it will be similar to that of ads you see for local businesses.

2. TV ads require careful preproduction work if you want to hold down editing costs. Plan out every part of your ad before you start shooting, as editing is very expensive. A storyboard is commonly used for TV ads.

This shows the visual image, the action that will occur, and the dialogue for each part of the ad.

3. Use music; it makes the ad more interesting.

4. Have action during the ad. Don't just have someone standing still or sitting down.

5. Have a strong opening and closing visual. People should be able to clearly remember the closing visual.

6. Match the style and tone of your ad to your customers' lifestyle.

ACTION STEPS

1. Coming up with visuals, story lines, and effective power phrases isn't easy. Always write down phrases you hear or see that might work for you. I've mentioned this before, but it is important, as it will make a big difference when you need an idea.

2. Start a photo file. If you see a view that fits your product, be sure to take a photo. You can use these photos to get people's opinion as to what visual is best, and they will help art directors and TV producers create better ads for you.

Chapter 16

Promotions—Another Way to Motivate

Cents-off coupons are a promotional tactic that everyone sees every day. But this is just one of dozens of promotional tactics that are available to industrial, consumer, and retail marketers. Promotions will motivate customers to buy, often without a negative impact on your profit margins. In addition, if used properly, promotions can reinforce the messages of your marketing program.

There are four basic types of promotions: (1) noticeable events, such as demonstrations, shows, or community projects; (2) promotions to help introduce new products, such as sampling, coupons, premiums, and loaner equipment; (3) non-price promotions, such as packaging, in-store displays, contests, seminars, celebrity visits, and co-op advertising; and (4) price-discount promotions, such as cents-off coupons, storewide discounts, back-end promotional programs, and package deals.

Industrial marketers often think promotions are just for consumer marketers, but that is clearly not the case. Industrial marketers run different types of promotions and avoid the use of price discounts, but a well-thought-out promotions program will increase the sales of most industrial suppliers.

NOTICEABLE EVENTS

Every year there is a big computer show in Boston that lasts a week. Journalists and customers come from around the world, and there are demonstration areas, classes, and workshops, along with an incredible amount of hoopla. The only company exhibiting at this show is Digital Equipment Corporation, and it pulls out all the stops. This is an event. It gets publicity. It's a great advertising tool. It increases the response to all of Digital's programs, and it starts people thinking that Digital is a company where something is going on.

Three Things Events Can Do for You
Build credibility
Customers are always a little skeptical of any company. They wonder if it really knows what it is doing and if it can be trusted. When a company runs an event with cooperation from other companies, community groups, and the media,

people get the impression that the company is trustworthy. People feel comfortable with companies that will run events that are subject to public scrutiny.

Communicating with customers
Finding something new to say is one of the challenges of keeping your name in front of customers. You need to give customers a reason to read your message. Events provide with you new facts, both before and after the event occurs. They give a reason not just to write but to call prospects.

Targeting customers
If you are a landscape designer who specializes in landscaping the yards of large homes and installing rock gardens, events are the ideal way to target customers. You could have a university professor give a class or demonstration. You and the professor could do a few radio interviews. You could have a rock garden class, or you could cosponsor a contest with a gardening club. All of these events could attract publicity, and all of them would target the right customer, build your credibility, and encourage people to buy your services.

Size of Events

Most marketers expect events to be big. Digital Equipment Corporation's one-company convention was a big event. The Mind Construction Co.'s space awareness promotion that I mentioned earlier was a big promotion. Large events scare marketers, as they are expensive and time-consuming.

But an event doesn't have to be big to be effective. There are three reasons for running an event: to create name recognition, to generate sales through the event's publicity, and to make contacts with key people. It's not the size of the event itself that's important, it's the results that you get from it that count.

Consider Hach Company of Loveland, Colorado, which sells over $90 million of water quality tests kits annually to several industries. Hach could arrange a seminar, with expert speakers, to explain water quality problems in Memphis, Tennessee. Would this seminar be a success if only five to ten people showed up? I'd say yes, for the following reasons:

1. Hach could publicize the seminar in trade magazines for a month or two before it took place. This would give Hach nationwide publicity, which typically will attract additional prospects.

2. Hach could run a direct mail campaign to appropriate companies in Memphis. The announcement of the seminar would be more widely read than a non-event-related mailing.

3. Hach could call current prospects and key industry personnel and invite them to attend the seminar. Even if these prospects don't attend, the event will build your credibility and generate sales. Incidentally, I've always received more event-related sales from people who didn't attend the seminar than from people who came.

4. Hach would have five to ten prospects at the seminar that could turn into good customers.

5. Hach could take photos and conduct interviews at the seminar, then use that information for additional publicity in newsletters and trade magazines.

Types of Events

There is an almost unlimited number of events that you could run. A jewelry store ran a promotion in which people came in to the store and melted ice cubes. Inside each cube was either a piece of glass or a diamond. The store showed people how they could tell the difference. The program was a huge success. Other possible types of events are:

• Classes or seminars
• Demonstrations
• Special clinics at trade shows
• Celebrity visits
• Promotions coordinated with community groups
• Theme events, such as Space Awareness Day
• Sponsorship of community events
• Craft days, or other events where people make something.

You can get other ideas by watching trade magazines and community newspapers for announcements of events.

Combine with Other Companies

When I marketed industrial products, I liked to use events as much as possible. The most effective way to do this is to combine with two or three other companies whose products are targeted at the same customer. This increases credibility, cuts expenses, and increases your publicity exposure, as your information will also go to prospects on the other companies' mailing lists.

I have cosponsored conferences on topics like electroless nickel processing, producing low-volume surface-mounted PC boards, and proper techniques for cleaning curved root canals. Attendance always at least doubles when you run programs with other companies.

For example, a retailer could arrange events in combination with other retailers, like Fridley Stockyard Days; combine with a supplier or distributor, to offer demonstrations on cost-effective retaining wall systems; or combine with accounting, legal, and advertising firms, on a seminar regarding new business trends for the 1990s.

ACTION STEPS

1. Events give you numerous marketing possibilities. You just have to be prepared to cash in on them. When you get ready to run an event, use this list to remind you of the action steps you should take:

   • Arrange for newspaper and trade magazine publicity.
   • Send letters to current and potential customers.

- Network with important people and groups.
- Coordinate the event with another company, a distributor, a supplier, or a community group. For example, a garden club is a great asset for a nursery or garden center event.
- Arrange for radio publicity, both before and during the event.
- Have in-store promotion with signs and displays.
- Prepare promotion sheets for salespeople to pass out to current customers or prospects.
- Send key customers invitations for both themselves and their friends. This tactic is especially effective when you sponsor community events.
- Take photos and interview people for after-event newsletter and newspaper publicity.
- Make up posters and other permanent publicity for future customers or for reception room or in-store displays. This is a key tactic if you sponsor a community event like a marathon run.
- Make sure you have large signs or banners promoting your name at any event you're involved in.

2. Start an event file with your ideas for events and magazine or newspaper stories about other events.

INTRODUCING NEW PRODUCTS

Gerald Tellis, a professor at the University of Iowa, did a study that concluded that TV advertising is not effective in getting people to switch brands. Tellis claims that TV ads just reassure people about the products they are already buying. While that is certainly a pessimistic view of TV advertising, I do believe you can get more people to try a new brand with samples, premiums, and coupons than you can with advertising.

Using coupons on established products can be dangerous because you run the risk that people will stop buying the product at full price. People understand that companies need to offer a coupon, premium, or sample to introduce a new product. They don't automatically assume that you will continue to make the same coupon offer.

Sampling

You have to be confident and proud to offer a sample. This tactic tells people, in effect, that your product is good and that you believe they'll like it, and keep buying it, if they just try it. That's a powerful message.

Some sampling tactics you can use are:

- Give away small samples.
- Offer a thirty-day free trial.
- Give away a retail-size product with the purchase or another product.

- Offer free services, such as a free diagnostic check.
- Set up demonstration areas where people can try a product out.
- Give out samples on street corners, at conventions or trade shows, or in retail stores.
- Run events, such as craft shows, seminars, and speeches. This is a favorite tactic of consultants.
- Give away samples in return for endorsements. This is an excellent tactic for industrial suppliers.

Don't think of a sample as something that's necessarily small. I have a friend who created a new way to make plaques, signs, and logo table tops for large companies. He gave one away (an $800 value) to a key contractor in town. He wanted to get an endorsement from the contractor, but he also wanted his product exposed to architects and other contractors.

Premiums

With sales of over $200 million per year, premiums are a big business. Marketers use them because they work. Premiums put your name in front of customers so that they will remember it, and hopefully try your product. There are four types of premiums: name recognition items, premiums tied to the product or service, a premium that is an incentive to buy, and premiums for the distribution channel.

Name recognition

Magnets, pens, and calendars are just some of the premiums companies give away to get you to remember their names. These premiums are ideal for businesses that people don't use often, such as insurance companies, real estate firms, dental offices, engineering services, or repair services.

Premiums tied to the product

When the video *Ghostbusters* first came out, video stores could get a free Ghostbuster phone with every order for six videos. The phone holder looked just like the Ghostbuster logo.

Industrial suppliers will sometimes give away premiums that show what their equipment can do. One machine tool manufacturer, for example, gave away a bronze miniature cutting tool. The premium had an interesting shape, and it elicited a lot of comments.

Another smart use of a premium is a toy store that gives a free subscription to its video game newsletter to anyone who stops in to try out a new game.

Premiums that encourage people to buy

Polaroid ran a camera promotion offering a 25 percent discount on any American Airlines ticket in the continental United States. Kids' meals at fast-food restaurants were introduced with small toys as premiums.

Other premiums can entice someone to buy one brand rather than another. For example, a store could offer a free can of shoe freshener or a free baseball or bat with the purchase of a pair of sports shoes. Industrial manufacturers often offer accessory equipment or product extensions as premiums. Companies will often offer a seldom-ordered option as a premium to help customers realize the value of the accessory.

Distribution channel premiums

You can often get a product off to a fast start if you offer premiums for your distributors, manufacturers' representatives, or your own salespeople. Dinners for two, weekend trips, cruises, monetary bonuses, or trips to Hawaii are all premiums that can motivate people to give a new product a little extra push.

Coupons

Consumer coupons, such as a bowling alley giving away buy-one-get-one-free coupons or a store offering a coupon for $1 off on a product purchase, are a tactic most people are familiar with. Industrial companies can give away coupons too. Free sample evaluations, free trial periods, discounts on machinery maintenance supplies, or one-year free maintenance contracts are all offers industrial companies can make.

Holding down coupon costs

You have to be sure that you are using coupons in a way that doesn't cost you too much. A bowling alley that gives away a free game isn't losing too much if it has open alleys available. But if an industrial supplier offers a 30 percent discount, it can wipe out the company's profits.

You need to be sure that a coupon isn't too expensive. If it is, you'd be better off using a sampling technique, which generally draws a bigger response. The best way to hold down coupon costs is to give something away you wouldn't normally sell. A typical example is buy a new suit and receive a free blouse. This is a tactic any company can use. Don't give away a product people would normally buy, give away something that's more of a frill.

Industrial suppliers

Companies often have unique products that requisitioners would like to have, but that are hard to justify. For example, we had a microscope measuring system for measuring semiconductor layers that was nifty to use. But it really only saved a few seconds of time, and so it typically was not ordered. That item was a great coupon offer.

You have to offer coupons to companies in a different way. Companies do not buy instantly. Instead, they have to go through a requisitioning process that can take six months to two years. So you have to give a coupon to the requisitioner that expires in about twelve months. Then the requisitioner attaches it to the paperwork.

This coupon gives you an enormous advantage. It gives the requisitioner a reason to choose your product, and it also puts a deadline on submitting the order. Every industrial company has had orders delayed year after year because of budget restraints. You'll get a lot fewer repeated delays if you put a deadline on a discount.

ACTION STEPS

1. Try to run promotions every time you introduce a new product. They increase your introduction success dramatically. The tactics you can use are:

   - Sampling
   - Premiums
     Name recognition items
     Premiums tied to the product
     Premiums that entice people to buy
     Distribution channel promotions
   - Coupon or price discount offers.

2. Watch competitors' introductions and see what types of programs they run. Don't be afraid to use another company's tactic if it works.

NONPRICE PROMOTIONS

Contests, sweepstakes, demonstrator models, video promotions, dealer displays, signs, point-of-purchase racks, and small samples are just a few of the types of nonprice promotions. You can use nonprice promotions in three ways: with your sales force, with your distribution channel, and with your customers.

Sales Force Promotions

Contests are one of the most common sales force promotions. If salespeople achieve a goal, they can win a vacation trip, a cash award, or an expensive item. I personally don't care for sales force contests because they don't pay off as well as distribution channel promotions. If salespeople work for you, they have only one product to sell. If they are doing a good job for you already, they really can't sell that much more. Manufacturers' representatives, distributors, and retailers are another matter. They may sell ten to fifteen or even more products. You will get a significant sales increase if you can get them to double or triple the time they spend selling your product.

Sales collateral materials

I do like to give a sales force sales collateral materials, which could include:

1. Models or demonstrators. Salespeople can get into a rut, and a model can liven up their presentation.

2. Videotapes. Include funny elements and nonsales materials. I worked with one company that had a short video that opened with a short sales presentation, then showed clips of TV shows talking about the company. The video was entertaining and gave customers a good feeling about the company.

3. Fliers, buttons, posters, free tickets, and other premiums. Salespeople enjoy having little items to give out to customers, and it helps motivate them.

Distribution Channel Promotions

Contests

As I mentioned earlier, contests for distributors can be effective because they have the potential to dramatically increase the time the distribution channel spends on your product.

You should coordinate a contest with your sales and other marketing objectives. Set a clear goal for a contest that includes your long-term as well as short-term benefits. For example, I ran a sales contest where distributor salespeople could win the free use of a Corvette for a year. The objective of the contest was to get salespeople to sell more packages of our products (which cost $15,000 to $20,000) rather than just selling individual items (which cost $3,000 to $5,000). Distributors typically combined products from several manufacturers to make up their own package.

Our support materials included a videotape and a demonstrator that showed how two of our exclusive features worked. The contest requirements were as follows:

1. Distributors needed to sell a certain number of packages.

2. Distributors had to bring in and display at least one complete package of our equipment.

3. A store display area had to be set aside for the video and demonstrator.

4. Distributors had to sponsor one evening sales seminar.

This promotion helped package sales shoot up 64 percent.

Support Materials

You can furnish point-of-purchase materials such as displays, posters, banners, selling cards, sales brochures, or signs to help promote your product. Distribution channels are often quite willing to use your materials if these materials will help them sell more.

Advisory Boards

Another tactic is to have an advisory board, or a distributor or retail council, based upon a contest or sales performance from the previous years. You can hold meetings in resort locations and make the position a reward for top performers. Boards and councils can also give input regarding promotional programs in the next year.

Consumer Programs

I've mentioned before that premiums are an effective consumer program. Other types of promotions you can use are packages, in-store displays, contests, and demonstrations.

Packaging

A product package sits on a store shelf, where people can look at it. Use your packaging every now and then for a promotion. Polaroid offered its discounts on American Airlines tickets right on its film packages. When you looked at the film, you had a big incentive to buy.

Other packages have premiums right on them. Photos of famous baseball players, a picture puzzle where you look for Waldo, contest information, and rebate offers can all be placed on packages. This is an effective strategy. Many more people will see your product's package than will ever remember your ad. And the people who see the package will be hot prospects.

Contests

Contests for consumers have a dramatic appeal, and they can be quite inexpensive, because the prize only needs to be given to one person. If you have a big or unusual prize, people will remember your name. Another positive point about a contest with one big prize is that you can have people enter it for a long time—as much as four to six months. This extends the contest's exposure and extends its benefit to you.

Some contests give prizes to many participants. Because they give away so many prizes, they have to have smaller prizes, but even with the smaller prizes, these contests are expensive. As a result, I don't think contests that give away small instant prizes are worth running.

Displays

In-store displays can be an effective way to motivate customers to buy. A retailer can use a large display in the front of the store to promote its business and to merchandise products. Manufacturers can furnish displays to stores or dealers, or use them at trade shows. Displays work well because they can provide a dominant image that will get people's attention.

Demonstrations

Many grocery stores have people either giving out free samples or demonstrating products every Saturday. That's a smart strategy. It exposes people to new products, and it generate immediate sales.

Demonstrations catch people in a buying mood and let you close a sale on the spot. Retailers should have demonstration areas and have employees, manufacturers' salespeople, or local inventors show off products as often as possible. Demonstrations create an action orientation that customers seem to like.

ACTION STEPS

1. Nonprice promotions are effective, do not cost very much, and are often easy to execute. Try to run two to three such programs each year. The programs you can choose from are:
   - Sales force promotional materials
       Contests
       Collateral materials
       Fliers, premiums, and models to pass out
   - Distribution channel promotions
       Contests
       Support materials
       Advisory boards

- Consumer programs
  Packaging
  Contests
  Displays
  Demonstrations.

PRICE DISCOUNT PROGRAMS

Price discount programs are dangerous for both profits and sales. Sears is an example of a company that had both of these problems. Discounts reduced its profits dramatically, and it started to have trouble getting customers any time it didn't have a sale. Sears was forced to switch to a low-prices-every-day strategy.

Economics of a Discount Program

New marketers often say, "I'll cut prices and then make it up with volume." Increasing sales enough to cover a discount is very difficult. For example, for a manufacturer of consumer products, the wholesale price is normally double the manufacturing cost. If the manufacturer makes a product for $1, it will sell that product for $2. If the price is cut by 20 percent, the manufacturer will make only 60 cents per unit instead of $1. It would have to increase sales 66 percent in order to make the same profits.

For example:

1,000 units times $1 profit per unit   = $1,000
1,667 units times $0.60 profit per unit = $1,000

That's a difficult, if not impossible, increase to sustain in a competitive market.

Best Types of Programs

1. Programs that offer a discount, but only if buyers meet a certain requirement. For example, customers get a 20 percent discount if they buy a package of products, such as a complete outfit. Hopefully, your discount requirement will get people to buy more than they otherwise would have.

2. Programs involving a special purchase of products that are then sold at a discount. For example, a manufacturer could sell one product at a 50 percent discount, provided the customer bought three other products. Service businesses can also use this tactic. An advertising agency might charge only $30 for copy and layout for a technical manual if the client placed its ad business through the agency.

3. Programs offering a discount on a high-end product that people might not otherwise buy. Dairy Queen will give you a $1 discount on a Blizzard when you purchase a hamburger or chicken sandwich basket. Normally people would buy a soft drink for 79 cents instead of a Blizzard for $2.25.

4. Back-end-loaded promotions. Rent nine videos and get the tenth free is an example. You don't get any discount until you have made nine purchases. Industrial suppliers of consumable products, such as plastics, of-

fice supplies, maintenance supplies, and boxes, use the same type of promotion to keep competitors away from their best accounts.

5. Programs offering discounts on just part of the product line. People must buy some products at full price if you are to have a chance of making money.

These types of promotions may not bring in as many sales as a gigantic storewide clearance, but the sales they do bring in will be profitable.

Action Steps

1. Choose at least four of these tactics to use over the next twelve months. Try to include at least three or four nonprice promotions for every price-oriented one.

2. Create a promotion schedule with some type of activity at least every eight to twelve weeks. Try to include at least two event-type promotions.

3. Keep experimenting with different types of promotions. Monitor how successful each one is so that you can find a strategy that works for your business.

Section 4— Conclusion

Motivation—More than a One-Time Affair

To be successful, you need to work at establishing a relationship with your customers, so that they know you and you know them. You need to look at motivation in this context. All your efforts must have a long-term impact. Few marketing tactics will have an immediate, strong, positive result. The results come when customers have a positive response to a large number of your activities.

Your job as a marketer is twofold. You must execute your program properly so that it has a positive impact. Also, you must maintain a consistency and a familiarity in your marketing program so that customers can remember it.

Section 5

Communicating with Customers

During the 1960s Alka-Seltzer ran a series of successful commercials that were played repeatedly on every major TV channel. They established Alka-Seltzer's brand name, and Alka-Seltzer is still a leading brand today. That strategy doesn't work anymore. In the 1960s there were just three or four TV stations, VCRs were not yet a common household item, and marketers could run a campaign that reached virtually every American. Today people can choose from over fifty cable TV stations, watch movies on VCRs, or read one of hundreds of specialized magazines.

Today's marketers have to find a group of customers, develop the right products for them, and then establish dialogue with them. That's the only cost-effective way for a small- to medium-size business to market its products. You need to learn how to communicate with customers so they stay with you for the long haul. That's the essential task of marketers in the 1990s.

Chapter 17

How to Communicate with the Skeptical Consumer

Three trends have changed the face of marketing forever. The first is market over-crowding: the steady stream of new products, new stores, and new services simply overwhelms consumers. Today there are more than 400 brands of beer, 300 types of cars, and 50 brands of detergents. There is just no way any consumer can keep up. The second trend is the growing number of cable TV outlets, specialty magazines, and other information sources. This trend makes it difficult for any marketer to reach more than a small percentage of consumers. The final trend is that experienced consumers, the aging baby boomers, are taking control of the buying process. People are moving in the direction of buying what they want, without any help from marketing or salespeople.

Skeptical customers like to receive information that is nonthreatening, convenient, and honest. This chapter covers seven how-to tactics for effective communication:

1. Create nonthreatening communications.
2. Convince people you are telling the truth.
3. Create a cluster communication format.
4. Use new electronic technology.
5. Catch a look that sells.
6. Talk to your customers through your distribution channel.
7. Give your customers some fun.

I have touched on some of these points earlier in the book, but this chapter puts them all together in a specific communication strategy.

NONTHREATENING COMMUNICATION

People are extremely wary any time they see a TV ad, talk to a pushy salesperson, or read a sales brochure. They are wary because they don't want to buy something they don't need. The three principles of nonthreatening communications are: (1) the sales message needs to be friendly, (2) the customer needs to make a choice, and (3) a connection needs to be made with the customer.

The Sales Message

People don't like being told what to do. You need to tell your message, but you need to tell it in a way that leaves the consumer in charge. You do that by having messages that are friendly and informative, and by making sure that your ad isn't preaching.

Compare these ad messages:

"Ask Phyllis her opinion of her antistroke drug."

"This part keeps our copiers running even during power outages."

Both messages communicate what the product is. The second message also communicates one of the product's advantages, fewer breakdowns. But the first ad sounds informational, whereas the second ad sounds like hard sell. Asking Phyllis seems like a more interesting thing to do.

Compare these two messages from companies selling financial services:

"Perhaps the one thing worse than dying is outliving your money."

"You have your own view of what's important."

The first message is preachy, whereas the second is friendly and puts the reader in charge.

Choice

Industrial applications

Giving customers a choice means making it clear where your product fits in and how it compares with other products. For an industrial product, this means explaining what a product does, what applications it is for, and why it is better. I once marketed a product that was used for measuring the layer thickness of electroless nickel. Our sales sheet explained the product's features and included a chart comparing the different methods of measuring electroless nickel. The sales sheet clearly stated that our product was best for layers less than 1 micron thick.

Consumer applications

About five years ago I worked in the electronics department at Macy's for about six weeks. One of the products the department sold was camcorders. At that time camcorders were fairly new, and their features confused both salespeople and customers. To help out, Macy's buyers put together a little booklet that explained the advantages and disadvantages of each type of camcorder and indicated which camcorders were best for each type of application. These charts were great for the salespeople, and we started to show them to customers. Customers loved them. They would look at the chart and say: "Those are the features I'm looking for." The charts cut sales time in half, and our closing ratio jumped dramatically. All we did was let the customers choose the product they wanted to buy.

Connecting with Customers

I have talked about being related to customers. They should feel you are communicating with them from a common ground. Testimonials are one way to connect. I like the "ask Phyllis" headline because it connects with people. Marriott hotel has a great message, "It's our version of a thank you note," for its stay-twelve-nights-and-get-one-night-free promotion.

TELLING THE TRUTH

Prego's campaign that showed it had a "thicker, spicier sauce" and Nike's cutaway shoe that helped raise its market share from 19 to 31 percent were mentioned earlier. Tell-the-truth marketing tactics are easy to execute and help your sales tremendously. There are four tell-the-truth strategies: providing visual demonstrations, offering convincing proof, giving clear information, and explaining a product's weak points.

Visual Proof

Nike and Prego are examples of marketers offering visual proof. Cutaways in furniture stores, mannequins with teeth in a dental office, or a picture of a heart full of heartworms in a veterinarian's office are also examples of offering visual proof.

When I was marketing dental equipment, we had a quality problem: Water wouldn't drain out of our cuspidor (the little sink next to a dental chair) fast enough. Dealers stopped selling the equipment because they had far too many service calls. We solved the problem, but we were unsure how to communicate this to dealers. Our solution was to take a five-gallon pail of water and pour it, as fast as we could, into the cuspidor. We gave this demonstration at trade shows, at dealer sales meetings, and at our training sessions. The water went straight through without a problem. The demonstration was dramatic. Dealers have told me years later that they still remembered that demonstration.

Convincing Proof

Toyota has been running an ad with the headline "We buy the best products in the world, no matter what state they're from." Toyota's ad has two objectives: to state that Toyota makes high-quality cars, and to state that its cars are not made exclusively from Japanese parts. In the ad Toyota lists the state of origin for forty-one parts. I don't know if anyone reads the entire ad, but that is not the important thing. What is important is that Toyota has parts listed to prove its claim.

Pepsi's comparison taste tests with Coke are another example of offering convincing proof. Other tactics include offering testimonials, showing publicity releases, having documented studies, or showing product comments from experts. In 1992 an independent service rated Buick as the highest quality car built in America. Buick immediately started using that rating as proof in its ads.

Clear Information

Aunt Jemima makes the claim, "Pancakes and syrup for under 200 calories." This claim is clear and specific, and much more believable than "low-calorie pancakes."

Ensure, on the other hand, ran a very unclear ad for a nutrition supplement drink. The ad's claim was, "Better nutrition for better health." Ensure's proof of its claim was that "Ensure is recommended #1 by doctors as a complete source of nutrition." But Ensure didn't say #1 compared to what. Is it better than a well-balanced meal? Probably not. Vague claims like this don't connect to customers.

Explain a Product's Weak Points

Products aren't perfect. Too often marketers try to hide their flaws, rather than admitting them. A surface mount assembly machine took 50 percent longer to set up than any of its competitors. The company did everything it could to hide this defect, with poor results. Then it changed its message to explain the defect: "50 percent more set-up time, for double the accuracy." That made sense to customers, and all of a sudden a perceived defect became an advantage.

When an insurance salesperson was trying to sell me an insurance policy, I complained about the high surrender charges. The salesperson told me that yes, the policy had a high surrender charge; that was because the product was meant for people who kept their policies for many years. The policy had a lower commission rate, which was a clear benefit to me, because of the high surrender charge. That explanation made sense. Don't try to hoodwink people; they will find out the truth sooner or later. Instead, be upfront, and explain how a drawback in one area allows you to have a benefit in another.

CLUSTERING YOUR COMMUNICATIONS

Most marketers have a competitive product chart that lists all the products in a market segment, and each product's strengths, weaknesses, features, and price. This is the information format that customers want: all the pertinent facts, all together, in one place.

Sears, after years of selling only its own brands, has now started to add more brand names. David Brennan, chairman of Sears at the time of the change, captured cluster communications with his comment, "When you walk into a Sears store, and you're shopping for a particular product, you're going to say, 'This is it. I've found the right place.'"

Shopping malls are one of the earliest forms of cluster communication, but this trend is now starting to take hold. Just look at some of the evidence.

- The number of specialty trade shows is rapidly expanding. These shows are ideal places for customers to look at and compare all or most of the available products in a particular field.

- The most popular trade magazine issues are those that feature informational charts about a product category. Customers don't want to be forced to do their own research; they prefer to have the information in one easy-to-find location.

- The highly successful *Consumer Reports* magazine publishes articles in a cluster-communication format.

- Prodigy touts its computer shopping service as a place where people can look at and compare a wide variety of products in any category.

This trend has two implications. One is that your sales brochures and product information sheets must explain how and why your products are different. You need to explain why one product has more features, what applications each product is for, and what type of customer should buy each model.

The second implication is that your product line has to make sense. You can't just cram every product into a category and still communicate in a cluster format. For example, Sony sells thirty-four models of Walkman radios. Thirty-four choices are too many for any customer to absorb, especially when the customer can't clearly differentiate between the models. Sony's line will make more sense to customers when it is pared down to a manageable, and relevant number of products.

COMMUNICATING ELECTRONICALLY

Electronic catalogs, complete product information on CD-ROMs, interactive videos, desktop multimedia presentations, and disc-based advertising are some of the techniques that marketers are starting to use. What makes these systems popular with consumers is that they put the consumers in control. They can ask the questions they want, then decide on their own whether or not to buy.

Catalog on Diskettes

The Canusa division of Shaw Industries, a manufacturer of heat-shrinkable pipe coatings, moved its product catalog from three-ring binders to a computer diskette. The diskette also includes a series of questions that help customers pick the best coating for a product application. Canusa started to send this diskette out to customers a few days prior to a salesperson's visit. Engineers looked at the diskette, decided what they wanted, and bought twice as often as they did before.

Interactive Videos

When you walk into a medical convention, you will find doctors congregated around any interactive video monitor. The monitor has product information on it. An entry pad lets doctors choose any information they want from a table of contents. They use the keypad to skip around, see back-up information, look at a bibliography, have information printed, or have a free sample sent to them.

CD-ROMs

An almost unlimited amount of information can be stored on a CD-ROM disc, including product catalogs, technical information, ordering choices, and repair information. With the proper programming, customers can find out everything they want to know about your product. Larger libraries have CD-ROM systems for magazine and newspaper articles, as well as for subjects such as the Civil War or the writing of the U.S. Constitution.

Disk-Based Advertising

When you respond to some ads for Buicks, you will receive a disk that gives the car model, its available options, and a spreadsheet that helps people calculate monthly payments. The disk also shows the car's features, but its biggest asset is a driving simulator that customers can use to get a "feel" for what driving the car will really be like. If you have an expensive product, disk-based advertising can be very effective.

Catching the Look

Every customer is going to react as if your company had a personality. They may feel that your business is bland, that it is cold and impersonal, that it is fun and exciting, that it is on the cutting edge of technology, or that it is a trend-setter.

The important point is that people are not going to think about how they feel or decide rationally what their feelings are. They are just going to react to their exposure to you. This exposure could include ads, brochures, the look of your store or equipment, your employees, and the tone and style of your radio and TV ads.

Consistency

People want to buy from people and businesses they like. You should decide how you want people to react to you. If you want to be considered technically advanced, every aspect of your business must reflect that. This means the way the phone is answered, the way products are packaged, the way a store is laid out, and every other small detail.

I once worked with a company that had an advertising manager, although it also used an advertising agency. Many people wondered why the company kept that person. However, he was worth his weight in gold. He made sure everything the company did created the right image. He checked technical manuals, fliers, brochures, the look of demo rooms, and everything else. That the company had a clear, memorable image was totally due to this one person.

Talking Through Distribution

Every marketer realizes that customers are becoming increasingly difficult to reach. The result has been a complete reversal of control in the distribution channel, with control switching from manufacturers to the channel. This has been bad for everyone. Manufacturers have responded to distributor demands by giving their product to anyone who wants it. And value-added retailers and distributors are having trouble competing with discounters that carry the same product.

Apple Computer, for example, used to sell its products exclusively through computer stores or its own exclusive outlets. Now Apple has announced that it will sell products through discount office products stores such as Office Max, Staples, and BizMart. This may help Apple in the short term by increasing sales, but in the long term Apple will suffer. The office stores' discount price will lower customers' perceptions of Apple's value, and Apple will lose the support of its current dealers.

Businesses are much better off returning to a partnership agreement with the distribution channel. The most important reason to do this is because distribution outlets are the spot where customers want to find information. When you want a new piece of production equipment, you probably contact a distributor or manufacturers' representative in your home town. When you want a TV, you go to a store that sells TVs.

Retailers, distributors, and manufacturers need to realign themselves with either their suppliers or their distribution customers. If companies work together, sales will be higher for everyone.

Nobody's interests are served if a product just sits in a catalog or on a retailer's shelves. Manufacturers need to provide some degree of exclusivity to the distribution channel, and distributors have to support manufacturers that give them an edge.

When I worked in Macy's electronics department, Macy's carried Panasonic telephones. Panasonic had twenty-five models of telephones, but Macy's could display no more than eight of them at any one time. Panasonic never knew what products Macy's would display or whether or not those brands would cover the whole range of Panasonic products. And Macy's salespeople never quite adjusted to a constantly changing product mix and a complete lack of sales materials for Panasonic products.

You should look at the distribution channel as not just the place to sell a product, but one of the major places where you communicate with customers. You need to make that communication count by working with all the companies in the distribution network.

GIVE CUSTOMERS SOME FUN

Americans will do almost anything to have a little fun. A friend of mine brought me a newsletter that had a football trivia contest on it. On one side were clues for teams' nicknames, such as "$1 an ear," and on the other side were team names, such as Buccaneers. I figured out every one of those answers, and I enjoyed doing it. I also read the newsletter. A little bit of fun went a long way toward familiarizing me with this business.

Some ways you can add fun to your communications are:

1. Contests, games, trivia questions, and puzzles.

2. Having a fun-looking store. F.A.O. Schwarz's toy stores are an example.

3. Product packaging, such as L'eggs's fun egg package rather than a flat rectangular package.

4. Giving a humorous look to ads or employees. Cahntal's is a manufacturer of pots and pans that always has employees in wild, funny hats.

ACTION STEPS

1. Pull out all of your ads, fliers, brochures, newsletters, and any other communications. If you don't have materials of your own, pull out materials from other companies that you have collected.

2. Look at each of these communications in terms of the seven tactics discussed in this chapter. Note which, if any, tactics you've already used, and then see which ones you can add. You'll be surprised at how much your materials can be improved if you follow these simple guidelines:

   • Create nonthreatening communications.

   • Convince people you are telling the truth.

   • Cluster all pertinent information together.

Chapter 18

Database Marketing — The Future Is Now

In the 1970s and 1980s, niche marketing replaced mass marketing as the predominant marketing philosophy. Sections 1 and 2 of this book, "Discovering Where the Money Is," and "Being Better than Everyone Else," explain the key niche marketing tactics of finding an underserved customer group, and then creating a product line to meet its needs.

In the 1990s, niche marketing continues to be refined. The two developing trends in marketing today are what I call informational marketing, which reformats communications according to customers' needs; and relationship marketing, where companies make an effort to develop a connection with their customers.

Today marketers are targeting smaller groups and using new and improved communication tactics, but they are still taking a scattershot approach when they try to reach customers in a targeted group. The newest emerging marketing trend, database marketing, takes niche marketing one step further by not just targeting a customer group, but using a systematic communication strategy to target people who have in some way had contact with the firm.

This chapter explains the database concept, shows what a database can do for you, explains how to set up a database file, shows how you can best use your database, and gives examples of companies that successfully use a database system.

A DATABASE—WHAT IS IT?

A computerized database is a collection of records on customers. Those records could include the prospect's name, address, and phone number; how and when the prospect contacted you; the prospect's sales potential; past purchase activity; current suppliers; past mailings; the prospect's salesperson contact; and the best time to contact the prospect.

A database is more than a glorified mailing list. A list just gives you a person's name to put on a label. A database is a file that contains information about customers; you can access this information, ask questions concerning it, and then pull off the names of people who have the characteristics you want. For example, if you want to host a seminar, you can decide which of the characteristics you have on file will make an individual an ideal candidate, then ask the database for the names of the people with those characteristics. With a mailing list you might mail out one or two pieces of information to everyone on the list. With a database, you might mail out five or six pieces to the ideal candidates.

Here are just a few applications for a database in your office:

1. You can send routine mailings to people every two or three months. Your database will tell you who to mail to and what to send on a daily basis.

2. You can send gifts or thank-you notes to your best customers.

3. You can determine when customers are due to order and call them up in advance. This cuts your sales cost and minimizes your chances of losing an order to a competitor.

4. You can run a special campaign directed only at prospects that are customers of competitors.

5. You can add a personal note, such as "Thank you for your recent order of 1950 widgets," on any mailing you send out.

6. You can call customers whose order rate has fallen off.

Everyone Should Use a Database

I believe that virtually every business should implement database marketing. Some industrial companies are starting to use it, but it works just as well for retail stores, restaurants, and service businesses. If you own a retail store and want to increase business, which do you think will work better: a blanket mailing to 10,000 people or personalized mailings to 800 people who have already contacted you? There is no question about it; the personalized mailing will be more effective.

Implementing database marketing is easy. I'm not a computer person by any means; I use a computer only when it is the easiest way to accomplish a job. Setting up a database system for a small- to medium-size company is something even I can do. I use the Q&A system on a 286-type computer, and that's the system I refer to throughout this chapter. The Q&A program has an Intelligent Assistant feature that is perfect for those who are not computer people. When you want a record or a mailing list, you request it in regular English. For example, I can ask for the names of everyone who has inquired over the last three months that lives in a particular Zip code. Q&A's Intelligent Assistant will write the program for me and print the list. If Q&A doesn't understand the command, Intelligent Assistant will tell me what else it needs to know. You can go out and buy an obsolete 286 or 386 computer, purchase the Q&A program, and be up and running in two or three days for as little as $1,200 to $1,500.

WHAT A DATABASE CAN DO FOR YOU

Numerous studies have demonstrated that 40 to 45 percent of a typical company's sales leads buy either that company's or a competing company's product within a year. Yet salespeople and marketers often report that leads are worthless. The reason for this discrepancy is that salespeople are oriented towards sales they can get today, not sales that might occur in twelve months. For most companies the result is that a lot of money is walking out the door. A database marketing system can stop that from happening.

Prospect Management

When I was in charge of marketing, I gave up trying to get salespeople to follow up on leads. They just were not going to do it effectively. I decided not to give a lead to a salesperson until that prospect was ready, or almost ready, to buy. At Philtec Instrument Co., a program that cost $2,000 per year raised our sales closing rate from 5 to 40 percent and cut sales costs almost in half. At Syntex Dental Products, a $24,000 "hot prospect" marketing program that could handle 400 leads per month generated over $1 million in sales.

Manual Database

Philtec used a manual database system. When a lead came in, a salesperson called the customer. If it was "just another inquiry," the salesperson gave the lead back to the marketing department. After two weeks we sent out a letter offering a free subscription to our newsletter, copies of three technical articles, or a free sample evaluation. We also asked prospects to tell us what their application was, what problems they were experiencing, and when they planned on buying equipment.

When the prospects responded, they went into a quarterly follow-up file. They received mailings from us every four to six months. The key to the sale was the free sample evaluation. When a prospect sent in a sample, we knew that that prospect had a problem that made him or her a potential customer. After we started this program, we began to get sales from leads that were a year, a year-and-a-half, and even two years old.

Simple Database Systems

At Syntex we used a simple computer program and a part-time telemarketer for our "hot prospect" system. The telemarketer called up every lead as we received it. She would ask the dental office when the doctor was considering purchasing. If the purchase was imminent, she turned the name over to a salesperson. If the dentist was not going to buy immediately, and over 90 percent weren't, she would record in the database the expected purchase date and what equipment the dentist intended to buy.

With that information, we started to mail the dentists updates, always asking if they were ready for a demonstration. We also called them back as their purchase date approached. Again, the prospects were there; they just weren't ready on our sales force's schedule.

Distribution Control

Database marketing is especially effective for industrial marketers that sell through a distributor network because they can learn about prospects before the distributor network does. The program at Syntex gave our sales force leverage with our dealer network because they knew about the prospect first. The salespeople would give those leads to the distributors, provided they pushed some other business their way.

Customer Relationships

Another use of database management is to strengthen a company's relationships with its customers. You can send customers regular mailings, thank-you notes, reminder notices, and special invitations. These small communications will give customers a good feeling about a company.

A database also lets you use the phone at a new level of effectiveness. Most salespeople don't enjoy making phone calls. A database helps get around that problem by always giving the salesperson a reason to call. "Hi, Judy, I was just noticing that you haven't purchased anything for two months. Since your last purchase we've gotten in two new lines of clothes that I think you might want to see." Your salesperson gets information like this right off the computer screen.

Telemarketing is one of the easiest ways for an industrial supplier to cut its marketing and sales costs. A telemarketer working with a database system can call customers when they should be ordering and get the order, follow-up on people who have stopped ordering, call and offer discounts to appropriate customers, and determine who should be interested in a new product. If a customer wants to see a salesperson, you can still send one, but often that won't be necessary.

SETTING UP A DATABASE SYSTEM

Databases are everywhere. When you go into a library, you check a database to find the book you want. For example, if you want to know whether the library has a certain book, you just ask the system, and it will tell you. The database system I will be discussing can be used to store customer records and then access those records. To do this, you need to establish a customer record and set up a record screen.

One of the reasons I like databases is that they are easy to use. When you look at a database record, it actually makes sense. You don't need to be intimidated about starting your own database. But you do need to buy software. *PC World* readers rated Fox Base/Fox Pro and Paradox as the two best, and easiest to use, database programs in 1992. I use the Q&A database program, which is an older system that I feel works well.

Setting Up a Record

The database you set up will contain a record for each of your customers and prospects. Each record will contain a number of fields in which information is stored. You need a field for every piece of information you may later want to use to segment customers.

List the information you want to put into your record then list the number of characters you need to record that data. For example, you might have a file with fields like those listed below:

NAME:	24 characters
ADDRESS1:	24 characters
ADDRESS2:	24 characters
CITY/TOWN:	24 characters
ZIP CODE:	12 characters
PHONE NUMBER:	13 characters, digits and dashes only
FAX NUMBER:	13 characters, digits and dashes only

CUSTOMER CODE1:	20 characters
CUSTOMER CODE2:	20 characters
CUSTOMER CODE3:	20 characters
PRODUCT PURCHASED1:	10 characters
LAST PURCHASE DATE:	10 characters
PRODUCT PURCHASED2:	10 characters
LAST PURCHASE DATE:	10 characters
SALESPERSON:	12 characters
LEAD SOURCE:	10 characters
MAILING DATES:	20 characters
ITEMS MAILED:	30 characters
LAST MAILING DATE:	10 characters
ITEMS MAILED:	10 characters
PHONE CALL DATES:	30 characters
LAST PHONE CALL:	10 characters

You may not need this much information in the record, or you may want more.

This layout is important. When you do a search, you don't want to search an entire record, as it takes too long. You want to search only the field where the information is. So if you want to mail to everyone who hasn't had a letter in ninety days, you want the computer to search the "last mailing" field.

Setting Up the Screen

To create a screen on the Q&A system, you start with a blank screen. Then you simply type the heading, including a colon, on the screen where you want each piece of information to go and then leave the number of characters (or spaces) after the heading for the entry. At the end of the spaces for entry, you place an angle bracket. For example, the screen heading for Name would look like this:

```
NAME:        >
```

Q&A will also let you use boxes to divide the screen into sections with labels such as purchase history or mailings sent. You can also leave a section at the bottom where you can write comments.

You may need to shorten certain fields to fit everything you want into a screen, but you should be able to put the screen together in less than one day. You can change it later on if it turns out that you have forgotten something. Another nice feature of Q&A is that once you change the screen of one record, Q&A will change the screens of all the other records for you.

The time required to enter new names into a database is a stumbling block to some people. It does take time to enter new names and information. But it is worth it. To enter a new record on the Q&A system, you enter the database file and enter the command "add a new record." Q&A will give you a new screen to fill in.

To access the database, you enter the database part of the program and ask for the names you want. The program will then either show you the information on the screen or print it out, depending on what you have told it to do.

HOW TO BEST USE THE DATABASE

To maximize your results from a database system, you need to develop a communication strategy, set up a system for weekly mailings, and create a mailing timetable for big events.

Setting Up a Communication Strategy

Figure 18.1 gives a communication strategy for a typical business.

Figure 18.1
Communication Strategy

HYDRAULIC REPAIR INC.

Customer timetable	Action
1 week after first purchase	Send thank-you note
1 week after major purchase	Send thank-you premium gift
6 weeks after last purchase	Send I miss you note
10 weeks after last purchase	Have salesperson call
14 weeks after last purchase	Send coupon offer

Call-in prospect timetable	
1 day after first purchase	Send introductory kit
10 days after inquiry	Send latest newsletter
20 days after inquiry	Send we hope to hear from you mailing
30 days after inquiry	Have salesperson call
40 days after inquiry	Send introductory coupon offer

Other prospect inquiry	
1 week after obtaining name	Send introductory flier
2 weeks after obtaining name	Send follow-up postcard
3 weeks after obtaining name	Send invitation to class
4 weeks after obtaining name	Send introductory coupon offer

Weekly Communications

You should access your database every week to get the names of people to contact that week, either by mail or by phone, based on your communication schedule. You can have the database print labels, or you can use a word processing program to print a personalized letter to each prospect. Personalized letters draw a better response, but they do take more time. I definitely think you should use them for customers. For prospects, send 200 prospects personalized letters and 200 prospects form letters, and see if the results are worth the extra time.

Event Communication

To run a successful event, you need a timetable for communicating with prospects. I've listed a sample seminar timetable in Figure 18.2.

Figure 18.2
Event Communication Strategy

HYDRAULIC REPAIR INC.

Four weeks prior to event:
Send out initial press releases.
Send first mailing to customers, call-in prospects, and other potential prospects.
Send out initial mailing to key people in your personal network.
Send out initial mailing to relevant trade groups.

Three weeks prior to event:
Send out second mailing to call-in prospects.
Send out free referral coupons to customers.
Call key people in your personal network and important people in trade groups.

Two weeks prior to event:
Send out follow-up press release.
Send out second mailing to customers and prospects.
Send out third mailing to call-in prospects with discount offer.

One week prior to event:
Phone follow-up on press releases.
Repeat free referral tickets to customers.
Send out fourth mailing to call-in prospects.
Repeat mailing to trade groups and personal network contacts.

Economics of a Database System

This may seem like a lot of work. But before you dismiss a database system, do two things. First, figure out what it costs you to get a prospect's name. What is your advertising cost for a lead? For example, if you spend $800 per month on advertising to get 60 leads per month, your cost per lead is $13.33. Most marketers will be surprised at how much they pay per lead.

Second, accumulate the names of fifty older prospects and fifty customers who haven't make a recent purchase. Send those people three mailings each, offering a class, a seminar, a newsletter, an update on your recent activities, a free gift or coupon, or another premium for either calling or stopping by to see you. My experience is that your database management system will bring people in at a cost that's only 25 to 40 percent of your current cost.

ACTION STEPS

1. Look through the mailings you've done in the past and pick out the ones you would use in your communication strategy.

2. If you don't have enough mailings, start a file of mailings you receive that you like. You can use those as samples to make up new communication materials.
3. Prepare a communication strategy. If you are reluctant to put in a database system, do the test discussed just before these action steps.
4. Plan a small event, such as a class. Set up and implement a communication strategy, again with a manual system and a small number of prospects.

EXAMPLES OF COMPANIES USING DATABASES

A personal computer with a database program provides plenty of capacity for virtually any small- or medium-size business. I have a Toshiba T310101/20 286 laptop computer and a Q&A program. It can hold more than a million bytes of information, which is more than I'll ever need. This section covers several examples to motivate you a little more to try a database system.

Fingerhut

Fingerhut is a mail-order catalog merchant that increased sales and profits during the recession of 1991 and 1992. All of Fingerhut's catalogs have a personalized message on the cover thanking the customer for the last purchase and suggesting other items that he or she, based on past purchases, might want to look at. Other tactics Fingerhut can use because of its database are:

* Sending out free gifts to good customers on their birthdays
* Calling customers before important anniversaries with special jewelry promotions
* Placing additional product inserts into catalogs based on past purchases
* Deciding what product inserts to include in people's monthly bills.

The result of all this effort is a 30 percent increase in per catalog sales without any increases in costs other than adding a database system.

Polaroid

Polaroid sells instant film to a wide variety of nonconsumer users, such as professional photographers, law enforcement departments, and science and research professionals. Polaroid decided it could maximize sales to these groups if it could separate customers by application, then target those groups with specialized mailings.

Polaroid set up a database system and started to send out three magazines: *Test* for photographers, *Instant Evidence* for law enforcement professionals, and *In Focus* for research scientists. In each magazine Polaroid includes a postcard that customers can use to request additional information. The card also includes a few additional questions to identify that customer's needs. Though Polaroid won't give out exact statistics, Kate McCaw, a senior advertising executive, states that Polaroid has significantly increased sales since starting this program.

Pioneer Seed Corn

Pioneer has a sophisticated database for its farm customers. It includes data about the types of crops they plant, their farm size, and the seeds they have purchased in the past. It uses that data to customize its mailings. As a result, Pioneer has been able to raise its mailing response rates to 20 percent or better (compared to most mailings' average of 1 to 5 percent). Pioneer looks at its database marketing system as a sales tool. More important, Pioneer looks at the database as a way to create a lifetime relationship with its customers.

Marilyn Miller Consulting

You don't have to be a big company to benefit from a database system. Marilyn Miller owns a career counseling firm. She uses a database program to collect and store the names, addresses, and phone numbers of leads she gets, whether from seminars, speeches, or referrals or in response to a direct marketing campaign. Marilyn's database allows her to send out targeted mailings to promote her events and seminars, from which she gets many of her clients.

ACTION STEP

Earlier I asked you to try a manual database system. If you did that successfully, or if you are convinced that you should start using a database, go out and buy a program and put your own system into use. The program that I like is Q&A; other programs that are rated highly are: Fox Base/Fox Pro, Paradox, Alpha Four, and DataPerfect, which works with WordPerfect software.

Last month I was talking to a woman who told me that she had received so many mailings that she just had to find out more about what we could do for her. I hear comments like that all the time, sometimes from people who originally inquired two or even three years ago. I'm convinced that every business has an enormous amount of revenue just sitting there waiting to be tapped. A database can help you bring that revenue into your company.

Chapter 19

Communications —
Tactics to Use Every Day

I believe there are two schools of marketing, the "hammer" method and the "bump" system. The hammer is the one-time close method of marketing. In this method, the salesperson gets a prospect's name, "nails him," and makes the sale. In the bump system, the salesperson moves along with the prospect, more at the prospect's pace, then gets the sale when the prospect is ready to buy. Marketers using this method work at developing a long-term relationship.

There is no doubt that companies that go after customers strongly will do better in the short term. Given 100 prospects, a one-time close method will secure more orders over the next thirty days than any other technique. But over the long term, nudging customers along will produce far more sales, and especially far more repeat sales.

George R. Markonic, Jr. is a marketing superstar. At the age of 29 he was running the Herman's Sporting Goods chain. At 35 he was the chief executive of Eyelab, and at 39 he is the head of Kmart's specialty products division, where he oversees Waldenbooks, Pac Membership warehouses, Builders Square, and Pay Less drugstores.

At Eyelab, Markonic boosted sales by collecting data on eyeglass purchasers, then sending them promotional material on a routine basis, even though it might be months before they needed new glasses. Now, at Kmart, he is gathering huge amounts of information on bargain shoppers, book buyers, and do-it-yourself homeowners. He is putting together a database system so that he can bump customers along until their next purchase.

Marketers have three distinct types of communication. The first type is used to find customers, the second to keep in contact with customers and keep giving customers reasons to contact you, and the third to motivate prospects to buy. This chapter is about nudging people along, keeping up your presence, and letting the customer decide when to buy. It covers the key strategy points; newsletters and brochures; radio, TV, and billboards; and low-cost tactics that people notice.

KEYS TO EFFECTIVE COMMUNICATION
Section 4 of this book talked about motivating customers, and Chapter 17 discussed some communication guidelines for today's skeptical consumers. I have

condensed that information into two charts. The first, Figure 19.1, is a communication worksheet that you should use when you prepare fliers, brochures, postcards, and other customer mail-outs. The second, Figure 19.2, is a checklist that you can use to review your piece when you have finalized its layout.

Figure 19.1
Communication Worksheet

Goal of piece _____

Attention devices. What two-minute bursts are being used? _____

What visual(s) is (are) used? _____

What is the headline? _____

What is interesting to the customer, i.e., what is new? _____

What is going to happen; what don't people already know? _____

How is desire created? Use of power phrases, emotion, etc. _____

What is your offer? _____

What action are you requesting—phone call, reply card, visit? _____

Figure 19.2
Mailing Piece Checklist

	Yes	No
Must Haves		
Style—is it personal, animated, and friendly?	____	____
Consistency—does the look match past materials?	____	____
Target customer—is it clear who it is?	____	____
Product—is it clear what it is?	____	____
Identity—is it clearly recognizable?	____	____
Look—does it capture the spirit of the message?	____	____
Things to Consider		
Invitation—does the piece invite the reader in?	____	____
Proof—do you offer proof for any claims?	____	____
Offer—is your offer convincing enough?	____	____
Emotion—are you appealing to any emotion?	____	____
Visuals—do they and the headline occupy 50 to 70 percent of the piece's space?	____	____

The Three Most Important Points

The points you need to pay particular attention to are the goal, the offer, and the photos or drawings.

The Goal

Setting a clear goal is the most important thing in any communication. If you don't know what you are trying to do, I can guarantee that your piece will not be effective. Your goal can be to announce a new product or service, to tell an interesting story about a customer, or to explain how customers can use your product.

Limit the number of messages you try to communicate to preferably one and certainly no more than two. People will not remember more than that, and if you try to give them more than two messages, you run the considerable risk that they will not remember any part of your message.

The Offer

Every mailing should have an offer of some sort. It could just be to be placed on a mailing list, to attend a special showing, or to reserve a seat at a class or seminar. Telling a customer to call and set up an appointment is still an offer.

You must create action on the part of readers right when they are reading your piece. That's the only time you have their attention. People are unlikely to remember a marketing piece after four or five hours, so you need an offer that will motivate them to call.

The Visual

People have to get the gist of your message by just looking at your headline and visual. If they can't, your message will not get through. Show customers, vendors, and business associates your visual and headline, without any other copy. Ask them what they think the message is. If they can't tell, you need to rework your visual.

You should also devote 50 to 70 percent of an ad's space to the visual and headline. People often decide not to read a marketing piece just because there is too much copy. Since your only goal here is to keep in contact with prospects and customers, you don't need much copy. What you need instead is a strong visual that catches the reader's eye.

NEWSLETTERS AND BROCHURES

Three Guidelines for Effective Print Communication

I know you are reading this book, and I'm glad you are. But the sad fact is that the written word is losing its impact as a method of communication. Since you can't hope to communicate too much at any one time, three points become important. First, the number of mailings you send is more important than the amount of information in each mailing. Second, mailings need to be entertaining and not overly informative. And third, your materials should be put in a format that lets readers find the information they are looking for in less than thirty seconds.

Newsletters

Now that I've told you that people just don't read much anymore, why do I recommend a newsletter? For several reasons:

1. Newsletters are a way to get people to ask to be put on a mailing list. They are an excellent tool for direct-response advertising.
2. People will take a look at newsletters when they get close to a buying decision.
3. Newsletters can be funny or have intriguing contests, which make them more readable than a direct-promotion piece.
4. Newsletters can contain offers that encourage prospects to contact you.
5. Newsletters can act as publicity releases, letting people know about either upcoming or past events.
6. Newsletters can function as premium give-away items. You can give them away when someone comes into your business, or hears a speech, or has any other contact with you.

The two most important parts of a newsletter
Your name and the layout are the two key points in a newsletter's design. The best names are ones that come from a customer perspective and that have a little humor. For example, *Byte Size News* is much better than *Personal Computer News*. *Clips, Pencil, and Paper* is vastly superior to *Office Supply Newsletter*.

Your layout is what gives your product eye appeal. Layout includes both your color scheme and the way your visuals and copy look on the page. Newsletters should have at least one color besides black and white. Printing in two colors (black and one other color) or three colors doesn't add much to the cost, and it can double or triple the readership of any piece.

Your newsletter also needs an inviting format. As in any other communication, you need to follow the two-second-burst rule. Prospects should be able to look at every page for only two or three seconds and still see something interesting.

To have an effective layout, you need a headline and visual on every page. On the inside pages, you might even want one visual to take up half to two-thirds of the double page. Once you have the visual in place, arrange your copy to balance each page.

Every newsletter should have the following items:

1. A customer-oriented publicity story
2. One easy-to-understand message about your company
3. Several photos, drawings, or other visual images
4. An offer the customer can respond to
5. One or two humorous articles
6. A story about something unique about your business.

You don't have to write the humorous pieces. You can buy them from syndicates. Here are some of the companies you can get pieces from:

JSA Publications	Crown Syndicate Inc.	American Int'l
P.O. Box 37175	P.O. Box 99126	Syndicate
Oak Park, MI 48237	Seattle, WA 98199	P.O. Box 46004
		Bedford, OH 44146

Brochures

Typically customers move toward a buying decision in steps. During the pre-buying stage, they just take in bits and pieces of information. Once they get closer to a purchase decision, however, they will often request, and read, a product brochure.

Two points that create ineffective brochures

First, unless you are selling through a direct-mail piece, a brochure's job *is not* to sell a product. A brochure's job is to get prospects to contact you. Too much information in a brochure gives people the idea that they know all there is to know about you. If you put in too much product information, people have no reason to call you.

Second, marketers often try to make brochures too sales-oriented. The prospect already has an interest in buying from you, or he or she wouldn't be reading the brochure. What customers want to know is whether you have a product that will work for them. Brochures need to include information clearly stating what each of your products can do and what applications it is designed for.

Make your brochures clear

Many brochures are confusing, primarily because they have two conflicting goals:

- To quickly and effectively communicate what the product is, who it is for, and why it is special
- To describe the product or service in just enough detail so that customers will know that it meets their needs.

Most brochures I see spend too much time on product details and not nearly enough on communicating what makes the product unique. You need to spend 50 to 75 percent of the brochure on what makes the product special. Usually one or two charts or graphs is enough to let people know that a product will meet their needs. If customers want more information, have them call you.

Three rules for effective brochures

1. In three seconds, the brochure should tell the reader what the product is and who it is for.

2. In less than fifteen seconds, the reader should know why he or she should contact you.

3. In less than two minutes, the reader should know enough about the product's features to know whether or not the product will work for him or her.

Rules 2 and 3 are tough to execute. You can't communicate that quickly with words, so you have to use pictures. I like a dominating visual on every page. Before preparing any copy at all, I hang the visuals I've chosen and the page's headline on the wall and ask people what the message is.

ACTION STEPS

1. Keep a file of stories and publicity releases that you can include in a newsletter.

2. Contact the syndicates mentioned in this section to see the kinds of stories you can use in newsletters.

3. Start collecting samples of newsletters you receive that you can refer to when you put together your own.

4. Start collecting ads, brochures, and other promotional materials that have an effective visual/headline combination.

5. Analyze the materials you have put together in the past using the forms in Figures 19.1 and 19.2. If your materials rate badly, redo them.

6. Run a contest for the best name for your newsletter. Give a nice prize like a dinner for two or a getaway weekend.

RADIO, TV, AND BILLBOARDS

Radio and TV ads are usually not cost-effective for communicating with customers unless a company:

- Can afford to advertise repeatedly
- Has an inexpensive product
- Could sell its product to a large percentage of the population.

For example, Budweiser, Coke, and manufacturers of candy bars are ideal candidates for radio and TV advertising.

When Mass Media Ads Pay Off

Radio, TV, and billboards are much more powerful than a mail piece. They make a strong impact on people, and they greatly increase a company's credibility. Circumstances when mass media ads are particularly effective are:

1. When your targeted customers are in a small town. The cost of ads will be much less, and you will have a good chance of reaching a high percentage of customers on programs with a strong local orientation.

2. When you can find a show to advertise on that is closely-related to your business and has many publicity possibilities. For example, a chain of fishing stores might sponsor a fishing show. It could put posters saying "Sponsors of Fishing Heaven" throughout its stores, as well as using the tagline in its customer mailings.

3. When you are supporting a well-entrenched database marketing program. Ads reinforce your other marketing messages and add credibility to your company.

TV Ads

1. Run the ad for fifteen seconds, or thirty at most. Your goal is just to keep your name in front of customers.

2. Remember that style is the most important aspect of an ad designed to keep your name in front of customers. Be sure the ad conveys the impression you want.

3. Make sure your ad's production is of TV quality.

4. Have your ad action-oriented.

5. Be sure the components of your visual identity are clear and obvious.

6. Don't run the commercial unless it is very effective. TV ads cost too much to risk running a so-so ad.

Radio Ads

1. The first few moments of an ad should have a strong hook to catch the listeners' attention. Use questions or dramatic statements to open the ad. "1880 cars are stolen every minute of the day" is a dramatic statement. "Do you know anyone who has ever had a car stolen?" is a strong question.

2. Your commercial should have a friendly, personal tone.

3. Be sure to repeat your call to action at least three or four times

Billboards

Billboards are a reminder-type of ad medium. Since your goal is to get people to repeatedly see your name so that they remember it, billboards are a good tactic for communicating with customers. To have an effective billboard, you need a clear, strong logo, so that people know who you are, and a strong visual to catch people's attention. You can use words, but the billboard should work without them. If you do use copy, limit yourself to no more than ten to twelve words.

The biggest problem with billboards is that sign companies don't like to rent space on just one. They want you to take several locations, many of which may not work for you. Get a billboard if you can get just one at a key location, but be careful if you need to commit to boards at poor locations.

OTHER COMMONLY USED METHODS

Communicating is really trying to grab a little piece of the customer's mind. You want to have a customer remember you, what you do, and why he or she should call you. You goal is visibility. Seminars, events, classes, and other similar activities, discussed in Chapter 15, are one way to maintain your visibility, and premium items, such as pencils, calendars, and refrigerator magnets are another. This section covers a few more tactics to keep customers thinking about you.

Phone Power

We all get so many calls from telemarketers that we often forget that the phone can be a friendly marketing tool. A personal call is effective if it is done properly. The key is to keep the call on a friendly basis. You want to call with some news that the prospect might want to hear, and you want to call after you have had a response from the customer.

You should try to call prospects if they haven't responded to three mailings after an initial response. Before calling, set up a call objective card similar to Figure 19.3.

Figure 19.3
Phone Call Objective Card

GOAL: To determine if the prospect is still interested in your business.
OPENING: Hi, this is John calling from the North Metro Electronics Cooperative. You contacted us a few months ago about a new product you were designing, and I'm following up to see if you are still working on it.

CUSTOMER RESPONSE
GATHER INFORMATION

OFFER: We are offering a free seminar on cutting the cost and time of new product design that might help you. What does your schedule look like?
CONFIRMATION: 1. When does it look like you'll need design engineering help?
2. Should we still keep you on our mailing list?

The opening of the phone call should finish with an open-ended question. Make it clear from the beginning that this is a conversation, not a sales presentation. You want the prospect to respond. Try to ask as many questions as possible based on the prospect's response.

Finish your call with an offer or a request for some kind of action. If the prospect doesn't respond to the offer, confirm that the person is still a prospect. There is no point in keeping someone in your database who is never going to buy.

Clubs

Sometimes a business will be able to pull a group of prospects together to form a club. This works for hobby clubs, but it also works if you sell to businesspeople. Clubs for design engineers, computer programmers, and tool and die operators are all possible.

If this applies to your business, you can sponsor such a club and help it get started. You can have meetings or carry out joint projects related to your mutual interests. The club would help your relationship with club members, and the publicity you can generate will attract more customers.

A club does several positive things for you:

1. It keeps your name visible to club members.

2. You can offer a free club membership in some of your mailings. That offer will both generate responses and increase your credibility.

3. You can cosponsor events with the club. This will help the event appear to be educational, and it will help attract more publicity.

Posters

Some businesses have posters with great-looking pictures that have the business's name on them. A semiconductor manufacturer sold a poster with the genealogy of all of the major chip manufacturers. The poster was unique, told a story people wanted to know, and was in great demand. A poster is also a good premium to offer in a letter, ad, or newsletter. A couple of color printers that offer a good price for posters are:

American Color Printing	U.S. Press
1731 N.W. 97th Ave.	P.O. Box 640
Plantation, FL 33322	Valdosta, GA 31603
305-473-4392	1-800-227-7377

ACTION STEPS

1. A communication strategy calls for a well-balanced way to communicate with customers. It should include:

   • Database mailings.

   • Production of new mailing materials, such as newsletters, postcards, brochures, and fliers.

   • Radio, TV, or billboard ads to communicate with customers.

   • Other tactics, including, but not limited to, seminars, classes, events, clubs, premium items, phone calls, posters, publicity, and trade shows.

   Prepare a communication strategy for your business on a monthly basis. See Figure 19.4 for an example for a wholesaler of gift products.

2. Keep looking for inexpensive ways to promote your business. Don't be afraid to copy another company's program if it looks like it would work for your business.

3. Make a commitment to find, within six months, a premium that you will sell or give away to your customers.

SECTION 5—CONCLUSION

Communication: A Key Part of the Marketing Strategy

There are four parts to a communication strategy that leads to a sale: (1) the message itself, (2) the style of the message, (3) the number of times someone sees a message, and (4) the way a business reinforces the message. When all four parts work together, the prospect will feel good about you, and more than likely is going to buy. The number of times you communicate is a crucial part of the strategy. If you don't communicate often, people won't remember your message and won't contact you when they are ready to buy.

Figure 19.4
Communication Plan

BJK WHOLESALERS

Month   **Action**

January   Prepare quarterly newsletter.
           Database mailings and phone calls.
           Attend gift retailers trade show.
February   Prepare announcement on new product line.
           Distribute magnets and catalogs to current customers and hot prospects.
           Database mailings and phone calls.
           Run classes on gift shop management in three local cities.
March   Work with vendors to obtain radio interviews to promote new product line.
           Database mailings and phone calls.
April   Prepare quarterly newsletter.
           Database mailings and phone calls.
           Cosponsor consumer gift show with eight retailers.
May   Prepare and distribute a report on a national trade show most local customers
           couldn't attend.
           Database mailings and phone calls.
June   Bring in vendors and craftsmen for retailer-sponsored craft show.
           Database mailings and phone calls.
July   Hold own trade fair showing customers new product lines for Christmas season.
           Prepare quarterly newsletter.
           Database mailings and phone calls.
           Offer premium items to retailers to remember company.
August   Conduct seminar, Eight Ways to Hold Down Inventory Costs for Christmas
           Season.
           Database mailings and phone calls.
September Prepare promotional selling sheet for additional winter products.
           Give customers last-chance order information for holiday season.
           Database mailings and phone calls.
October   Prepare quarterly newsletter.
           Database mailings and phone calls.
           Phone calls to every customer and prospect regarding holiday orders.
November   Prepare premium calendars for retailers.
           Furnish holiday buying posters, with BJK Wholesalers name, to promote in-store
           sales.
           Database mailings and phone calls.
           Prepare sheet with holiday shopping tips.
December   Phone calls to check on resupply orders.
           Database mailings and phone calls.
           Send out seasons greetings cards to customers.

Section 6

Making the Sale

Salespeople have been resented at every industrial supplier, distributor, and wholesaler I've worked with. Other employees always seem to think that salespeople are paid too much for what they do. I've heard this comment hundreds of times: "They really don't sell anything, they just take orders." The reason salespeople often make a lot of money is that sales is hard work.

This section is especially important for industrial suppliers. Sales is also essential for consumer-oriented companies, but these companies typically appreciate the value of a top salesperson. That is not always the case with industrial suppliers. I believe that 60 to 80 percent of new manufacturers, consultants, and service firms fail because they don't put in enough sales effort. Selling in a retail store has problems, but selling to other companies is much more difficult.

The salesperson's job is to give the customer the last push into buying from you. In a retail or consumer environment, the customer evaluates his or her needs against your product. In a business-to-business setting, customers usually do not buy on the spot, so they evaluate their needs against your products and your competitors' products.

This section covers how to make the customer comfortable; how to sell through relationships; how to close a sale; how to use catalogs, direct mail, and telemarketing to support your sales efforts; and selling products through radio, TV, and magazine ads.

Chapter 20

Making the Customer Comfortable

When people buy products, they have an intuitive sense that governs many of their actions. As a rule, people have to trust someone before they will do business with that person. Therefore, you have to work on setting up a comfortable environment in which customers are likely to buy. You can do this through your literature, your in-store layouts, your customer service, or your actual sales approach, or in dozens of other ways.

To gain people's trust, you need to make sure you don't give prospects a reason not to buy, have a consistent message, put your customer in charge of the buying decision, back up whatever claims you make, and have a quality sales force.

ELIMINATING REASONS NOT TO BUY

According to some reports, most successful entrepreneurs have started a business similar to the one they just left. Part of the reason is that they know what to do, but another part of the reason is that they know what not to do. Back in Chapter 5 I mentioned that you should learn why people won't buy as a way of learning about customers' desires. This section looks at why people won't buy to find aspects of your business that stop a sale from occurring.

You can discover obstacles in the sales process by realizing that people's reasons aren't logical, setting up an advisory board, developing key contacts in the distribution channel, reading trade magazines, and being a member of trade associations.

Customers Aren't Always Logical

Prospects may not buy because they once had a bad experience, they have heard a rumor or misinformation in the past, the product doesn't seem right, they mistakenly think that a part is poorly constructed, or any number of other reasons. I introduced a tire cutter about four years ago. I found out that another company had introduced a similar product a few years earlier. That manufacturer had had quality problems and had gone out of business without issuing any refunds. The product we had was vastly superior, but that didn't matter. Most prospects still wouldn't touch it, and we took it off the market.

You can find out about some of these red flags by asking people what problems they have had in the past, by listening to people's comments, and by checking with people in your distribution channel. Don't dismiss comments because they don't make sense. Instead, question the person a little further to see if some past event has inspired the comment.

Advisory Boards

I've already mentioned the advantages of an advisory board several times. An advisory board is a group of customers or prospects who meet with you every two to three months to discuss how they view your business. They can give you feedback about potential features or advertising programs, and also about whether or not they will react negatively to any of your planned activities.

You should also ask your advisory board about any moves your competitors may be making. Its members will be able to point out both your competitors' mistakes and their smart moves, which will give you more information about reasons people may not buy.

You can also set up an advisory board of people in your distribution channel. If you are a retailer, you can ask some manufacturers' representatives, distributor salespeople, or members of a manufacturer's marketing and sales force to serve on your board. These people will know what tactics have backfired in the past, especially if some of them have years of experience.

Trade Magazines

Read the magazines for your industry and look for articles about companies' successes. Often an article will explain problems the company had and how it overcame them. Note and keep a record of those problems so that you don't make the same mistakes.

Association Roundtables

If you are a member of an association, you will find that they are always looking for topics for their quarterly or monthly meetings. Suggest to the association's president a roundtable, class, or seminar on companies' biggest mistakes or errors companies should never make. Some of the association's more experienced members can probably tell quite a few horror stories about things to avoid.

I know that most readers are busy and that it is difficult to find the time to join an association. You need to look at that time as an investment. You'll have a chance to meet contacts in the distribution channel, you'll meet competitors who have a great deal of experience, and you'll have a chance to pick up tidbits of information that can really help you.

ACTION STEP

Start a file on mistakes to avoid. Include in it:

* Magazine articles
* Stories from customers or distributors
* Advisory board evaluations of your program and competitive programs
* Notes from meetings with associations.

AN INTEGRATED MARKETING APPROACH

Consistency gains a customer's trust, and consistency comes from an integrated marketing approach that enhances the marketing message with pricing and promotion, emphasizes your message through the distribution channel, and reinforces your message with every customer contact.

Enhancing the Message

Pricing and promotion can both be used to communicate your message. Pricing can reinforce product features, and it can also help target customers. Promotions and advertising can help enhance the message by their tone, where they are run, what features they are promoting, and what the materials look like.

Pricing

Pricing is a strong marketing tool that is often overlooked. Most marketers worry too much about low prices. Instead, they should be worrying about whether or not their pricing supports their marketing strategy.

The Saturn car from GM sells for $12,000 to $15,000. That price tells people that the Saturn is a practical, economical car. GM's pricing positions the car at the high end of the economy car market, and the car's stylish look targets it toward young adults. People wouldn't believe GM if it started boasting that the Saturn was a powerful, fast car. That claim wouldn't fit the car's price. If the Saturn was priced at $18,000, customers might believe the high speed claim.

To a large degree, price determines a product or service's perceived value. If you price your product at $20, that's what the market will value it at. If your competitors all price their products at $25, customers might believe that your product is inferior, rather than that it is a better value. Cost Cutters sells haircuts for $8.95. Is that a good value or a cheap haircut? Most people will believe it's a cheap haircut. $8.95 is a good price only if people think the product is worth $12 or more.

Promotions

An image can also be affected by promotions and advertising. What is your reaction to a car manufacturer's offer of a $1,000 rebate on a car? Probably that this is a low-priced economy car. People will have a more positive reaction to an offer of free leather upholstery. That offer suggests that the car is worth $20,000 or more.

Guidelines for promotions:

1. People associate coupons and dollar-off sales promotions with low priced products.

2. People associate upgrade promotions, such as receiving a deluxe picture frame with any print purchase, with more expensive products. This guideline is crucial for industrial suppliers. They need to stay away from sales discount offers.

3. Don't run dollar-off promotions until you have established a price for a product.

4. The quality of promotional material also contributes to perceived value. Cheap, black-and-white materials indicate low quality products. Glossy, four-color brochures indicate a higher-quality product.

5. The magazines or radio and TV shows you advertise on also contribute to your image. An ad in *Time* magazine is more prestigious, and adds more credibility, than an ad in *Income Opportunities*.

Emphasizing Your Message through the Distribution Channel

Where you are located or the type of sales channel you sell through can: (1) identify your target customer, and (2) reinforce your product's price point. You can also emphasize your message through display materials that you provide to manufacturers.

Target customers

Retail stores, manufacturers' representatives, distributors, and even your own sales force all come with an image and a way of doing business that will reflect on your product. If you sell to department stores, you are targeting high-income shoppers. If you sell through a rack-jobber distributor, you are targeting small five-and-dime stores and convenience stores. If you sell through a low-end distributor, you are targeting economy-minded shoppers. If you sell through a sales force of engineers, you are targeting large companies with complex problems. If you sell through manufacturers' representatives, you are probably targeting small- to medium-size companies.

Price point

The distribution channel you choose also implies a pricing strategy. Technical sales forces imply a higher price. When company principals, such as design engineers, call on prospects, that usually implies a lower price.

Using display materials

Take the time to talk to other people in the sales channel to find out what materials will help both of your companies' sales. A retailer could ask a manufacturer for displays that would help it establish an image as a knowledgeable source or as a store with the latest technology. A manufacturer will often find that a retailer will offer premier sales space if it will furnish a certain type of display.

Manufacturers or service companies using manufacturers' representatives definitely need to supply as many sales and display materials as possible. That will enhance your stature in the customers' eyes, and it will improve the representatives' presentation.

Enhancing the Message with Every Customer Contact

A store layout can convey key information to customers. Consider a record store that promotes itself as being in tune with today's "hot music." The store could have the week's top eight albums prominently displayed, a jukebox where people can play the latest songs for a quarter, a display featuring three local disk jockey's choices of up-and-coming albums, a part of the store set aside for local bands, and an event center with upcoming music events.

A service business connects with customers in different ways, including:

- A waiting room
- Invoices and statements
- Advertising
- Sales materials
- Service repair people
- Sales personnel
- Receptionist
- Customer service.

A manufacturer has its package and after-sale support to promote its message. Have the package look like the communication pieces from your business. You want your common look to be obvious.

ACTION STEPS

1. Write down the image that your business should create.

2. Take a critical look at your operations and make three lists. The first should include aspects of your business that strongly support your image. The second should be aspects that actually hurt your image. The third should be aspects that are neutral, not helping or hurting your image.

3. Most marketers will end up with a list of ten to twenty, or even more, items that need to be improved. Pick out four negative aspects every three to four months and work to improve them.

PUTTING THE CUSTOMER IN CONTROL

You want to make customers happy when they do business with you. At least half of the reason people buy is that they have been put into a buying mood. You put them in the right mood by showing customers that you care about them, making it clear that you are an expert, and putting the customer in control.

I Care about You

There are three ways to show that you care about people. One is to be friendly and courteous, another is to take time with each customer, and a third is to be sure you listen to what customers tell you.

Be friendly and courteous

The biggest obstacle to courtesy is employees with a downbeat attitude. Much of the time this problem is caused by management, and if it isn't, management can correct it. Here are five tips to keep employees upbeat:

1. Discourage negative comments like "I'm tired" or "nobody has any money." Tell employees things aren't so bad and to be positive.

2. Allow your employees to be flexible. Difficult circumstances will develop, and your employees will have to deal with them as best they can. Tying people up with too many rules is demotivating.

3. Don't get upset by an employee's mistake. If you give employees the room to be flexible, they will make mistakes. In the end, the benefits you'll get from upbeat employees will outweigh the cost of any mistakes.

4. Don't make employees look to you for every answer. If employees can't make decisions, they can't care about customers.

5. Praise employees when they do something well. Keep reminding them of the things they do that help your business succeed.

Give customers time

Most people resent being constantly rushed. If you take just a little extra time with each customer, you'll find that customers will buy more, and more often. Rushing customers is a fault that most industrial suppliers have. Many industrial companies get just a few large orders or inquiries per day. As a result, incoming calls are often treated like an intrusion rather than a source of income. This is especially true when incoming calls from prospects are outnumbered by calls from other companies' sales forces.

Some of the ways you can make a little extra time for customers are:

1. Have your receptionist give the caller a warm, friendly greeting, ask for the caller's name and company, then ask how he or she can help.

2. Have knowledgeable people available to handle customer questions.

3. Let employees know who your important customers are so that they will recognize these customers when they call.

4. Have an incoming call tracking form so that you know what happens to a caller. This also emphasizes to employees that incoming calls are the lifeblood of a business.

5. Have coffee and donuts available so that you can take some time to talk to customers.

6. For retailers, show customers in-store displays, posters, color charts, or magazine reprints to take a little extra time.

Listening

The last thing you can do to show people you care is just to listen to them. I always recommend that anyone talking to a customer or prospect take notes. It shows that you care about what the person is saying. Try to ask as many follow-up questions as you can to learn more about the customer. Simple questions work best. For example, if a company calls you about an accounting service, ask how the company is getting the work done now.

You Are the Expert

You want to project your business as an expert when you explain purchase options to prospects in order to give these prospects confidence that they are making the right decision. Being an expert does not mean telling people what to do, like the stockbroker I discussed earlier in the book. What it means is that you, as the expert, will be reinforcing people in the belief that they are making the right purchase decision.

Establishing Credibility

One way to show that you are an expert is to have outside documentation about your background and experience. Here are some tactics you can use:

- Have publicity releases published about you, even if they are just published in a company newsletter.
- Attend relevant courses in your field.
- Document extensive work experience.
- Provide customer testimonials.
- Have a publicity sheet showing various employees' background.
- Cosponsor key events.
- Be a member of relevant associations.

A second way to show that you are an expert is to competently explain your position to customers. A maintenance manager took in some electronic testing equipment for repair. The service person told the manager that the machine needed to be overhauled. When the manager asked why, he was told that the equipment was just due for an overhaul.

Well, electronic components don't wear out like brake shoes, and the manager took his equipment to another shop. There, the service person showed the manager which parts were defective, then explained why it was easier just to replace the entire assembly. This service person sounded like an expert because he was willing to explain the action he recommended. Product knowledge is important, but a true expert also knows how to explain what he is doing and why it is important to customers.

Putting the Customer in Control

People like to feel that they are capable of making a smart purchase decision. Your job is to explain what options customers have and then let them choose which product to buy. You can actually do this several times during a sale.

For example, I had a request for consulting services from the state of Minnesota. The first thing I did was tell the state that there were three ways I could address this problem. I then explained each way briefly, in about two minutes, and asked the requisitioner which approach was preferred. The requisitioner told me which fit her view of how the job should be done, and I proceeded to offer three ways in which I could implement the approach. We kept going until we had finalized a bid proposal.

Now I certainly slanted my explanations to encourage the person to choose certain options. And I recommended certain actions when she wasn't sure which approach to take. But despite my steering, the customer didn't buy my product, she chose the product she wanted. That is the way customers truly like to buy.

ACTION STEP

Have three or four people you know contact your business. Have them start as prospects and go through all the steps to a purchase. Then ask them to answer these questions about your business:

- Were people considerate?
- Did people take the time to understand your needs?
- Do you feel that people helped you choose the product that was best for you?

BACK-UP DATA

In the first chapter I talked about people who bought my last book only after they looked at the index. These people wanted to be sure that the book discussed their particular problem. They were doing something that almost everyone does when buying a product: subjecting it to their own special reality checks.

Every customer has a few particular things that he or she checks before buying. These could be things their parents told them, things they learned in school, or a piece of information they picked up on a radio talk show. If you can't satisfy prospects' own reality checks, they won't buy. The way to satisfy them is to have back-up data available to address their concerns. You can do this with three-ring binders or through electronic data retrieval. You won't need the material all the time, or even most of the time, but it will be necessary to close some sales.

Three-Ring Binders

Here is some of the information you should have in a binder:

1. Any required financial bonds and appropriate business licenses
2. Magazine articles or excerpts from books that support product claims
3. Photos of events held in the past, including pictures of prominent attendees
4. Literature from competing companies (you may need this when prospects overvalue competitors' features)
5. Detailed testing reports on various products' reliability
6. Quality reports, both from the factory and from independent consumer magazines
7. A company organizational chart
8. Testimonial letters
9. Resumes of key employees
10. Operation, installation, and repair manuals.

Electronic Data Retrieval

In the future this type of system will be essential for almost any type of complicated sale, including industrial, medical, and dental products and most services. Any of the following systems is a possibility:

1. Electronic storage on a CD-ROM system that can be directly queried.
2. Computer storage with access through a series of menu questions.
3. Either of the previous two systems accessed by a company salesperson or a customer through a laptop computer and modem. Pharmaceutical companies are already moving in this direction.
4. A fax retrieval system. These systems have a variety of data stored on a computer that can send a fax. Salespeople can call the number and have certain information faxed to them at their customers' location.

Ask for the Order

As a rule, customers use their reality checks only when they are considering buying, and customers will have a positive feeling about you if you pass their reality checks. So always ask for the order right after you show the materials.

I've also closed many orders by just telling people that the back-up material was available. "Mr. Jones, I know you are concerned about this point [whatever the objection is]. Would you like to see some documentation that shows why our product is best in this area?" Many people will state right then that no, they don't need to see, they're ready to buy.

ACTION STEPS

1. Start a three-ring binder with the back-up materials you have. Be sure to use tabs to index the information so that it is easy to find.
2. Start a 3 by 5 index card file of the questions you get from prospects. Then find materials to support your answers and include that information in your three-ring binder.

THE QUALITY OF YOUR SALES FORCE

For most businesses, putting together a great marketing plan won't put people into a perfect buying mood if you don't make an effort to have a quality sales force. The salesperson has to gain customers' trust, motivate them to buy, and then actually close the sale. Good salespeople can do that; bad ones can't. You need a strategy that includes hiring the best people, keeping them at their jobs, training them so that they know what they are doing, and finally giving them an opportunity to advance.

Hiring the Best People

Compensation, support, and flexibility are the three factors that attract quality salespeople. You need to take the time to hire the right salesperson not just to increase sales, but because hiring and training a salesperson can cost anywhere from $15,000 to $50,000.

Compensation

You don't need to offer people a higher salary than anyone else, but you should include a commission or bonus structure that gives them a chance to earn more if they perform well. You can ask your local Chamber of Commerce, a local personnel (or human resource) association, or your local trade association for average sales salaries.

Support

Support is a subjective term. Every company says it supports its sales force, but good salespeople can immediately tell if you value them. You show support when you have a sales force advisory board that provides input that you listen to and take action on. You also show support when most of your sales materials are prepared in response to a salesperson's request.

Flexibility

Good salespeople like to have the flexibility to adjust a presentation to their personalities. Don't try to force salespeople into a rote way of doing things. There is a commercial I like that has a salesperson ask an owner, "How should I treat someone who wants to make a return?" The owner's answer is, "Treat them the same way you'd like to be treated." You do need rules for salespeople to follow, but you should make them guidelines, not rigid doctrine.

Sales tests

I highly recommend that you give people a written test before you hire them. Quite a few companies sell products for screening salespeople, and some of these tests are incredibly helpful. You can't tell from an interview how positive or how persistent a person is, but these tests can tell you. Don't use them exclusively, however, as they are not always right. You can find companies that sell tests in the Yellow Pages, or by looking in magazines like *Inc.* or *Sales and Marketing Management*.

Keeping People at Their Jobs

Respect is the most important thing you can offer a top salesperson. Salespeople are really out on their own. They need self-confidence to succeed, and they won't have it if they feel that someone is looking over their shoulders. Set goals for salespeople, explain to them what you need them to achieve, but then respect their abilities to get the job done.

Compensation, flexibility, and career advancement will also help you keep, as well as hire, good salespeople. But it is your attitude towards the salesperson that is most important.

Training

Your training program tells a salesperson exactly how important the job really is. If you expect salespeople to represent your company well, you should emphasize that point by having a training program. If you don't have such a program, salespeople aren't going to think their job is important. With salespeople, what you do is much more important than what you say.

Besides the psychological benefits of a training program, you also need to show people how you want them to sell—i.e., relationship selling rather than a hard closing sale—and you need to give them the product and company knowledge they need to close sales.

Opportunities for Advancement

In most companies, there aren't many opportunities for salespeople to advance into sales or marketing management. But you can still build promotional moves into your sales force. Sales Representative can be an entry-level position. Sales Consultant could be the next step up, once a person has proved he or she knows the product line and can offer expert advice. Senior Sales Consultant could be another step up, and Sales Trainer could be a salesperson who mentors new colleagues.

It irritates experienced salespeople to have a new, untrained, unproven person join the company at the same title position as theirs. It doesn't show respect for experience. Having a few advancement opportunities in the sales force gives you a way to reward performance and keep your sales staff motivated.

ACTION STEPS

1. Prepare hiring and promotion guidelines for your company. This helps salespeople see that a sales position is important, and it helps you develop a coherent strategy.

2. Prepare a training program for new salespeople. Make training a top priority for either you or someone on your staff.

3. Conduct exit interviews with people when they leave the company. If you feel uncomfortable doing this, develop a questionnaire. Find out if the people felt appreciated, if they felt they had enough training, and if they felt they had opportunities for advancement.

Chapter 21

Closing — Sales Built on Trust

Before you start reading this chapter, try to forget any negative feelings you have about salespeople. You don't have to be pushy, manipulative, or devious to be a salesperson; you can be helpful, friendly, and relaxed. You don't have to cater to every prospect's whim; you just need to be honest and fair.

In reality, everybody is a salesperson. We all try to persuade someone to do something virtually every day. You are being a salesperson every time you give someone the support to make a decision, try to persuade someone to do something, or reinforce a choice someone has made. Don't ever say you can't be a salesperson; you started out on a sales career when you were about two years old.

Your marketing program encourages people to buy from you. Now it's your job or your sales force's, to help the customer make the final decision to buy. Don't minimize this challenge. Most people are reluctant to make a major purchase, even if they really want the product, because they are afraid of making a mistake.

Your goal is to help customers decide to buy the things they want. If you don't do that, you won't have any profits. But you want to make those sales in a way that creates a trusting relationship between you and the customer. This chapter will help you develop that relationship. It covers the key elements of making a sale, the sales opening, the presentation, handling objections, overcoming stalls, and closing the sale.

Before continuing, I want to warn you that some of these ideas are going to be different from what you may have previously read or heard. This is a different way of selling that not only sells more, but keeps customers coming back, because it is a system designed to build relationships that last.

PRINCIPLES OF A SALE

Control

Chapter 20 discussed putting the customer in charge by giving him or her options to choose from. When you do that, customers will feel like they made the decision to buy. But you still need to keep control of the sales process.

What you do want to give up is center stage. You want to let the customer do most of the talking, but to direct the conversation with your questions, comments, and answers. A good rule to remember is that the person doing all the talking dominates the conversation, and the person doing all the listening controls the conversation. Just watch the *Tonight* show. Jay Leno, and before him Johnny Carson, talks only 20 to 30 percent of the time. But he still controls the conversation.

Try to have the customer talk 60 to 70 percent of the time. Customers will give you the information you need to close the sale, and you won't be talking about points that bore the customer.

Reinforce Positive Points

Prospects will make statements to you that are positive for your sales efforts: "I think my business would run more smoothly if I got a better handle on my cash flow." To an accountant, that's a positive statement, and he or she should answer, "That's very perceptive of you, Jim. You'll probably be able to spend more time selling if we can control your cash flow." Customers buy for their own reasons, which can be different for each buyer. Give prospects a chance to tell you why they'll buy, then reinforce their thinking.

Never Disagree

Salespeople are often trained to handle objections by providing reasons why the objection isn't true. That's really arguing with the customer, and it isn't a tactic that works well. Instead, you should either agree with the customer or give a clarifying probe. For example, if a prospect says, "Your product is expensive," you could either agree—"you're right, it is"—or give a probing statement like, "oh, really?" or "why do you say that?"

When the customer answers a probe, you can get more information that will allow you to respond appropriately. For example, the prospect might answer a probe with "Jensen's sells a snowblower for less." You can agree—"You're right, they do,"—then ask a question that will reveal your product's advantages. For example, you could ask, "How long do you want your snowblower to last?" and follow up by asking, "Can I show you a few features that enable our snowblower to last longer than Jensen's?"

Probes

There are two types of probing questions. One is an open-ended probe like "oh," "really," or "hm." You are just asking prospects to keep talking, and usually they will. In a more directed probe, you ask a specific question: "Why do you think the price is high?" You can get more information with an open-ended probe, but you should use directed probes if people aren't responding.

Silence

I have had sales calls where no one has talked for two to three minutes. That doesn't bother me, and usually it doesn't bother a customer. When you ask a question, wait for the customer to respond. Just because someone doesn't answer right away doesn't mean they are ignoring you. Sometimes they are trying to decide what to say. People who don't talk right away like to make clear, meaningful comments, and they don't like to ramble on. They also won't listen to what you have to say if they are thinking. So just wait; the customer will answer eventually.

Questions

You have to ask people questions if you want them to keep talking. Prospects often look at a sales presentation as an exercise of "You talk, and I'll listen, and then I'll decide what to do." That's not what you want, since when you talk, the customer is in control. Instead, you want to keep asking questions to keep the customer talking.

I like to have a note pad when I give a presentation so that I can write down people's comments. For some reason, people seem more receptive to questions when you write down their answers. You can ask questions about why a person is thinking of buying a product, how he or she intends to use it, and what features are most important. If you follow up answers with probes, you'll know exactly what the customer is looking for.

THE BEGINNING

At the start of a sales call or presentation, you must build trust, understand what the customer is saying, and explain your goals to the prospect.

Opening Comments

There is a famous quote from Dale Carnegie: "You'll make more friends in two months by being really interested in other people, than you will in two years by trying to get people interested in you." Start out your conversation by asking people questions about themselves. You can get conversation cues from the way people look, when you are talking to them, and what is on their walls or desks. There is something interesting about everyone. Try to find out what it is for every customer.

The Opening Question

One of a salesperson's biggest mistakes is to talk too much. Often when a customer approaches a salesperson ready to buy, instead of taking an order, the salesperson starts a sales presentation. To avoid this, ask three questions before starting a presentation:

1. Why have you decided to buy a(n) _____?
2. Why did you decide to call us?
3. Have you decided which model to buy?

If you have done a good job of marketing, people will say yes, they've decided to buy, and yes, they've decided to buy from you. Don't give these people a sales presentation: just congratulate them on their choice and take the order. You can start your presentation if people say that they haven't yet decided whether or not to buy.

Understanding

You ask questions and use probes so that you can understand what customers want. Don't start a sales presentation until you understand what the customer wants. I was at a car dealer where the salesperson asked a prospect, "Why have you decided to buy a van?" The prospect answered that he was a soccer coach and he needed more room. "What kind of a van are you looking for?" The prospect wasn't sure which model would work best for him. "What features are important to you?" The customer wanted a V6 engine, as many seats as possible, and storage room for three bags of equipment. This simple exchange let the prospect know that the salesperson understood his needs.

Tell People What You Are Going to Do

"My goal today is to persuade you to start work on your invention. At the end of our conversation, we'll choose a program that will work for you. Once we do that, I'm going to ask you to sign up. Will that be all right with you?" I have never yet had someone say no to that question. I also use it at the start of seminars, and nobody has yet to say, "No, you can't ask me to buy."

You can't relate well to prospects if there is tension between the two of you. Not knowing what to expect at the end of a conversation produces tension. "At the end of this demonstration, I'm going to ask you to tell me if you think the product will work for your application. If it does, I'm going to ask if I can help you prepare your requisition. Is that O.K. with you?"

I started using this type of opening after we received some publicity that produced more leads than we could handle. Our goal was to screen out people who weren't serious buyers. But no one ever told us we couldn't ask the question. Our closing rate went way up, and our call time went way down. Salespeople stopped worrying about asking people to buy, and customers were happy to know where the conversation was going.

THE PRESENTATION

As a rule, I don't believe in sales presentations. I even dislike the term, as it implies that the salesperson talks and the customer listens. It also implies that the salesperson is going to say what he or she wants to say, not what the customer wants to hear. Some sales managers say that a presentation builds product value; I say that a presentation bores the customer and can kill a sale.

There are three facts that you need to have crystal clear in your mind before you give a presentation. First, customers buy products for their reasons, not yours. Second, features and benefits don't add value unless they are important to the customer. And third, people buy on emotion, and they respond emotionally to things that are important to them. The real key to an effective sales presentation is for you to help the prospect realize that your product is exactly what he or she wants.

You should have a conversation with a prospect, not give a presentation. But the conversation needs a format or you won't get the sale. You have opened up the conversation; now you need to move forward towards your close and the sale.

A presentation is actually made up of dozens of small presentations. Each one has four stages: a short benefit statement, customer feedback, a choice, and, if necessary, a request for a new decision.

A Short Benefit Statement

People remember only a few things at a time, so there is no use overloading them with information. You want to make a short point, then see what the prospect thinks about it. I'll use a microwave oven as an example simply because it is a product everyone is familiar with. These principles apply to any type of sale, including industrial, service, consumer, and retail sales.

Our prospect is a working couple with children whose microwave has given out. In the opening, Gail, the salesperson, discovered that the couple was looking for a microwave big enough to cook their meals and simple enough that their children can use it. A simple benefit statement for this couple is, "This is a large-capacity microwave. It's large enough to cook a twelve-pound turkey."

This is not an exciting statement, but it gives a benefit and turns the conversation back to the prospect. You need about fifteen short benefit statements that you can use during a presentation, so be sure to prepare them in advance.

Feedback

Once you make the statement, you want a response: "That's about the size I want," "Do you have a bigger size?" or "We don't need something quite that big." That tells you if you are on course.

Or the customer might say, "I can't see how a twelve-pound turkey would fit in there." This comment could be either an objection or a request for a larger model. Objections are explained later in the chapter. But don't always assume that a comment is an objection; instead, assume that it is not an objection. Ask instead, "Do you want a bigger model?" and then see what the customer says.

You also have to be alert to nonverbal signals. If people look distracted, it may mean that they do not care about the feature or that they do not like the way it is. Just ask, "Is this feature important to you?" If it is not, ask what features are important. If the customer doesn't like your feature, he or she will tell you why.

Choice

After you have made a point and have some feedback, you want to offer a choice to see whether the customer is ready to buy or to better identify what the customer wants.

Gail might say to our microwave buyers, "Would you like me to explain this model's controls, or would you prefer to find a larger model that will fit your needs?" The customer will do one of three things:

1. Ask Gail to explain the controls, which means that she zeroed in on the right model.

2. Ask Gail to find a larger model.

3. Reject both choices, at which time Gail should probe by asking for the order: "Is this the model you want?"

Asking for an order, in a friendly, conversational way, is one of the very best probes you can make. Some people will say yes. Others will comment on what they are thinking: "I think so; I'm just wondering about your repair policy." "I don't know. I just can't afford to spend this much money." "I really want a unit that exhausts air out the front." Whatever the response, it will lead you to the next part of your presentation.

Make a New Decision

Nobody likes to be told they're mistaken, and people don't like to change their minds. Therefore, when a prospect voices an objection, you have to show that prospect new information so that he or she can make a new decision. If a prospect has a problem with your benefit statement, you may have to overcome that objection.

One of the advantages of a short benefit statement is that it leaves you a lot of room to let people make a new decision. If someone voices an objection, you can furnish more information, then ask the customer to make a new decision. For example, if the customer voices an objection about the microwave's cooking capacity, the salesperson can simply ask, "Can I show you some features you might not be aware of?" After explaining those features, it would be time for the salesperson to move on to the next benefit statement.

Once you and the prospect are back on the same wavelength, you can again offer the prospect a choice.

HANDLING OBJECTIONS

The reason salespeople are well paid is that they need to resolve objections people have before they buy. People may be hesitant to buy your product because it doesn't have a feature other products have, because the product works differently than they expected, or for a host of other reasons.

Only one type of customer objects: Someone who is considering buying your product. A person who offers objections is a hot prospect. People who are indifferent don't object, they stall you with comments like "I want to talk to my wife" or "I'm just looking today." So smile when you get an objection, because it means you have an excellent chance to get a sale. To handle an objection, you need to relax and be comfortable, probe for the real reasons for the objection, understand what the customer is looking for, paint a picture, and provide more information.

Relax

The manner in which you handle an objection is often more important than your answer. If you are tense and nervous, the prospect will pick up on that immediately, and think, "Oh, oh, there's a big problem here." Intuition will take over, and the prospect will never buy. Remember that people who object want to buy, so there is no need to worry.

Probe

Don't jump in and answer an objection until you understand it. Use nondirective and directive probes to get the customer to explain what he or she is worried about.

Understand What the Customer Wants

Often your customer's objection is not related to why he or she wants to buy the product. So ask again. "Why did you want to buy a new microwave?" "I want to prepare big, nutritious dinners for my family." Then you need a directive probe like, "Are you starting to think that this microwave won't be able to do that?" This will give you a better idea of how to approach the customer's objection because you will know how it relates to the prospect's objective.

Paint a Picture

You will have a ready answer for some objections: Your product easily does what the person wants. Other times, the objection might concern a feature or benefit your product does not have. In either case, it pays for you to go back and reinforce the reason the customer wants to buy the product. The best way to do that is to paint a picture. For example, you might say to the microwave buyer, "I understand you completely. You want to be able to cook a roast with potatoes and carrots, even on nights when you get home late. Is that right?"

Provide More Information

The last step is to provide information the prospect isn't aware of so that he or she can make a new decision. You might show additional features or give product back-up information. In some cases you may want to show that your product has other features that help the prospect meet his or her goal. You finish by asking something like, "Does that make sense to you?" If it does, you move on. If not, you have to start over, probing for what the customer wants, or you need to decide if the prospect is stalling.

OVERCOMING STALLS

A stall occurs when a customer won't decide to buy. Sometimes the customer is indifferent and has decided not to buy, and sometimes the customer just can't make up his or her mind to go ahead. People who stall are a salesperson's biggest challenge.

One way to tell a stall from an objection is that people who have an objection are usually animated and are still interested in what you have to say. People who are stalling are indifferent and are not listening to you. They have decided not to buy that day, or ever.

The best way to head off a stall is to face it head on at the beginning of a presentation. I recommend that you ask these three questions when you start a presentation:

1. Why have you decided to buy _____? (name of product)

2. Why did you decide to call us?

3. Have you decided which model to buy?

Some people will tell you from the beginning that they are "just looking." You should still give a sales presentation, as many times people who say this will buy. But other people are really not going to buy. After you explain your product, if people still don't want to buy, set up another appointment or suggest some further action.

Most stalls occur when people who are prospects turn indifferent. These are definitely lost sales, and you need to head these prospects off before they decide not to buy. The best way to handle a stall that I have found is to say at the first moment I see the customer is getting indifferent, "I have the feeling that you've just completely lost interest in what I have to say." Then be quiet and listen to the customer. He or she will usually give you an objection, tell you he or she is still interested, or say that he or she just doesn't want the product. You can then probe to see what changed the person's mind.

If you are encountering too many stalls, you are probably: (1) not spending enough time getting to know prospects, (2) talking too much during presentations, and (3) too nervous or tense when answering objections.

CLOSING THE SALE

You don't have to wait until the end of your presentation to ask someone to buy. You can do it at any time. The best time is right when the customer has decided to buy. You will lose sales if you continue to talk after the customer has made a buying decision. So if a customer says, "This is what I want," stop, get your order pad, and write up the order. If the prospect is in agreement with you, just ask a simple question to get the order:

- "Which model did you want to buy?"
- "How soon did you want the equipment delivered?"
- "How did you want to handle payment?"

Sometimes you do get to the end of the presentation and need to close. The closes I feel work best are the presentation close, the question close, the choice close, and the don't delay close. If these closes don't work for you, read any of Zig Ziegler's books. He is truly the master of sales closing techniques.

The Presentation Close

The presentation close works well when you aren't quite sure if a prospect is ready to buy. In this close, you repeat what has happened in your conversation.

1. Start by repeating why the customer came in to see you. "I know you came in today so you could get a microwave capable of cooking an entire meal."
2. List the features the prospect said were wanted. "You told me that you wanted a large capacity microwave with easy-to-use controls."
3. List three to five reasons why your product meets the customer's needs.
4. Recommend that the person go ahead and buy or requisition your product.

The prospect will either buy, offer an objection, or give you a stall.

The Question Close

This is an effective close when people are in agreement with you or after you respond to an objection. All you do in this close is ask the prospect if what you said made sense. If it did, just ask a direct question like, "Did you want to buy this model?" If the prospect isn't ready to buy, he or she will say so.

The Choice Close

This is another simple, easy-to-use close. Here you just tell the customer that he or she can buy any of three products, then ask which one he or she wants. For example:

1. You can simply list the products available. "Do you want to buy our mid-speed model, or would you prefer to go with our high-speed production unit?"

2. You can state the choice by listing the products' main benefits. "Do you want to get our easy-to-use inspection system for your production unit, or did you want the unit that can also offer you more flexibility so that it can be also used by the research department?"

3. You can offer a choice with options. "Do you want the unit with the built-in electronic counter, or do you prefer the manual system?"

The Don't Delay Close

Some people are constantly putting off their purchases. Often they will really want to buy a product, but just not today. If this happens, first verify that the prospect really likes the product: "You're saying you really do want the product and would like to buy it?"

There are two approaches to take with a don't delay close. One is to ask how long the prospect has thought about buying the product. If it has been a while, and it usually has been, say, "Look, you've spent more than enough time thinking about this purchase. The more you delay your purchase, the more time you'll waste over a decision you've already made. Since you want the product, why not just buy it today?"

Another choice is to say, "It's a lot of work getting ready to make a purchase. You think about it for days in advance, and now you've gone to the trouble of talking to me. Since you've already decided you want the product, why go through the buying process again? Do yourself a favor and buy today."

ACTION STEPS

1. Start a sales file on 3 by 5 index cards of the following:
   - Openings
   - Short benefit statements
   - Word pictures
   - Objections
   - Closes
   - Ways to overcome stalls
   - Open-ended probes
   - Statements with emotional appeal
   - Reasons people buy
   - Points to make when responding to objections
   - Effective statements

2. All salespeople fall into a rut, using the same tactics over and over again. This takes the enthusiasm out of your speech, and it tends to make you

less focused on the customer. Every few weeks, take out two or three index cards and vary your approach.

3. Start reviewing your presentations and those of your sales force. Note what went well and what went wrong. Don't be afraid to change something if it isn't working for you.

4. Institute a sales call follow-up procedure. Send out thank-you notes both to prospects and to people that actually purchased. Be sure to put these people on your mailing list for events, newsletters, and product announcements.

Chapter 22

Selling Through Direct Mail, Catalogs, and the Telephone

The methods companies use to sell their products are changing rapidly. Telemarketers are selling industrial systems that cost millions of dollars. Direct mail sales are giving way to catalog sales, cable TV ads, TV shopping networks, and card pack promotions. One of the biggest trends in the 1990s will be a shift towards advertising that asks for a customer response.

Your success in the 1990s will come from finding a core group of supporters and selling to them through a wide variety of cost-effective tactics. This chapter covers three such tactics: catalogs, direct mail, and telemarketing. Don't think of these as stand-alone strategies. Think instead of how you can take advantage of the trust and relationships you have built to sell customers products in as many ways as possible.

CATALOGS

The nation has more mail-order catalogs than ever before, and marketers keep adding more every day. You can certainly set up a traditional mail-order business that relies almost exclusively on mail-order sales, like Harriet Carter's, Fingerhut, or Sharper Image. You can also use a catalog to supplement the way you do business now. This is one of the most profitable marketing tactics emerging in the 1990s.

Traditional Mail-Order Catalogs

Product requirements

To market through a mail order catalog you need a unique product line that is not readily available anywhere else. Ideal mail order catalogs are ones that are aimed at small target markets where the customers are easy to reach. For example, a product line of replicas of antique household fixtures is an ideal mail order catalog product. Owners of old, expensive homes are easy to find through specialty magazines, and the market is so small that it's unlikely there will be stores where people can buy the products.

It is important that your products are not readily available. I read comments that the reason that catalogs are taking off is because people want the convenience of shopping at home. That's true to a degree. People don't want to shop all over to find a special item. But on the other hand, many people won't buy from a catalog if they can buy the same product at a nearby mall. People still prefer to touch and see a product before they buy it.

Rules for an Effective Catalog

1. The catalog has to look like it's from a well-financed company.
2. Tell something about your company on one of the first three pages. Show a picture of your factory, your showroom, or your employees. This will add to your credibility.
3. Hire a photographer to do all the pictures, so that your catalog will have a unified look.
4. Offer money-back guarantees.
5. Have each page laid out by a graphic artist. The products have to look great in order to motivate people to buy.
6. Have a separate order page, but also include an 800 number for customers to call.
7. Add some personal touches to your catalog. For instance, you could add helpful hints about how products can best be used.
8. Try to make the catalog pictures action-oriented. Don't just have products in still shots; put in photos of people using them.

As with all direct-mail tactics, the mailing list is all-important. Chapter 11 discussed several ways to put together an effective list. One additional tactic, which Fingerhut uses, is to run a magazine ad offering a popular item at a low price. The names of the people who order can then be added to your mailing list.

Using a Catalog to Supplement Your Business

A catalog can do three things for virtually any business: it can improve customer service, it can improve sales, and it can improve the company's visibility. Those are pretty compelling reasons for any company to consider a catalog.

Office Max is a large office supply retailer, similar to Staples or BizMart. It has large stores with a wide variety of products at discount prices. Office Max also has a catalog that it passes out to customers. This catalog does several key things for Office Max:

1. Because it is at the customer's location, it reminds the customer to shop at Office Max.
2. It allows customers to look at a series of products and decide which ones they want before coming to the store.
3. It encourages people to look in the catalog for a solution to a small problem that they might not otherwise take the time to solve.
4. It enables Office Max to list many more products than it can carry in its store. This tactic lets Office Max provide better customer service, and it also increases sales.

Catalogs can also offer companies three more benefits:

1. It allows customers to interface with and order from an inbound telemarketer. This is a tremendous cost saving benefit for industrial marketers.

2. It allows customers to call in and order immediately, rather than waiting until the next time they see a salesperson or visit a store.

3. It puts information into a cluster communication format that people like, and it also cuts down on your need for brochures and other sales materials.

You don't need a great-looking catalog if you're using it to support your business. People already know your business, so you don't have to use the catalog to tell them who you are and why they should buy from you.

Include in your catalog unusual items that people might buy only occasionally. There might not be enough demand for these items to justify a special promotion or brochure, but if they are intriguing enough, people will keep your catalog in case they decide to buy them.

Action Steps

1. Decide to put out a catalog to support your standard sales tactics. Start by watching for products that are unusual. One of the benefits of a catalog is that you don't have to stock a heavy inventory of a featured product. You have three to four weeks to ship the product, and you can order it after you receive orders.

2. Start to collect catalogs for products similar to yours. Try to get catalogs from companies that use them to support a store or distribution channel, rather than from mail-order-only companies.

3. Subscribe to one of the two magazines below to start building a file on companies that prepare or print catalogs:

Catalog Age	*Catalog Business*
Six River Bend Center	Mill Hollow Corp.
P.O. Box 4949	19 West 21st St.
Stamford, CT 06907	New York, NY 10010

Direct Mail

Direct mail can be either directed to an established customer base, which was discussed in Chapter 19, or to a purchased mailing list. The key components of a direct mailing are the envelope, proof statements, a relatedness piece, the offer, benefit statements, the letter, and the reply card.

The Overall Package

The copy and layout rules for direct mail communication are just the same as those for any other communication material. Visuals are still important. Two-second bursts are still the key that will get people's attention. Copy still needs to be clear and snappy, and full of word pictures and visual appeal.

An effective direct-mail piece walks people through the whole program with two-second bursts in thirty to forty-five seconds. People will not read most of your material, but they want to know it's available. Every page has to have a visual focus and a message that people can pick up in two to three seconds.

The Envelope

The envelope's job is to get people to open it. There are three tactics you can use to do that.

1. Use precanceled bulk mail stamps or a meter reading, instead of having the bulk mail symbol printed on your envelope.

2. Avoid using standard labels for people's names. Either have the name printed right on the envelope or use the translucent labels that are now available.

3. Print teaser copy on the envelope. On the last mailing I did, I used a quote about my last book from *Income Opportunities*: "The surest way to take your invention to market."

Proof Statements

Testimonials, test results, explanations of why your product works, newspaper and magazine quotes, and information about your past successes are all tactics you can use to support your claims. Have a separate sheet with proof claims, rather than burying them in the copy.

The job of proof statements is to raise your credibility. Guidelines for an effective proof piece are:

1. Don't crowd statements together. Use two sides of a piece of paper if necessary. People should be able to glance at a page and see how many statements you have.

2. Put white space around each statement so that readers can quickly go from one statement to the next.

3. Use visuals whenever possible. Action photos of people work best. The logos of magazines or newspapers that have run stories on your company are also effective visuals.

4. Have a dominant visual. Your best proof source should take up a third to half a page.

5. Use a strong headline. Examples are "the nation's number one show," "two hours you can't afford to miss," "the most widely-praised system in years."

A Relatedness Piece

In some cases the people on your mailing list won't know your company, and you will need to explain who you are. You should explain your company's background and why you are selling the product. Follow the same guidelines you used for your proof statements. Include a visual of your corporate offices or a picture of the company founder. Write in friendly, natural tones, and be sure to use "you" language.

The Offer

You should include three offers in a direct mail piece: the product offer; an offer, or reward, for an immediate response; and a guarantee offer.

The product offer

You need to tell people what you are selling and what you are selling it for. But you should do both together, or people won't read the letter telling them why they should buy. Follow these three rules when making your offer:

1. On the cover of a four-page letter, or on a separate piece of paper, put a picture of your product with one or two powerful benefit statements. Your goal is to be sure that in the few seconds before they throw your information away, prospects realize that the product is directed at them.

2. If your price is extremely low and prospects will realize that, put the price next to the picture of the product.

3. If you don't have a low price, put your price at the end of your letter and on your order reply card.

The offer for an immediate response

Here you have to offer something free or at a big discount, or give customers some other big incentive. Since this offer is very positive, you want people to see it right away. I recommend that you put the immediate offer on a half page that will be the first thing a person sees upon opening the envelope. This way you get off to a fast start with the reader.

You should also mention the immediate response offer at the end of your letter and on your order reply card. Always include some reward for a quick reply. It will have a huge impact on your response rate.

Guarantee

Include a guarantee with your product offer. Tell the readers they can get their money back for thirty days if, for any reason, they want to return the product. Include the guarantee at the end of the letter, right after you ask for the order.

Benefit Statements

Your letter will highlight your product's benefits with a one- or two-paragraph explanation of each. Include these points for each benefit:

1. Start each sequence with a bullet or some other mark to make it clear that you are starting to talk about a new benefit.

2. Paint a picture of what the benefit will do for the reader. "Are you tired of spending your afternoons following up on a quality problem?" People buy products to meet a goal, to solve a problem, or to make life easier. A word picture helps them see the benefit. Put the word picture in italics, or in an indented paragraph, so that people will notice it.

3. Explain why your product provides the benefit and offer some proof.

Don't make your benefit statements too long. Six to eight sentences is ideal.

The Letter

The letter will take up the bulk of your mailing package and will include both your offer and your benefit statements. Effective letters keep people reading. Here are some points you should remember:

1. Write in a personal style.
2. Personalize your salutations (Mr. Jones).
3. Put a box in the top corner of the front page of the letter with a question indicating the problem whose solution you will supply. For example: "Are you having trouble selling your ideas?" "Do you want to start making money from home?" "Are you tired of spending so much time in the kitchen?" You can also ask a question that promises a reader information: "Would you like to cut your direct mail costs by 50 percent?" These types of questions invite readers into your letter.
4. Vary the way your letter looks. Use bullets, bold copy, indented paragraphs, and italicized sentences to make your letter appear more interesting.
5. Use testimonials to support benefit statements. It's okay to duplicate a testimonial you used in your proof piece.
6. Ask for the order at the end of the letter. Have a closing statement that summarizes why people should buy and why they should buy today.
7. Add a postscript at the end of the letter. It should give a benefit statement or a reason for the reader to buy.
8. Use two-color printing for your letter, with the second color blue. Highlight important points in blue, and have your signature in blue.
9. Leave a space between each paragraph, and keep your paragraphs short. Six or seven lines is as long as any paragraph should get.

The Reply Card

You need a separate order card that people can send in with their money. Here are some tips to make the card work better:

1. Include a toll-free number. You will always get a better response if people can call up and order with a credit card.
2. Make your offer clear. Have people check a box that states, "Yes, I want to order _____(your product)." Also, have them check a box that states that they are ordering by _____ (the immediate response date) in order to receive _____ (whatever your free offer is).
3. Include your company's name, address, and phone number on the form, and state who you want the check made out to.
4. Include an envelope to return the reply card in.

Credit Card Payments

Banks are reluctant to give a merchant credit card account to a company selling through direct mail for the first time. Banks have suffered losses when direct mailers have gone out of business and people wanted to return their purchases. Unless you have a proven track record at the bank, it probably won't give you a merchant account.

You can still take credit card payments by using a fulfillment house that will handle payments, shipments, and other aspects of mailing out products. You can find the names of fulfillment houses in magazines like the ones listed below:

DM News Mill Hollow Corporation 19 West 21st Street New York, NY 10010	Mail Order Digest National Mail Order Assn. 5818 Venice Blvd. Los Angeles, CA 90019
Target Marketing North American Publishing 401 N. Broad St. Philadelphia, PA 19108	Direct Marketing 224 Seventh St. Garden City, NY 11530

Action Steps

1. Start collecting direct mail packages that you find effective. In particular, save packages for products similar to yours. Observe whether the products are unique or whether products like them are readily available.

2. Buy something from a mail order catalog that sells products in your product category. Once you buy a product, you'll get plenty of direct mail packages to review.

3. Try out a direct mail program. Wait until you have a unique product that sells for at least $25, then do a test mailing to 300 to 700 people.

Phone Calls

Phone sales have gotten a bad reputation from all the telemarketing calls people get at home. But phone sales are a tactic that companies, especially industrial suppliers, should be using. A phone call is much more effective than a direct mail piece with prospects that have already contacted you.

Phone sales efforts can do three things: They can help you follow up with prospects to turn them into customers, they let you sell products to past customers, and they can help you get reorders from current customers.

A telephone presentation is similar to a regular sales call except in the opening and the close. You need to build credibility in a phone call opening, and you need to offer more closing alternatives.

Opening

Your initial opening should be short and simple so that you can start a conversation as quickly as possible. Follow this four-step approach to introduce yourself and to start your contact talking. You can change the wording if you like, but keep the same format:

1. Say hello and ask for the person you want to talk to.

2. Give your name and the company you represent.

3. Say either: "I'm calling because you responded to (then state how you obtained the prospect's name)" or "I'm calling because our records show it's about time for you to order (whatever the product is)."

4. Ask a relevant open-ended question, such as, "What have you done to resolve your production delays?" or "How much inventory do you have in stock?"

Don't ask a question that can be answered with a simple yes or no. Your goal is to get the person to talk. If someone gives you a short answer, pause for about five seconds and give the person a chance to talk. Often he or she will start talking again and give you more information.

Building Rapport

You need to work much harder to build rapport over the telephone. If people are being distant and not overly cooperative, tell them a little bit about your background with the company: "I joined the company three months ago. I've finished the sales training program, and I'm now starting to call people." Your background doesn't have to sound impressive; it just has to sound real.

Next, tell people why you're calling. "I'd like to tell you about our new accessory, which I'm going to recommend that you order." Don't stall around about the reason you are calling. Tell people what you want right away and they will be more receptive.

The Presentation

When you talk to someone in person, you can point to features of your product, give a little demonstration, and show back-up data. On the phone it's just you and your voice. So you can't rely on questions as much; instead, you have to be ready to give a formal presentation.

Good phone presentations are not based on product features or benefits. They are based on a concept. To illustrate, consider General Electric's new CarPro service. For $49.00 a year you can receive free consultations with an expert mechanic who will tell you what is probably wrong with your car, a recommendation of an auto repair business you can go to for a repair, and a chance to talk to CarPro's mechanic again after you receive a estimate, but before you authorize the repair.

A feature/benefit presentation would talk about how a CarPro presentation can help you make sure you are getting the right repair. "CarPro will help you be sure that you know what's wrong with your car, then send you to a repair business that has been carefully screened. The benefit to you is that you will know you are getting the right product for the right price." The problems with a feature/benefit presentation on the phone are that you will tend to talk too long and that your comments will be focused on the product instead of the customer.

A concept presentation doesn't focus on the product: instead, it focuses on the customer's needs or lifestyle. "I hope to convince you to sign up for CarPro's no-hassle car service. It will help you save money, and make sure your car is properly repaired. But what CarPro really does is give you the time to do what you enjoy doing."

The core of a concept presentation is something related to customers that makes their life better. That's a topic that people want to hear about.

Closes

People are more suspicious on the telephone than they are in person. The best phone closes are straightforward benefit closes. Use a short benefit statement, make a recommendation, and then ask for the order. "Joe, I think the CarPro system is going to make your life easier. I recommend that you become a member. Do you want to join?" If objections come up, respond to them as you would in person, then simply ask: "Joe, does that make sense to you? Can I start your membership today?"

The big difference between phone and in-person sales is what I call an alternative close. This is used when a person turns down your original offer and you then offer an alternative. For example, "If you won't take a one-year membership, would you try a three-month trial membership?"

Alternative closes don't work that well in person, because it sounds as if you didn't explain some low-priced options in your original presentation. People don't expect you to be as thorough on the phone, and so an alternative close seems more natural and is an effective technique.

ACTION STEPS

1. Do a test in which you call fifty people who have contacted you just once and fifty people who haven't purchased for some time.

2. For each call, record the following information:
   - Contact's name
   - Company's name
   - Address
   - Phone number
   - How the client originally contacted you
   - What you are going to try to sell
   - Whether the person is still a prospect
   - Whether the person bought
   - Whether the person will buy in the future.

3. You should have a positive result from your efforts. If you do, set up a routine phone sales system and include it in your database system.

Chapter 23

Selling with Magazine, Radio, and TV Ads

Radio and TV ads can be effective in selling consumer-oriented products. Weight-loss products, auto safety devices, tapes, videos, cooking sets, fishing gear, and a host of other products are sold either through thirty-second to two-minute ads or on half-hour-long infomercials. Magazine and card pack advertising can be used to sell industrial supplies and equipment, services, and consumer products.

There is no doubt that all these tactics work. TV shopping networks such as QVC and the Home Shopping Network do close to $2 billion a year in sales. Look through any TV section and you will see half-hour blocks of time dedicated to infomercials. Radio commercials helped build million-dollar sales for The Club, an antitheft device for automobiles. And magazine ads have built empires for a variety of companies such as NordicTrack, a home fitness equipment manufacturer.

For some products, especially those that customers won't immediately understand why they want or need, these ads can be the best way to create sales. A good example is The Club. It locks around a car's steering column and makes it impossible for a thief to turn a car's wheels. A person seeing The Club on a store's shelf won't immediately grasp why it works, but a radio or TV ad can drive home its benefits and persuade people to buy.

The drawback to all three tactics is that they cost money, both to produce the ad and to run it repeatedly. The safest way to try them is to start in smaller towns or in low-circulation magazines, where costs will be low. If an ad produces enough sales, you can keep running it and expand to larger markets.

RADIO ADS

If you listen to the radio, especially late-night radio, you'll hear ads promoting and selling products. Some informational products, such as workbooks for attending government auctions, are reported to have sold millions of dollars worth of products over the radio. With the right product and the right strategy, you can make radio work for you too.

This section covers what kinds of products to sell, how to target the right customers, when to run the ad, what the ad should be like, and when to use radio representatives.

What Kinds of Products

The four requirements for a successful radio product are: (1) it is unique, (2) it is goal-oriented, (3) it costs between $25 and $100, and (4) it can be understood without a visual image.

Unique

People have to do a lot of work to buy from a radio ad. They have to listen to your ad, get a pencil and paper, write down your 800 number, call the number, give a credit card number, and wait four to six weeks for delivery. They won't do that unless you have a product that is difficult to find anywhere else.

Goals or emotions

Products commonly sold on the radio are ones that will make or save you money, like a course in buying real estate with no money down. You need a product tied to a bigger benefit than its cost would indicate. For example, spend $49 to take a course that could make you rich. Or buy a $9 fuel economizer that will save you hundreds of dollars on gas every year.

You can also appeal to people's emotions. For example, The Club's sales pitch involves dark and dangerous areas where you wouldn't want to find your car missing when you came back. Again, the cost of the product is tied to a more expensive benefit: You spend $50 to save your $20,000 car. That type of cost/benefit ratio is always compelling.

Product costs

A product for radio ads should cost at least $15 to $25. Only a small percentage of people will buy from a radio ad, so you need to be sure that you can make enough from each sale for this relatively small number of sales to cover the cost of the ad. You just can't sell enough $5 products to make an ad pay off.

Visual image

Customers need to see some products before they will buy them. For example, Ronco sells products such as miracle knives and all-in-one fishing poles on TV. These products have to be seen to be bought. People can't understand the product without seeing it. To work on radio, products have to be either known or easily understood, or else be informational products such as workbooks, audio tape series, or videotapes.

Targeting Customers

You want to advertise on radio stations that your target customers listen to. This can be difficult if you serve a niche market. One of the problems with radio is that stations concentrate on a format, such as news and talk, rock, country, or easy listening. Those categories may not correspond to your target customer. Targeting customers is actually easier on a radio network that offers specific programming that appeals to a certain target market, such as business, cooking, or health and fitness shows. You can find out information about networks from the following groups:

Radio Network Assn.
1440 Broadway
New York, NY 10017
212-382-2273

Radio Information Center
675 Third Ave.
New York, NY 10017
212-818-9060

One last point about targeting customers: You need to have people call an 800 number and order a product. They can do that only if they have a credit card. Don't advertise on the radio to sell a product unless you expect your target listeners to have credit cards.

When to Run Ads

Most of the ads selling products that you hear are on nighttime talk shows. There are three reasons why nighttime ads are the most popular:

1. Talk shows require active listening. Many people use music stations for background noise, and so music stations don't work as well.

2. People are often home listening at night. If they like your ad, they can write the number down and call you. In the morning and afternoon, listeners are often in cars, where they can't always write your name down.

3. Nighttime ads are cheap. That means you can run your ad over and over again, giving you a better chance to motivate someone to call you.

I recommend that you start by advertising in the evenings on stations your target customers are likely to listen to. Commit to at least a two- to three-week ad program and see how well your product sells. You can always move to other times if the ads are successful.

Key Components of a Radio Ad

1. Your ad needs an opening that grabs people's attention immediately. This statement should tie into the customer goal you are targeting, not your product. For example: "Your car could be stolen tonight." "You can buy a new home for only $5 down." "How are you going to look in your swimming suit this summer?"

2. Use music and sound effects in your commercial. The music relaxes the listener, and sound effects can grab people's attention.

3. Repeat your telephone number at least three times.

4. Sell your product based on the customers' goals and the product's benefits.

5. Use thirty second commercials if possible. They are almost as effective as sixty-second spots, and you will be able to run more ads.

6. Have your ad sound a little different from the radio station's format. Some commercials blend right in with the station, so that people don't even know a commercial is on.

7. Offer a money-back guarantee.

Using Radio Representatives

Radio rates are typically highly negotiable. Once an ad time slot is gone, it is gone forever, and stations would rather receive some money than none at all. So you can negotiate with a station to get a first-time advertising discount or some other price break.

If you want to advertise nationally or if you haven't advertised before, you should consider contacting a radio representative firm. These companies sell radio time for a wide variety of stations that could be right for your product. This will save you having to search for the best station in every market. Radio reps can also help you find stations that will run an ad on a per inquiry basis, where you pay only for leads you actually get. I've listed one radio rep firm and the Radio Advertising Bureau, which can help you find others:

Katz Communications
125 West 55th St.
New York, NY 10019
212-424-6000

Radio Advertising Bureau
304 Park Ave. S.
New York, NY 10010
212-254-4800

TV Ads

Many products are sold directly to consumers through TV ads. Food processors, cosmetic formulas, exercise equipment, and videotapes are just a few of the products sold on TV. Some of these products are sold through one- and two-minute commercials, some are sold on home shopping networks such as QVC, and others are sold through thirty-minute infomercials.

TV lets marketers use a tactic they can't use anywhere else: a demonstration. Showing how a product works and what it does is an effective way to motivate people to buy. TV ads also have an instant element to them. People see the ad, then call up and order. They can't wait, or the ad will be gone. Magazines don't have that "right now" quality. People can put the magazine on the table and "order later."

TV advertising does have drawbacks. One is that people are skeptical of a product they can't touch and feel. On a couple of talk shows recently, people talked about the worst TV product they ever bought. That's bad publicity. Another drawback is the cost of TV advertising. You have to be prepared to spend several thousand dollars for a good ad, and up to $25,000 for an infomercial.

TV Shopping Networks

One TV avenue open to every company is QVC and Home Shopping Network. Before you decide to use one of these channels, watch them to see the types of products they sell and the way they sell them. In general, the products they sell are unusual, and they spend five to ten minutes explaining how each product works. They prefer products for which they can do a snappy demonstration. Both companies will take a look at products from virtually anyone. Their addresses are:

QVC Network Inc.   Home Shopping Network
Goshen Corporate   Park P.O. Box 9090
West Chester, PA 19380   Clearwater, FL 34618

What Type of Products

Products that can make money with TV ads should have a built-in demand, be unique, be hard to buy elsewhere, demonstrate well, and sell for over $20.

Built-in demand

Products for losing weight have a big built-in demand. Everyone wants to be thin. Diet drink formulas, exercise machines, and fitness videos can be sold on TV because of this demand. Time-Life books, music videos, kitchen products, and entrepreneur courses are other products in which most people have an interest.

Some products are sold on TV shows directed at their target audience. Gardening, fishing, and home repair shows all have sponsors that promote and sell related equipment.

Unique

One of TV's advantages is that people have to purchase right now. That advantage does not count unless the product is available only on TV. If people can buy the product in a store, they will procrastinate, and you will lose a percentage of your sales.

Demonstrations

A product that demonstrates well can take advantage of the TV medium. Examples are food processors, exercise videos, and fishing tackle.

Key Components of a TV Ad

1. Run one- or two-minute ads. You need to ask people to order three or four times, and your ad needs to be long enough to do this.

2. Have an action-oriented ad. Have people moving around, doing something with your product.

3. Demonstrate the product—not only what it does, but what the result is.

4. Use testimonials. Have current users give short quotes praising the product.

5. Repeat your 800 number throughout the ad. Also superimpose the 800 number on the screen.

6. Have a strong opening. Base the lead-in on what your product accomplishes. For example, ads for exercise videos start with a picture of trim, athletic-looking men and women.

Buying TV Time

You can buy ads directly from TV stations, but you will often end up paying more than you have to. You can also buy TV time through companies that help you get the best buy. You can find help by looking in the Yellow Pages under the categories: Media Buyers, Television Station Representatives, or Television

Show Producers. You can also find ads for companies that can help in *Advertising Age* and *Adweek*. Larger libraries will carry current issues of both magazines. If you just want to test an ad, you can call up a local cable company and work out a deal. Cable companies will typically go out of their way to help out a new advertiser. You might even be able to pay on a per inquiry basis rather than paying a flat fee.

MAGAZINE ADS

The big advantage of a magazine ad is that you can aim precisely at your target customer. You can advertise in a consumer or trade magazine where most of the readers are potential buyers of your product. Another advantage is the staying power of magazines. People may cut an ad out and order the product months after the ad first appeared. The disadvantages of magazine ads are that they don't have urgency, they don't have the persuasive power of radio or TV ads, and they can be quite expensive.

Where to Advertise

To find magazines you can advertise in, go to the library and look in *Gale's Source of Publications* for magazines that would appeal to your target audience. This book lists magazines by state and by interest area. Once you get a list of magazines, get the *Standard Rate and Data Service* directory, which lists the cost of ads in each magazine. Start with a smaller magazine or buy space on a small regional basis (for example, *TV Guide* will let you buy ad space limited to a metropolitan area) until you can be sure the ad will sell your product.

What Kind of Products

Radio and TV ads work best for products with broad appeal. Magazine ads work best for products that solve specific problems. For example, one company sold a pattern viewfinder for a shotgun. A magazine ad doesn't persuade people to buy, so the product has to do that on its own. Again, your product should sell for at least $15 to $25 in order to recoup your costs. You can sell products that are as expensive as $500 to $1,000. The only time you can sell a product for less than $15 is if you are selling the product to get the names of prospects.

Key Components of a Magazine Ad

1. Don't be too cute. Sell your product in clear terms. Your headline and visual should make it clear what the product is. People have to recognize the problem your product will solve before they will buy it.
2. List an 800 number to call. It adds urgency that will increase sales.
3. Use testimonials and other proof statements.
4. Offer a thirty-day money back guarantee.
5. Try out quarter- to half-page ads, as they will often draw as many responses as a full-page ad.
6. Show the problems you are solving rather than the product's features. Statements that start with the word "eliminates" are often effective.

Saving Money

Magazine ads can be expensive, but, as with most ad costs, you can usually negotiate a lower price. You can save money if you buy leftover (also called remnant) space. If a magazine costs too much and won't give you a discount, ask the advertising representative to call if he or she can ever offer you remnant space.

CARD PACK ADVERTISING

There are more than 700 card packs now being distributed throughout the country. These packs advertise a wide variety of products and services and provide a viable way for companies to sell products. The most common card pack order tactic is to offer a fifteen-day free trial. Customers have fifteen days to either return the product or pay for it.

A card pack has the advantage of having a very low cost per respondent, usually only 1.5 to 2.5 cents. Another advantage is that card packs usually generate a fast response. You'll have 80 percent of your responses within three weeks.

Types of Products that Sell

There is very little room on a postcard, so you can't really persuade people to buy your product. You need to have a product people can understand, a product that is priced below the competition, or a product with a special feature that cannot be purchased anywhere else. For example, we recently bought mailing labels from a card pack ad. The labels' price was about 50 percent lower than what we had been paying. What caught our attention was the low price. Other products sold through card packs directed at small- to medium-size companies include office supplies, convention displays, printing for color catalogs, posters, and advertising specialties.

Targeting Customers

Card packs are effective only if they go to your targeted customer group. Your public library may carry the *SRDS Card Pack Rates and Data Directory*, which lists more than 650 card packs and their advertising rates. If you look through this directory, you should be able to find several card packs that will work for you.

Key Components of a Card Pack Ad

1. Lay out the card horizontally so that its format is the same as that of the other cards.

2. Always use at least two-color ads, and consider three-color. Additional colors will add to you response rate without costing much more money.

3. Your headline is all important. Spend extra time on it to be sure it connects with customers.

4. Include an 800 number for people to call.

5. Offer a free trial. You will probably not be paid for 10 to 20 percent of the orders, but you will double or triple your response rate.

ACTION STEPS

1. This is the one chapter where I don't want you to start a program this week. You need to be careful when choosing radio, TV, and magazine advertising for products. Instead, start collecting print ads and taping TV and radio ads for products similar to yours that advertise repeatedly.

2. Start collecting the names of magazines, radio stations, and TV shows that might be ideal advertising vehicles for you. Consider advertising if one of them offers you a deeply discounted rate.

3. Card pack ads are easy to prepare, and they can be effective and inexpensive. Check whether any of the various card packs in your market are aimed at your target customers. If one of them is, either ask for remnant space or ask to place your card in the pack on a per response advertising basis, where you pay only for the responses you get.

Chapter 24

Writing a Marketing Plan

I recommend that you sit down and write a marketing plan at least once a year. Writing a plan helps you in four ways:

1. It forces you to sit down and evaluate your business. You need to take the time out to check on how well your business is doing and whether you are missing any significant trends.

2. It gives you a marketing action plan that you can share with employees and investors so that everyone knows what you are trying to accomplish.

3. It provides you with a timetable that you can follow throughout the year. This timetable will keep you on schedule and provide a detailed listing of your expected expenses throughout the year. It tells you, in advance, how much money you will need to spend. You may have to adjust your marketing plan several times to bring your expenses in line with the money you have available.

4. It allows someone else to come in and take over the marketing activities. A marketing plan will let a new person come in, understand what you are trying to accomplish, and implement the tactics in the timetable.

The marketing plan has two contradictory objectives. First, it has to be brief enough to be quickly and easily read by people who just want to know the essence of your marketing activities. Second, it needs to be specific, with an action timetable. To meet both objectives, the marketing plan should begin with a brief overview of the rationale behind the strategy and conclude with a detailed timetable.

When you are working on a marketing plan, remember that there are dozens of potentially successful strategies for any business. Don't spend months trying to find the one perfect strategy. You are better off moving into action with tactics that will help your business than you are continually reworking your plan until you feel it's perfect.

Your first consideration in a marketing plan is consistency. You want this year's plan to fit in with successful programs of the past. Customers relate to a consistent marketing program. Don't be afraid to change your program if it's not working, but don't change it unless you need to.

MARKETING PLAN FORMAT

Objectives

Sales dollars	_____
Gross profit dollars	_____
Gross margin percent	_____
Net profit dollars	_____
Dollar market share	_____

The opening section gives a capsule view of the product's sales objectives and profit position. Here is a brief description of each item:

- *Sales dollars.* This is your expected sales for the next year.

- *Gross profit dollars.* This is total sales dollars less the cost to buy or produce the product. This money is what you use to pay marketing, overhead, and administrative expenses.

- *Gross margin percent.* This percentage is calculated by dividing the gross profit dollars by the sales dollars. In most industries there is a typical gross margin percent. This percentage is different for different industries. For example, pharmaceutical companies' gross margin is usually 60 to 80 percent, whereas the figure for heavy equipment manufacturers is 40 to 45 percent. Listing this figure here helps you see how your profitability compares to the industry average.

- *Net profit dollars.* This is your gross profit dollars less marketing, sales, administrative, and overhead expenses.

- *Dollar market share.* This tells the reader how important you are in your relevant market. For example, if you sell clothes to teenage girls in a mall, your market share might be based on similar stores within a one-mile radius. If you are a manufacturer of clothes for teenagers, your dollar market share would be based on clothes sold through specialty mall retailers.

Sales History

	Last Three Years			Next Two Years	
Total market size ($)	____	____	____	____	____
Your dollar size	____	____	____	____	____
Dollar market share	____	____	____	____	____

The last three years should be your actual sales history. The next two years are your estimates of what sales will be.

If you don't have a sales history, this section should explain how you predicted your first-year sales. For example, my wife and I liked the educational toys in a Philadelphia toy store and considered opening a similar store in Minneapolis.

We found out the Philadelphia store's sales volume and the number of mall visitors per day. Then we found a similar mall in Minneapolis with the same number of visitors. But the sales per square foot in the Minneapolis mall were 25 percent less than those in the Philadelphia mall. Therefore, I projected sales at 75 percent of the Philadelphia store's volume.

You can estimate sales volume even if you don't have a similar store or business to compare to. I once worked on the introduction of a unique piece of electronic assembly equipment. Here are some of the steps I took to determine the first year's sales volume.

1. To estimate the market size, I talked to industry sources and checked magazine articles to determine the number of manufacturers that could use our equipment. There were 3,000 potential customers, and each could buy two to five units, for an estimated market size of 7,000 units.

2. I determined that over the past three years, about 950 units of the equipment we hoped to replace had been sold, 400 of them in the last year. The sales projection for the next year was 700 units. I obtained these estimates from manufacturers' representatives and a trade association article distributed at a trade show.

3. I examined first-year sales of other equipment products that had been introduced to our potential customers. Successful new products usually sold between 200 and 400 units.

4. I talked to about fifteen potential customers and found that a third of them would prefer our equipment to the existing product.

My final sales projection was 200 to 225 units, based on 700 potential units times 35 percent. This number was also consistent with past introductions of new products.

Market Share Trends

	Last Three Years			Next Two Years	
Your market share	___	___	___	___	___
First major competitor	___	___	___	___	___
Second major competitor	___	___	___	___	___
Third major competitor	___	___	___	___	___
Others	___	___	___	___	___

The value of market share trends is that they indicate how you are doing compared to your competitors. They also show whether any of your competitors are increasing their share rapidly. You don't want one competitor to jump ahead of everyone else, as that company's momentum will soon hurt your sales.

Commentary

This section should give an overview of the events of the last year or two that have led to your current market position. List major events, trends, and competitive developments that either have happened or are expected to happen.

Competition

This section should list your major competitors and their current position as you see it, including any significant strengths and weaknesses.

Your competitors aren't necessarily all businesses just like yours. They can also be stores or products offering a similar benefit or service. For example, if you have an athletic shoe store in a mall, a sporting goods store that also sells shoes could be a competitor. If you sell a word processing typewriter, you might want to consider a low-cost computer with word processing capabilities as a competitor.

Price Comparison/Price Value

This section includes a chart comparing your and your competitors' prices. After you list the prices, you may want to note any significant features that explain the price differences; for example, one color TV doesn't have remote control, which would explain its lower price. Also list subjective features, such as product quality, if they are areas of significant difference among competitors.

Problems/Opportunities

This section should contain a brief description of any problems or opportunities, either short-term or long-term, that are facing your business.

Major Marketing Thrusts

I prefer to use the word "thrust" rather than "effort" or "strategy" because it is an action word that implies that you are going to get the job done. Among the dictionary definitions of thrust are "to push or drive with force," and "to put forcibly into a course of action." That's exactly what I want you to do.

There are three major types of marketing thrusts. The first is a thrust designed to make you better than anyone else by creating a sustainable advantage. You might be targeting a new customer, repositioning your product so that it meets the needs of a specific application, or adding and changing product features to meet the needs of a certain customer segment. You might also decide to pursue a new market channel, or to add new services to help your distribution networks. For this type of thrust, you want to state the change you are making and the tactics you are going to use to make that change.

For example, you might decide to reposition your product so that it will be used for a new application. Your tactics might include changing your name, creating a new slogan, printing new fliers and brochures, attending certain trade shows, joining key industry groups, starting an advisory council, and running three events cosponsored by a community group. You want to state your message and the strategy you are pursuing, then explain in detail how you are going to implement that strategy.

You also want to make sure to explain how your efforts to create a sustainable advantage are going to solve your competitive problems. For instance, suppose one of your problems is that your prices are considered too high given the customers' perception of the value of your product. If your marketing thrust is to specialize in one application, explain why that thrust will improve your perceived price/value relationship.

The second type of thrust involves the way you find or communicate with customers. You might be adding a computer bulletin board, starting an active network and referral program, or putting in place a publicity strategy. Again, you want to list the major actions you are going to be taking, then explain the tactics you will use to implement your strategy.

The third type of thrust is in your sales strategy, whether it be adding distributors, starting to sell through direct mail, instituting a new sales training policy, providing more sales back-up materials, or implementing a co-op advertising program. Again, you want to list what you are going to do and what tactics you will use.

Minor Thrusts

You cannot have more than two or three major thrusts in any given year. If you do, you will never be able to implement them. If some of your thrusts are not major, such as providing retail displays, list them here rather than in the "Major Thrust" section.

Positioning Statements

A positioning statement indicates who your customer is, what your product is, and why people should buy from you. For instance, some sample positioning statements are: "ABC Office Supplies carries every office supply a doctor's office will ever need"; "The Record Revolution is a low-priced neighborhood record store that caters to teenagers"; or "Jaguar sells high-income professionals the world's most elegant family sedan."

A positioning statement is not a marketing slogan. A marketing slogan conveys a message to a customer, whereas a positioning statement is for internal company use. It makes clear to every employee what the company is trying to accomplish. It is listed in the marketing plan because you want to be sure your plan supports the positioning statement.

Tactics

List in detail all the tactics you plan to implement in the next year. You may have already prepared a detailed analysis for some of the tactics. If that is the case, give a brief description of the tactic in this section and include your analysis as an attachment.

Where Will the Business Come From?

This section justifies your sales projections. If your projections in the first section of the plan call for a 20 percent increase in sales, you should explain how your marketing thrust and tactics will generate that increase.

For example, a manufacturer of industrial cleaning equipment might project a 40 percent sales increase. The first marketing thrust calls for the manufacturer to specialize in cleaning equipment for chemical plants. The company is going to reconfigure two products and add one totally new product to better meet the needs of chemical plants. The company's other thrusts are to attend two trade shows, to participate in a seminar focusing on cleaning corrosion-resistant, glass-lined storage tanks, and to add two additional manufacturers' representatives. To achieve a 40 percent sales increase, the company would need to sell twenty-four new pieces of equipment. The manufacturer expects to get six new customers from each trade show, three from the seminar, and five from each new manufacturers' representative. These numbers are in line with sales picked up in the past from trade shows and new representatives. Does the 40 percent increase make sense? Yes, based on the company's past experience.

This is the one section of my marketing plan format that differs from most other published formats. I like it because it forces you to prove that your sales objectives are reasonable and obtainable. I have changed many plans because they don't pass the "where does the business come from" test.

Timetable

This section lists a timetable that you can refer to throughout the year. It also allows you to determine marketing costs on a monthly basis. Here is an easy-to-follow format:

	Action Items	Key Dates	Quantity	Costs	Person Responsible
1.	_____	_____	_____	_____	_____
2.	_____	_____	_____	_____	_____
3.	_____	_____	_____	_____	_____
4.	_____	_____	_____	_____	_____

The key dates are the months in which the program will be implemented. Some programs may have several key dates, such as an ad campaign that has to be introduced to key retailers a month before its general release. In that case list all the key dates in the timetable.

Marketing for the 1990s

GETTING READY FOR THE FUTURE

This book is a marketing survival guide for the 1990s. When I started to write this book, I had four objectives in mind:

1. To give a strategy, the six steps for marketing success, for you to follow.
2. To share with you the philosophy of relationship marketing, which will allow you to keep your customers for life.
3. To help you understand what customers will be like in the 1990s and what you will have to do to communicate with them.
4. To show you a wide variety of tactics you can use to implement these strategies.

Time-Life Books' marketing strategy is a good example of the marketing tactics you'll need in the 1990s. The company sells a large number of multivolume collections on topics such as the Old West, World War II, human behavior, and foods throughout the world.

Time-Life Books follows most of the key steps needed for 1990s marketing:

1. It has a clearly chosen target audience: people who like to read magazines like *Time* and *Life*.
2. It has the right product for its target group: easy-to-read, heavily illustrated, informative books.
3. It has one of the few series of books of its type.
4. It has a competitive edge from the large number of photos and stories printed over the years in *Time* and *Life* magazines.
5. It has an active program to find customers, using magazine and TV ads and direct mailings to *Time* subscribers.
6. It has a large number of products to sell prospects. Once it has a customer, it can keep contacting that customer to sell additional products.
7. It continues to contact past customers with offerings of new products.

You should now be prepared to go out and succeed the same way that Time-Life Books has. The first key step, as always, is to get started. Make a commitment to yourself that you are going to improve your marketing performance this year. Then decide what tactics you are going to use, and start using them. The only thing that can keep you from success is a lack of desire and effort on your part. I'm sure that's not the case with you, or you wouldn't be reading this book. Good luck, and I hope you succeed beyond your wildest dreams.

Appendix A

The Marketing File Drawer

This appendix lists some of the key sections on your marketing efforts that you should keep. They will give you an easy-to-refer-to source that you can use when you develop a project. These files have been referred to throughout the book, but this appendix lists them all in one place.

THE KEY SECTIONS

These sections provide the key marketing information—such as your target customer, your identity, and your marketing thrust—that you will need before you start any program.

1. Customer Needs/Possible Strategies

   This chart has four headings: Customer Needs (pp. 65–68 and 71–72), Possible Product Strategies (pp. 75–84), Specialization (p. 87), and Specialization Present Now (p. 90). Figure 6.1 gives an example of the first two headings. This chart helps you look for openings where you can redirect your efforts.

2. Proprietary Features (pp. 84–86)

   First, list on this chart any proprietary features you have, such as patents, trademarks, proprietary manufacturing processes, or copyrights. Second, list product aspects that you could turn into proprietary features.

3. Distribution Channel Options (pp. 43–44)

   This chart should list all the distribution channels you could use to market your product, including location, distribution support, and any other distribution method that sets your product apart.

4. Distribution and Sales Strategy (pp. 93–98, 101)

   This chart should list the various distribution and sales strategies you are planning to implement over the next twelve to fifteen months.

5. Marketing Strategy Thrust (p. 109)

   Also see Figure 15.1.

6. Marketing Strategy Budget (pp. 107–108)

7. Guidelines for Finding Customers (pp. 118–119)

8. Company Identity Statement (p. 156)

   Also see sample statements in Figures 13.1 and 13.2.

9. Promotion Schedule (p. 184–194)

   This is your schedule of events for the next year.

10. Communication Strategy (p. 210)

   See Figure 18.1. This gives you a week-by-week strategy for following up on sales, sending out prospect mailings, and communicating with customers. Also see Figure 19.4.

11. Event Communication Schedule (Figure 18.2, p. 211)

   This is a schedule of mailings prior to events.

12. Communication Worksheet (p. 215)

13. Mailing List Checklist (p. 215)

   This item and the preceding one are forms that you should use prior to every mailing.

14. Customer Confidence Chart (Figure 14.1, p. 167)

15. Six Guidelines for Effective Ads (p. 175)

   Put these six guidelines on a chart and refer to it every time you do a communication piece.

THE MARKETING FILES

Customer Files

Customer Segmentation: Different Ways to Find Target Customer Groups
- Articles
- Suggestions or comments from customers
- Your comments

What Do Customers Want?
- Relationships, features, services
- Why do they buy?
- Buying modes

Possible Strategies
- Articles
- Suggestions
- Your comments

Product Files

Possible Product Features
- Product features
    - Articles
    - Suggestions
    - Competitor's features

- Product support
  - Articles
  - Suggestions
  - Competitors' tactics
- Service options
  - Articles
  - Suggestions
  - Competitors' tactics

Pricing

- Competitors' prices for various features
- Demand-based pricing for various market options. Use product directories or trade magazine buying guides for pricing information (p. 45)
- Cost-based pricing for features. Calculate a feature's cost, then multiply it by your standard industry markup (p. 143)

Product Questionnaires

- Questionnaires you have used in the past. Never throw them out. You can get key information years after a questionnaire was taken
- Competitors' questionnaires, samples, or articles

Proprietary Features

- Your features
- Competitors' features
- Articles

Lead Product Strategies

- Your lead product
- Competitive products
- Articles

Distribution Files

Possible Strategies

- Your strategies (pp. 93–96)
- Articles
- Competitive moves, plus comments from advisory boards

Locking Up Distribution

- All possible tactics listed in Chapter 7
- Articles on implementation
- Key contacts for locking up a channel

- Important companies to contact
- Other companies, suppliers, and vendors you can partner up with

Finding Customers

Networking Files

- Key names in the industry
- Key vendor or customer names
- Key names at other companies you could work with
- Key contacts that could help you later

Getting Customers' Names

- Successful past programs
- Programs you have seen used by other companies
- Suggestions or comments from salespeople and customers
- Articles and other information

Referrals

- Names
- Successful programs
- Articles and competitive programs
- Suggestions and comments

Classes

- Potential topics
- Places to teach
- Sample programs and class guidelines

Classified Advertising

- Samples of effective ads
- Samples of past ads
- Magazines and newspapers where ads could be run
- Products with potential as classified ad products

Publicity File

- Your past publicity
- Competitors' past publicity
- Ideas for future programs
- Articles
- Organizations and businesses that might run joint promotions
- Magazines and newspapers to which mailings should be sent

• Key editor names for follow-up phone contacts

Card Pack File
• Names of appropriate card pack vendors
• Samples of ads that you think are effective
• Past ads that you have run, plus a short report on how effective each ad was

Yellow Pages and Directory Ads
• Past ads and competitors' ads
• Effective ads of other companies
• List of key directories, along with yearly deadlines for placing ads

Trade Shows
• Potential shows, along with rates and past years' programs
• Photos of other booths at shows you may attend
• Interviews with attendees from other companies
• Any data about sales from the convention that you are able to obtain

Seminars
• Topics
• Seminar locations
• Seminars by other companies

Newspaper and Magazine Ads
• Magazines or newspapers in which your ads could run effectively
• Samples of effective ads
• Results of past ads, including your original objectives

Direct Mail
• List of companies that furnish mailing lists
• Other companies or organizations that will do joint mailings or trade mailing lists
• Other sources of qualified lists
• Samples of effective pieces by other companies

Electronic Communications
• Names of computer users and clubs that are familiar with the process of setting up a bulletin board
• Articles, stores, and other information
• Product information regarding available database programs

- Names of companies you can use to exchange electronic mail and to access databases
- Companies through which you can set up a database

Radio Publicity

- List of radio and TV show contacts
- Tapes of past publicity/tapes of competitive publicity
- Ideas for "publicity-worthy" events from articles and magazines
- Magazines, such as the *Radio and TV Interview Report*, where you can advertise to key people

Identity, Layout, and Copy

Identity

- Potential names
- Potential slogans
- Possible logos, along with people's reactions
- Visuals that convey the product's benefits

Brochures

- Past brochures
- Competitors' brochures
- Articles
- Story lines
- Power phrases
- Customer "hot buttons"
- Photo files
- Ratings of past ads and brochures (each page rated for clarity, impact, visual appeal, and relatedness)

Print Ads

- Past ads, including ratings for clarity, impact, visual appeal, and relatedness
- Competitors' ads
- Ads you find particularly effective
- Ads with color appeal, or where key elements are separated well by outlines, boxes, or some other visual device

Newsletters

- A "next newsletter" file containing letters from customers, short publicity stories, and any recent photos
- Potential names, headlines, and slogans

- Articles that you could reprint in your newsletter
- Names of syndicates from which you can buy articles of humorous pieces
- Samples of newsletters you like

Promotions

Events

- Past events, including results
- Potential events
- Other companies or groups that might cosponsor events
- Articles on potential events, including articles on other companies' activities, comments, and suggestions
- Possible speakers or presenters
- List of items you could use for giveaways

Contests/Sweepstakes

- Articles
- Past contests, with results
- Competitors' programs
- Brochures, etc. from awards companies and sweepstakes promoters

Giveaways (Premiums and Specialty Items)

- Past programs, with results
- Competitors' programs
- Articles
- Brochures, comments, and suggestions

Sales Collateral Material

- Articles on new, upcoming materials
- Articles on how to use videotapes
- Information on doing your own video editing
- Past materials
- Competitors' programs
- Suggestions for new materials

Displays/Demonstrations

- Past programs
- Competitors' programs
- Other programs you have liked
- Brochures from suppliers
- List of customers or vendors that have requested displays in the past

Advisory Board
- Possible members
- Results of past meetings
- Topics to discuss
- Promotions and company strategy to discuss
- Incentive ideas
- Articles, information, comments, and suggestions

Database Marketing
- Articles on database use at other companies
- Brochures, etc. on companies supplying database software
- Lists of people who can modify the database program
- Letters, articles, and fliers that you send out to prospects and customers
- Results of past database mailings
- Database and event communication strategy (see pp. 210 and 211).

Sales Strategies
Mistakes to Avoid
- Your mistakes
- Competitors' mistakes
- Advisory board comments
- Customer input

Sales Representative Promotion Guidelines
- Written policy, past communications
- Articles, reports on past programs, or analysis of competitors' sales promotion strategy
- Training programs
- Tests
- Past results
- Articles, etc.
- Improvement suggestions
- Exit interviews

Catalogs
- Samples of catalogs from other companies
- Past catalogs of yours
- Unique products that would work in a catalog
- Low-cost printing sources

- Ads that generate requests for catalogs
- Samples of past ads
- Mailing list sources for catalogs, including lists of magazine subscribers, mailing list compilers, other companies, and trade show attendees

Telephone Sales
- Call records for each salesperson (see p. 221)
- Articles
- Strategies for both you and your major competitors
- Phone strategy on outgoing calls, when to call, etc.
- Written company policy for handling incoming calls
- Monitoring system, and results, for incoming calls
- Articles
- Past efforts, with results

Appendix B

Glossary

Ad-slick. Camera-ready art for a magazine or newspaper ad. Once you have had a slick prepared by a printer, you can reuse it. Sometimes a magazine will prepare an ad slick for you; if so, you should get a copy for future use.

Advertising Allowance. The amount of money a manufacturer will give a retailer towards the cost of advertising its products. An advertising allowance differs from a co-op advertising program in that a co-op program will only pay up to 50 percent of an ad's cost, whereas an allowance may cover most or all of it.

Advertising Rates. Published costs for an ad or card pack.

Aftermarketing. The efforts you make after a sale is complete to retain customers.

Aftermarket Products. The additional products you sell after the main product is sold. Auto parts stores sell many aftermarket products.

Afternoon-drive. For radio, the time from about 3:00 p.m. to 7:00 p.m., when people listen to the radio while driving home.

Agency Commission. The 15 percent discount from the price of ads they place that advertising agencies receive from radio, and TV stations. If you place an ad for $10,000 through an agency, the agency receives a $1,500 discount, which in whole or part covers the agency's expenses.

Aisle Advertising. In-store advertising displays, such as point-of-purchase displays, end-aisle displays, island or free-standing displays, or shelf displays.

Assortment. A retailing term relating to the number of products sold.

Audience Profile. Data regarding a magazine, radio station, or TV station's audience, including characteristics such as age, income, interests, and so on. You should insist on seeing this data to be sure your advertising is going to magazines or stations that your target customer reads or watches.

Back Cover. The back page of a magazine. This is considered the best ad spot because half of the time it will be facing up.

Backdoor Selling. Calling on engineers or quality control technicians rather than purchasing agents in order to sell products.

Base Rate. The magazine, radio or TV station, or newspaper ad rate for a one-time user.

Benefit Segmentation. Differentiation of customer groups on the basis of what benefits they want from a particular product.

Bill Insert. A little flier for a new product that comes with monthly bill statements.

Bingo Card. A card with a number for each ad that is inserted in trade publications. Readers can circle as many numbers as they wish, and the material offered in those ads will be sent to them. All your ads and publicity releases should be published with a bingo number if the magazine offers this service.

Black-and-white. Black printing on white paper.

Blow-in. A technique used for inserting pieces or postcards into a magazine. They are blown in, and they fall out into your lap.

Body Copy. The main part of an ad or brochure's copy, as opposed to headlines, slogans, and captions.

Bonus Pack. A product package that contains two items, but the consumer only pays for one. An example might be a free razor blade with the purchase of a can of shaving cream.

Bounce-back Offer. A selling offer for the same product that was just purchased or for a related product. For example, you might get an offer for more envelopes with the purchase of five boxes, or you might be asked to order another product. Bounce-back cards are an effective tactic.

Box-top Offer. An offer of merchandise, either free or at a discount, if a consumer sends in the box top and a proof of purchase.

Brand. The combination of names, slogans, or words that differentiates a product from other similar products.

Broadcast Media. Radio, TV, cable TV, and satellite broadcasts. This term usually refers to TV and radio news reports or programs during which advertising appears.

Bulk Mail. Mail that is grouped by Zip codes and states and shipped at savings that start at 9 cents per piece. You need only 200 pieces to qualify, so bulk mail is a possibility for every company.

Burst Advertising. A tactic whereby large amounts of advertising are concentrated in a short time span. For instance, you might run in one week all the ads that you would usually run in one month.

Business Reply Card. Postal materials that can be mailed back to you at no charge to the sender (45 cents charge to you). These envelopes or postcards say "No postage necessary if mailed in the U.S."

Business-to-business. A term referring to companies whose customers are other companies rather than consumers.

Buyer's Market. A situation in which the supply of a product, from a variety of companies, is greater than the demand for that product.

Buying Committee. At a company, a group of people who are to jointly recommend and requisition a particular piece of equipment. At a distributor, a buying committee might select the products to be distributed.

Buying Signals. Verbal and nonverbal cues that show that a person is ready to buy. For example, questions regarding delivery or a positive, friendly manner are buying signals.

By-line. A name identifying the author of a publicity release or newspaper or magazine article.

Callbacks. A follow-up attempt to contact someone. If you tried to call someone and that person wasn't in, your next call would be considered a callback.

Camera-ready. A layout of an ad or brochure that is ready to print. When the ad or brochure is actually printed, a photograph is taken of the page; the photograph is then used in the printing process. This term simply means that the layout is ready to be shot by a stat camera.

Campaign. A series of ads or brochures with a common theme.

Caption. A word or phrase describing the action in a picture.

Cash Discount. A reward for prompt or immediate payment. For example, 2/10, n/30 means that the company will offer a 2 percent discount if payment is received within ten days, and that the full payment is due in thirty days.

Catalog. A book, often with large graphics and visuals, that details all of a company's products or services.

Celebrity Endorsement. Recommendation of a product by a celebrity. It can be a great sales tool.

Center Spread. An ad that covers the two facing center pages of a magazine or newspaper.

Chain Stores. Groups of stores or businesses that are very similar and spread across a large geographic area.

Channels of Distribution. Businesses that help a product get from the manufacturer or service provider to the consumer.

Cheshire Labels. Paper labels that have to be cut apart and affixed to packages. Avoid them at all costs. Buy pressure-sensitive labels no matter how much more they cost.

Circular. A one-page sheet with large visuals and headlines. Circulars can be hand-delivered, sent through the mail, put on cars, or put in with other mail, or a whole range of other delivery options can be used.

Circulation. The number of people that subscribe to a magazine.

Classified Advertising. Small (usually two- to five-line ads) that appear by category in the back of newspapers and magazines.

Clipping Service. A company that monitors newspapers and magazines for articles on certain types of products and events.

Closing. The end of a sales presentation where the salesperson asks for the order.

Closing Dates. Last dates for getting an ad into a magazine or newspaper. For example, all ads for the December issue must be in by October 20th.

COD. Abbreviation of Collect on Delivery.

Cold Call. Making a telephone or personal visit to someone you haven't met or contacted previously.

Collateral Materials. Sales brochures, kits, and other printed materials you can use with customers.

Color Separations. Color printing is actually done with four printing processes using the colors black, red, yellow, and blue. Each color is printed separately, and so each color needs its own plate. An expensive process.

Combination Rate. Some publishers have two magazines aimed at the same target audience, and may give you a combination rate if you run in both magazines.

Commission. An amount paid to a salesperson or an advertising agency. A 5 percent commission, means a salesperson gets 5 percent of the total amount of sales. Agencies typically get a 15 percent commission based on the amount of their billings, which is the total of the published rates of magazine space or radio and TV time where the product is advertised.

Competitive Bid. A situation in which a customer asks for bids or proposals from two or three companies.

Compiled List. A mailing list that has been gathered from a variety of sources, such as directories, telephone books, or membership lists.

Comp List. A list of people who get a free (comp as in complimentary) subscription or a free ticket to an event.

Computer Letter. A personalized letter laser-printed by a computer.

Consignment. A tactic whereby a retailer or wholesaler pays for a product only after selling it, rather than buying it and taking ownership of the goods.

Co-op Advertising. An arrangement whereby a manufacturer will pay up to 50 percent of the cost of a retailer's or wholesaler's ad. The amount of the manufacturer's commitment is usually limited to the size of its order; for example, there might be a 15 percent co-op advertising allowance for the first 15,000 units ordered.

Co-op Mailing. A direct mail tactic in which you combine forces with another company.

Copy. Words used in an ad or brochure.

Copyright. A legal procedure that stops other companies from using your layouts and copy in their ads. You can copyright any published piece for no charge simply by placing (1) the word "copyright," (2) the year, and (3) the name of the person or company holding the copyright—for example, Copyright ©1994, DSD Marketing. You should do this on every piece of literature.

Cost Per Thousand (CPM). An advertising measurement that lets you know how much it costs you to reach a certain size audience. For example, a magazine ad might cost $3,000 to reach 40,000 readers, for a cost per thousand of $75.

Cost-based Pricing. A pricing method in which a product's cost is increased by an average industry or company markup to determine the selling price.

Cross-selling. Trying to sell complementary products to a customer who has already purchased one product. The complementary products could be from the same company or from a different company.

Customer Profile. Listings of key customer aims, goals, or characteristics that will help you target customers and develop the best marketing programs to reach them.

Database. Focused information about a certain customer group or topic that is compiled for easy access.

Dealer. A retailer, or part of a distribution channel, that takes ownership of the product lines it handles.

Dealer Loader. A promotion program that encourages dealers to bring in a large stocking order. Discounts for packages, large volume discounts, and other such programs encourage stocking.

Demand-based Pricing. A pricing technique in which customers are charged what they think a product is worth—for example, if people think a product is worth $15, then that is what you should charge.

Density. A popular direct marketing term that indicates how many prospects there are in a certain mailing zone. High density indicates that a large percentage of the population are prospects.

Desktop Publishing. Using a computer to prepare a layout and typeset copy for newsletters, brochures, circulars, and other print media.

Differential Advantage. A situation in which one unique aspect of a company's business makes that company better than anyone else.

Dimension Marketing. A direct marketing term that means that the product doesn't lie flat, but instead has some height, or dimension, to it.

Direct Distribution Channels. Distribution that goes from the manufacturer to the consumer without any intermediaries such as distributors or retailers.

Direct Marketing. Manufacturers taking their message directly to customers through mail or the phone.

Direct Selling. A sales approach typically associated with salespeople calling on people in their homes.

Display Ads. Ads that are dispersed throughout magazines or newspapers (as opposed to classified advertising).

Distributor. A company that serves as a redistribution source, providing its customers with products from several manufacturers. It takes ownership of products, and adds value by packaging together products that stores and consumers want.

Door-opener. Anything that will stop customers and get them to pay attention to what you say.

Drop Date. The date on which a promotion is given to the mail system. You should track your response rates versus the drop date to see how the promotion is doing.

Drop Shipment. A method of distribution in which the retailer or distributor never touches the product. For example, when you buy a new bike from a retailer, it might be drop-shipped directly to you from the manufacturer.

Economy Pack. A sales promotion technique in which several items are packed together in order to cut costs.

Editorial Calendar. For a magazine, calendar of stories to be featured each month. Marketers can advertise in issues that are of particular interest to their customers.

Electronic Mail. Messages exchanged between people on a computer network.

Endorsements. Advertising in which well-known people praise the product.

Events Marketing. Using major events as a sales and publicity tool.

Exclusive Agreements. Agreements with other companies that preclude you from making the same type of arrangement with another firm.

Exposure. The number of times a prospect will see or hear a marketing message.

Fact Sheet. A one- or two-page informational document that is included in publicity and sales kits.

Family Brand. A brand name that applies to a whole line of products. For example, Campbell is used for soup, baked beans, and a host of other products.

Flat-rate Pricing. A pricing tactic in which every customer is charged the same price, no matter what the buyer's volume.

Flier. A one-page promotional piece, generally on 8½-by-11-inch paper. It is generally cheaper to produce and of lower quality than a brochure.

Focus Group. A group of people from a targeted customer group who are brought together to consider one or two aspects of a business or product. There are usually six to twelve people in the group.

Format. The content of a radio station's programming, such as country and western.

Four-color Printing. A process that uses four colors to reproduce all the colors in any photograph or graphic illustration.

Freelancer. A person who is hired on a per-job basis. This arrangement is especially popular among advertising artists, graphics designers, and photographers.

Free-on-board (FOB). The point from which buyers will be responsible for freight. FOB St. Paul means that buyers will pay the charges from St. Paul to the customer's destination.

Frequency. The number of times an ad is heard on a radio or TV station. It can be given as times per hour or times per day.

Fulfillment. The process of taking orders, approving credit cards, shipping, and other billing procedures. The physical act of taking and shipping an order.

Galley Proofs. The first copy of printed material, not made up into pages. They are used for proofreading before the final pages are made up.

Generation. Indicates how far a product is from its master, or original copy. An audio tape made from a master is first generation. Tapes made from first-generation tapes would become second generation, and so on.

Generic Products. Product names that don't refer to a specific brand, such as Folger's coffee, but instead just give the product description, such as automatic drip coffee.

Graphic Design. Creating the visual look, or element, of a printed communication.

Green Marketing. Capitalizing on consumer interest in recycled products.

Gross Profit. Net sales less cost of goods sold, which is the cost of manufacturing a product.

Growth Strategy. A strategy that sacrifices short-term profits for market share growth.

Halftones. Printed reproductions of black-and-white photographs. This process gives the best reproduction for black-and-white ads. A black-and-white photograph is shot through a screen and the result is used for printing.

Handling Allowance. An incentive to retailers and distributors to handle promotions or contests.

Hard Goods. Hard products that last a long time, such as refrigerators or TVs; also called durable goods.

Heavy Users. People who buy a great deal of a product.

Hit List. A salesperson's list of people that should buy soon.

House List. A list of customers and prospects that have contacted the company. This is the best mailing list any firm can have.

Illustrations. The visual element of print materials. Could be artwork, photographs, cartoons, or diagrams.

Image. Consumers' perception of a company, individual, product, or service.

Image Advertising. Ads that try to create an image, rather than trying to sell a product based on features and benefits.

Implied Warranty. An unspoken promise to customers regarding a product's performance and what customer remedies are available.

Impulse Buy. A spur-of-the-moment purchase created by product packaging or a floor or aisle display.

Inbound Telemarketing. Salespeople and telemarketers that handle incoming calls on 800 numbers.

Indicia. The graphic in the top right-hand corner of an envelope that indicates that postage has been paid.

Industrial Products. Products that are sold to companies that make other products.

Infomercial. A thirty- to sixty-minute paid advertisement that explains the benefits of a product in a TV-show format.

In-pack Advertising. Materials placed into product packages.

Inquiry. A consumer's request for information.

Insertion Order. An order for print advertisements.

Interactive Television. A system that allows consumers to receive manufacturers' information at home on their TV screen.

Jingle. A song created for a TV or radio commercial.

Jobber. A small-scale wholesaler.

Joint Venturing. Two companies combining forces to exploit a marketing opportunity.

Justification. A typesetting term meaning to make the right side of a page flush, at a certain margin.

Keyline. For print advertising, an outline drawing that shows the exact size of the type, artwork, and layout.

Layout. A rough design of a brochure, ad, or other printed material that shows where visuals, headlines, and copy will go.

Lead Generation. A company's program for finding new prospects either for or by the sales force.

Logo. A design, or series of words, that identifies a product or organization.

Make-good. Occasionally an ad will have a mistake, or it will be run in the wrong section. Then you'll receive another ad free.

Mall Intercept Interview. A technique in which researchers stop people in a mall and ask them questions regarding a product.

Manufacturer's Brand. Products with a manufacturer's name on them, such as Whirlpool, as opposed to store brands, such as Sears.

Manufacturers' Representative (or Agent). Carries products for several manufacturers, typically five to twelve, that he or she sells to a limited geographic area.

Margin. The percentage of profit as compared to costs. For example, if you make $35 of profit on a $100 sale, your margin is $35/$100, or 35 percent.

Markdown. A reduction in selling price.

Market Demand. The amount of products that a targeted group of customers will buy within a certain time frame.

Market Development. Opening up, usually through a distribution plan, new markets, either by geography or by application.

Marketing. Any activity a company undertakes to create strong links between itself and its prospects and customers.

Marketing Budget. The amount of money the company has allocated for marketing expenses.

Marketing Channels. The wholesalers, distributors, or retailers you might work with to take your product to the market. The difference between marketing channels and distribution channels is that a marketing channel always involves outside companies.

Marketing Communications Mix. The different ways you take your message to customers. It could include trade shows, brochures, fliers, radio ads, TV ads, publicity, and so on. How your marketing money is allocated would determine your communications mix.

Marketing Information System. All the various reports the marketing department will receive to monitor sales and marketing performance. It can be a set of five manual reports, or a list of 250 computer-generated reports.

Marketing Mix. The four variables that marketers are supposed to take care of: price, promotion, place (more commonly called distribution), and product. The term represents an old-fashioned view of the marketing process.

Marketing Myopia. A common marketing phenomenon whereby marketers look at what a product can do, not at what customers want.

Market Niche. A narrow market segment that a company targets because it has clearly identified needs and is free of competition.

Market Orientation. The process companies use when they look at customer needs as a starting point to create new product ideas.

Market Profile. A method of breaking a market down so that it is easier to understand and attack. For each major customer segment, it usually will give the percentage of sales, expected growth, key customer needs, key suppliers, important unmet needs, and developing trends.

Market Segmentation. A strategy of separating markets by some aspect or characteristic, such as application, behavior, psychology, or benefit.

Market Share. Your sales divided by the total market size. For example, if your sales were $10 million and the market size was $100 million, you would have a 10 percent market share.

Markup Pricing. The common retail tactic of setting a product's retail price based on a wholesale price and a predetermined markup. For example, with a 50 percent markup, a store would price an item with a wholesale price of $1 at $1.50.

Mass Marketing. Trying to sell a product to everyone in a market, as opposed to niche marketing.

Mass Media. Radio, TV, and magazines that reach a broad spectrum of potential customers.

Media. A catch-all phrase for methods for disseminating information. The term "print media" and "broadcast media" are also used. Note: Media implies impartiality.

Media Kit. A kit a magazine or newspaper puts together for potential advertisers, as opposed to a press kit, which is a kit people and companies put together for the media.

Media Relations. Keeping up good working relationships with the press both to get stories published and to have a chance to comment on negative articles; a new requirement for marketing departments.

Merchandising. How visible or attractive products in a store look. A store that does a good job of merchandising has products displayed well.

Morning Drive. The rush hour traffic time from 6:00 a.m. to 11:00 a.m., when radio stations have the largest audience.

Multimedia. Presentations or ad campaigns that use print, radio, TV, and other media.

Narrowcasting. Hitting a small, narrowly defined customer group by advertising on specialized radio or TV shows.

National Accounts. Common term in industrial companies for large companies with facilities across the country. Rather than having many different salespeople calling on the same company, one salesperson from headquarters will call on all locations.

National Brand. A brand sold nationally, as opposed to a regional brand.

Neck Hanger. A tag hung around a bottle's neck with a coupon offer of some kind. This is a common tactic with one-gallon soda containers.

Net Profit. The amount of money left over after all expenses are deducted from total revenues.

Network. A group of radio or TV stations that are affiliated and that broadcast the same programs.

News Conference. A publicity event where the news media are invited to attend an announcement of some type.

News Release. A short informational clip sent to newspapers, radio and TV stations, and magazines to promote some company activity.

Niche Market. An identifiable market or market segment that can be easily reached and sold to.

Nonprice Competition. A tactic whereby products are differentiated in terms of promotion, packaging, delivery, or other product support rather than by price.

Objection. A prospect's reason for not responding favorably to a salesperson's request for an order.

OEM (Original Equipment Manufacturer). A company that sells products that are then used as components in others' products. A manufacturer of compressors for construction equipment would be an OEM manufacturer.

On-pack Premium. A free gift or coupon attached to a product's package.

On-spec. Work done by an advertising agency or other service company without payment in hopes of convincing a company to do business with it.

Open Account. A situation in which a company can purchase products and then pay for them thirty days later. This term is also used to refer to a past debt.

Outbound Telemarketing. A sales tactic whereby people from a firm call prospects and customers. The tactic can be used to qualify prospects or to sell products.

Outer Envelope. A direct mail term for the wrapper that holds all of a mailing's promotional material.

Overruns. For printed material, products produced over and above anticipated demand. Overruns are used to cover printing mistakes, requests for old issues, free samples, and so on.

Packaged Goods. Small consumer products sold in small packages, typically in drugstores or grocery stores.

Package Insert. A promotional piece placed in a package designed to sell other products.

Page Proof. The last proof before printing of a booklet or pamphlet. It shows the sequence in which the pages appear. Note: *Don't skip a page proof.* I have had some real horror stories by not doing one.

Panel Research. A group of consumers or users that gives attitudinal information rather than specific product research.

Pass-along Circulation. The number of readers who get a magazine from a friend or fellow worker, or who read it at a library.

Paste-up. Finished mechanical artwork, including photos, copy, and headlines. Desktop publishing is replacing most paste-up jobs.

Personalized Ad. An ad, bound in a magazine, with each subscriber's name on it.

PIMS (Profit Impact of Marketing Strategies). A term coined by the Strategic Planning Institute for information that explains a company's profit performance under certain conditions.

Planogram. A diagram prepared by retail store buyers that shows where products should be displayed. K Mart, for instance, will do a planogram for two or three months that will detail what products go on what shelves in every store. Very important term to retailers.

PMS Colors. Standard shades of colors for printing purposes.

Point-of-purchase Advertising. Also called P-O-P. Advertising at the same point as the product.

Positioning. Trying to influence the way customers perceive a product. For example, a marketer will try to position a car as a value leader in the luxury car class, both through its product features and its advertising and promotional material.

Preferred Position. A requested advertising location in a magazine, such as the back page.

Preprint Advertising. A common tactic whereby copies of print advertisements are given to retailers prior to the ad's running. Stores can use copies to support the ad's message. Customers do appreciate this small courtesy.

Presorting. Sorting mail by Zip code in order to take advantage of bulk mail savings.

Press Kit. Photos and information about a new product or other company event that are distributed to key magazines and retailers.

Pressure-sensitive Label. An easily removed and reapplied label for direct mailings. It usually costs only 1 cent more per label, and it is worth the extra cost.

Price Competition. A situation in which companies in the market compete primarily on price, rather than on nonprice factors such as packaging, product support, and service.

Price Leader. A company that typically is the first one to raise or lower its prices. Also occasionally used for products that have an extremely low price to generate store traffic.

Price Lining. Tactic where products in a similar price range are grouped together. For example, one area in a toy store might have $50 items, while another has toys from $15 to $20.

Print Run. The quantity of material to be printed; i.e., a book might have a print run of 10,000 copies.

Private Brand. Products owned by a reseller, such as Sears, rather than by the product's manufacturer.

Product Differentiation. The marketer's task of presenting products to customers so that they will appear to be different from competitive products.

Product Liability. A company's legal obligation to ensure the safety of the products it sells.

Product Life Cycle. The four stages of a product's life: introduction, growth, maturity, and decline.

Product Line. A group of products that have similar characteristics and are all aimed at the same target audience.

Product Mix. Usually refers to all of the product lines a company sells.

Product-oriented Sales Force. Sales forces divided on the basis of product lines rather than geographic areas.

Professional Services Marketing. Marketing for groups such as dentists, doctors, accountants, lawyers, engineers, and management consultants.

Promotional Allowance. An incentive given by a manufacturer to a retailer or wholesaler to handle the paperwork of a specific promotion.

Pulling Power. The ability of an ad to create the desired response.

Pull Strategy. An effort by manufacturers to get prospects and customers to request their products from dealers and retailers.

Push Money. Money given to retailer or dealer salespeople to push a certain product. For example, a salesperson might get an extra $10 for every unit he or she sells.

Push Strategy. A strategy where sales are created by pushing as many products as possible onto retailers' shelves. Similar to a load program.

Qualifying. The process of deciding whether or not a sales prospect is actually a bonafide potential customer.

Quota. A specified number of sales that might need to occur for a salesperson to receive a bonus, or for a retailer to qualify for a promotional allowance.

Rack Jobber. A type of wholesaler that furnishes products on consignment for small racks in drugstores, convenience stores, and some small five-and-dime stores.

Rate Base. The circulation numbers a magazine or radio/TV station bases its rates on. For example, a magazine's rate base might be 250,000 subscribers.

Rate Card. A listing of charges for advertising for any media source.

Referral. A sales tactic that gets the names of new prospects from current customers.

Release Date. The date on which you want publicity to be published or broadcast by the media. A release date of July 31 means that the release should be only used after that date.

Remainder. Merchandise, or ad space, that has not been sold because of lack of customer demand.

Repeat Rate. How often people are rebuying your product. An indication of consumer satisfaction.

Reply Envelope. Direct mail term. An envelope, with your name on it, for customers to return with an order form or request for further action.

Reprint. The reproduction of an ad that has already printed. Highly recommended, as reprints help establish credibility.

Resellers. Companies and people who purchase and resell products to make a profit. Wholesalers and retailers are both resellers.

Rollout. A marketing term used for introducing a new product and putting all its programs into effect.

Sales Budget. Money allocated to finance salesperson training, compensation, and travel expenses.

Sales Forecast. A projection of the quantity of goods that will be sold over a time period. Its preparation is one of marketing's most important tasks, as the forecast dictates a company's manufacturing and financial plans.

Sampling. A market research technique where you might go in and sample every tenth buyer of your equipment to see if it is performing well.

Scanner. An electronic device that reads bar codes.

Scratch-off Promotions. A popular game device where people scratch off labels to see if they've won any prizes. A favorite of McDonald's.

Segment. A small customer group within a market.

Seller's Market. A situation where the demand for a product is greater than the supply.

Service Bureau. A company that provides support services such as accounting and secretarial work to individuals or other companies.

Share of Mind. How often customers will think of your product when they think of the category you are in. For example, Pitney Bowes has a very high share of mind for mailing machines.

Shrink-wrap. A clear plastic film that can be used for product packaging and also for direct mailings.

Skimming. A new product pricing strategy in which the product is initially high priced, in effect skimming a high margin from early buyers.

Soft Offer. A sale offer that lets people try a product out for two weeks to a month before they have to buy it.

Specialty Store. A retail store with a very narrow target market, such as a store selling rope climbing equipment.

Speculative Pitch. Similar to doing work on spec. A service company prepares a sample of work for a company, hoping to get its business.

Spokesperson. A person hired to promote a product or service.

Sports Marketing. Company sponsorship of sporting events in a community as a method of promoting a product or company.

Staple Goods. Products that are constantly bought and consumed and that are bought with little thought. Also called commodity products.

Stock. Another word for inventory.

Storyboard. A series of drawings that depict the sequence of visual events in a TV commercial. Copy typically appears next to each visual.

Strategic Alliance. A fancy way of saying that two companies are combining to attack the same opportunity.

Strategic Business Unit. A division of a company that is independent of other operating divisions. This term is common in big companies.

Strategic Window. A short-term marketing opportunity.

Subculture. Similar to a small market segment. A subculture is a small group, such as teenage Asian dropouts, with characteristics that are both the same as and different from those of the larger culture.

Super. Common term in video editing that means to superimpose words or a phone number over a TV view.

Superstores. Starting to be called category killers, stores that are much larger than previous stores and typically sell products at a lower price.

Syndicate. An organization that supplies specific types of programming to newspapers or TV and radio stations. Your best bet for targeting radio ads at specific groups.

Tag Line. The final line of copy at the end of a print, radio, or TV ad.

Take-one. A print ad that features coupons, refund blanks, or entry forms to fill out and send in.

Target Audience. The people that a marketer wants to reach with his or her message.

Team Selling. Used on complicated products. Engineers, marketers, and salespeople may be combined in various ways to give the company a better chance of making the sale.

Test Group. A group in a research sample that gets either more or less than other people in the survey.

Tie-in Advertising Promotions. Activities where companies are tied together, both promoting the same concept. Examples are offering coupons with other companies or a manufacturer who runs an ad with a retailer.

Top-of-mind. The product people think of first when they think of a certain product category.

Touch-screen Video. A video system that activates a response once a viewer touches the screen next to a menu listing.

Tracking. A direct mail term for monitoring a program so that you know how it's working.

Trade Advertising. Advertising directed at wholesalers or retailers, or other companies in the trade, rather than consumers.

Trade Associations. Groups of people in an industry that meet to address common problems.

Trade Magazines. Magazines targeted at people in a trade rather than consumers.

Trademark. Legal protection for a brand name or a clever phrase that describes a product. Most brand names are trademarked, which means that the name cannot be used again by another company. Only costs $175.

Trade Promotion. A promotion directed at the trade rather than at consumers.

Trade Shows. Conventions attended by retailers and distributors in a particular trade.

Trial Offer. Allowing a customer to try a product out before buying.

Turnover. The number of times inventory needs to be sold. For example, if a manufacturer wants to turn its inventory six times per year, its inventory should equal two months' sales.

Unique Selling Proposition. A selling proposition that your company and only your company can provide. This is the reason people should buy from you. Occasionally abbreviated to USP.

Universal Product Code (UPC). A code assigned to every product. It is printed on the outside of the product's packages.

Value-added. Strictly, what a company does to a group of raw materials to make them ready for the market. A more common definition is finding features, product support, or service that a marketer can add to give a product more value.

Vertical Market. A situation in which a market only has a few possible customers, but all of them need the product. For example, a computer operating chip might only have twenty customers, but every one of them needs a lot of chips.

Videotex. An interactive video system that can send information to consumers through their computer screens. Increasingly used for advertising messages.

Wraparound. A decorative banner that circles a display.

Zone Pricing. A pricing policy for heavy items that bases the product's price on the buyer's geographic location.

Appendix C
Helpful Sources

DIRECTORIES

Directory of Conventions, 633 Third Ave., New York, NY 10017.

Encyclopedia of Associations, Gale Research Corp., Book Tower, Detroit, MI 48277.

Encyclopedia of Business Information Sources, Gale Research Corp., Book Tower, Detroit, MI 48277.

Mail Order Catalogs and Directory, Grey House Publishing, Bank of Boston Bldg., Sharon, CT 06069.

Directory of Manufacturers' Representatives, Manufacturers' Agents National Association, P.O. Box 3467, Laguna Hills, CA 92654.

Standard Rate & Data Services, 3004 Glenview Road, Wilmette, IL 60091.

The Sourcebook, Sumner Communications, 2025 Eye Street, N.W., #916, Washington, DC 20036.

Thomas Registry of American Manufacturers, Thomas Publishing Companies, One Penn Plaza, New York, NY 10001.

U.S. Manufacturer's Directory, American Directory Publishing, Omaha, NE 27347.

MAGAZINES

Direct Marketing, 224 Seventh St., Garden City, NY 11530.

Sales and Marketing Management, Bill Communications, 633 Third Ave., New York, NY 10017.

Successful Meetings, 633 Third Ave., New York, NY 10017.

Trade Show and Convention Guide, 49 Music Square West, Nashville, TN 37203.

Trade Show Week, 12233 W. Olympic Blvd., Suite 236, Los Angeles, CA 90064.

BOOKS

Best Sales Promotions, 6th Ed., by William Robinson. NTC Business Books, Lincolnwood, IL. 1987.

Bulletin Board Systems for Business, by Lamont Wood and Dana Blankenhorn. John Wiley & Sons, New York, 1992.

The Business-to-Business Direct Marketing Handbook, by Ray Ljungren. AMACON, New York, 1988.

Cash Copy, by Jeffrey Lant. Jeffrey Lant Associates, Cambridge, MA, 1989.

Encyclopedia of Telemarketing, by Richard L. Bencin and Donald J. Jonovic. Prentice-Hall, Englewood Cliffs, NJ, 1989.

How to Start and Operate a Mail Business, 4th ed., by Julian Simon. McGraw-Hill, New York, 1987.

On the Air, by Al Parinello. The Career Press, Hawthorne, NJ, 1991.

Publishing Newsletters, 2d ed., by Howard Penn Hudson. Charles Scribner's Sons, New York, 1988.

Tested Advertising Methods, 4th ed., by John Caples. Prentice-Hall, Englewood Cliffs, NJ, 1981.

COMPUTER RESOURCES

On Line Computer Resources, 4330 J. Clayton Road, Concord, CA 94521; BBS # 415-687-0236.

Computer Readable Databases, American Library Assn., 50 E. Huron St., Chicago, IL 60611.

The North American On Line Directory, R.R. Bowker, 245 W. 17th St., New York, NY 10011.

ACCESS TO DATABASE SYSTEMS

Bibliographic Retrieval Service, 1200 Route 7, Latham, NY 12110.

Dialog, 3460 Hillview Ave., Palo Alto, CA 94304.

A SAMPLING OF DATABASE SYSTEMS

AP News, 90,000 current articles, as recent as forty-eight hours old.

Arthur D. Little/On Line, Extensive listing of research articles prepared in the past by this premier consulting company.

Bizdate, A business news format with information culled from a variety of sources.

D&B, Dun's Financial Records. Profiles of 2 million companies, 90 percent of which are private.

Electronic Yellow Pages. Ten million listings from 4,800 telephone directories.

FIND/SVP Reports and Studies Index. Listing of major research reports.

Moody's Corporate News—U.S. News and information about 13,000 U.S. companies.

MRI Business-to-Business, Data on purchases of products and magazines by 4,000 professional managers.

NEXIS, Series of databases of new articles in papers, magazines, and broadcast media.

Simon's Study of Media and Markets, Product usage information on 3,900 brands in 800 categories from 19,000 U.S. adults.

Index

Don Debelak has marketed over 250 products ranging from consumer-oriented videos to semiconductor equipment. He is the author of *Total Marketing: Capturing Customers with Marketing Plans that Work* and *How to Bring a Product to Market for Less than $5,000.* Don is president of DBD Associates, New Brighton, Minnesota.